WEBSTER'S DICTIONARY

This book was not published by the original publishers of the Webster's Dictionary, or by any of their successor.

©1989, Text Copyright: K. Nichols

RULES OF SPELLING

(1) The most common way to form the plural of a noun is to add an s (Example: girl, girls; town, towns; hall, halls).

(2) The plural of nouns which end in y following a consonant are formed by dropping the y and adding ies (Example: country, countries; baby, babies; family, families).

(3) The plural of nouns which end in y following a vowel are formed by adding an s (Example: toy, toys; boy, boys; attorney, attorneys).

In this quick reference dictionary, a double dash (--) indicates a hyphenated word, and a single dash (-) indicates syllablization.

Abbreviations Used in This Dictionary

abbr.	*abbreviation*
adj.	*adjective*
adv.	*adverb*
conj.	*conjunction*
Elect.	*Electric*
Gram.	*Grammer*
interj.	*interjection*
Mus.	*Music*
Naut.	*Nautical*
n.	*noun*
pl.	*plural*
pref.	*prefix*
pron.	*pronoun*
suff.	*suffix*
v.	*verb*

A, a the first letter of the English alphabet

aard-vark *n.* anteater

aard-wolf *n.* hyena-like mammal that eats carrion

ab-a-ca *n.* plant for the Philippines that is the source for Manila hemp

a-back *adv.* unexpectedly

ab-a-cus *n.* counting frame with beads

a-baft *adv.* toward the stern or aft of a ship

ab-a-lo-ne *n.* a type of a sea mollusk

a-ban-don *v.* desert; to forsake; to withdraw **-er, -ment** *n.,* **-ed** *adj.*

a-base *v.* lower in rank, position; or estimation **abasement** *n.,* **abasing** *v.*

a-bash *v.* to disconcert; to embarrass; to make one ashamed or uneasy

a-bate *v.* to make something or someone smaller **abater, abatement** *n.*

ab-be *n.* French title that is given to a priest

ab-bey *n.* a kind of monastery, or a convent

ab-bre-vi-ate *v.* shorten; make brief **-tor, -ation** *n.*

ab-di-cate *v.* to relinquish something **abdication** *n.*

ab-do-men *n.* stomach; belly **-inally** *adv.,* **-inal** *adj.*

ab-duct *v.* carry away wrongfully as by force **abduction** *n.,* **abductor** *n.*

a-beam *adv.* right angles to the keel of a ship

a-bed *adv.* to be on a bed

ab-er-rant *adj.* straying from the right way; to be wandering or varying from

a-bet *v.* incite or encourage **-ter, -tor, -ment** *n.*

ab-hor *v.* dislike intensely; to loathe or to hate greatly **-rent** *adj.,* **-rer, -rence** *n.*

a-bide *v.* tolerate; to last **-biding** *adj.,* **-ance** *n.*

a-bil-i-ty *n.* state of being able **abilities** *n., pl.*

ab-ject *n.* sunk to a low condition **abjectness, abjection** *n.*

ab-jure *v.* renounce solemnly

abjurer, abjuration *n.*

ab-late *v.* to be cut

ab-la-tion *n.* as in surgery, the removal of a part of the body **ablative** *adj.*

a-blaze *adv.* on fire

a-ble *adj.* having sufficient ability; talented or capable **ablest** *adj.,* **ableness** *n.*

a-ble--bodied *adj.* having a sound strong body

ab-lu-tion *n.* cleaning something with water

ab-ne-gate *v.* to deny; to refuse; to renounce

ab-nor-mal *adj.* not normal **abnormality** *n.,* **-ly** *adv.*

a-board *adv.* on board a ship

a-bode *n.* dwelling place

a-bol-ish *v.* put an end to **-ment, -er** *n.,* **-able** *adj.*

A--bomb *n.* an atomic bomb

a-bom-i-na-ble *adj.* being detestable; being loathsome **abomination** *n.,* **-bly** *adv.*

a-bort *v.* to terminate

a-bor-tion *n.* an induced termination of pregnancy

a-bor-tion-ist *n.* a person who aborts something

a-bound *v.* to have plenty of something

a-bout *adv.* approximately

a-bove *adv.* to be higher or greater than

ab-ra-ca-dab-ra *n.* a word which is believed to have magical powers

a-brade *v.* to wear or to rub something off; to grate off **abraded, abrading** *v.*

a-breast *adv.* to be located side by side one another

a-bridge *v.* make smaller **-ment, -er** *n.,* **-able** *adj.*

a-broad *adv.* widely

ab-ro-gate *v.* to repeal; to cancel; to put an end to **abrogation** *n.,* **abrogated** *v.*

ab-rupt *adj.* to be happening or occurring suddenly

ab-scess *n.* type of swollen pus filled sore **abscessed** *adj.*

ab-sence *n.* being away

ab-sent *adj.* being not present; gone **absently** *adv.*

ab-sen-tee *n.* person who is not where they should be; one that is absent

ab-so-lute adj. to be unconditional **absolutely** adv.

ab-solve v. to release from duties, guilt or debt **absolver** n.

ab-sorb v. to take in **absorbency, absorbent** adj.

ab-stain v. to refrain from doing something

ab-ste-mi-ous adj. to be showing moderation

ab-sti-nence n. the forebearance one has voluntarily **abstinent** adj.

ab-stract v. to remove something **abstraction** n.

ab-struce adj. being hard or difficult to understand

ab-surd adj. clearly untrue; ridiculous; unsound **absurdly** adv., **absurdity** n.

a-bun-dance n. large quantity; an ample supply; enough; fullness; wealth

a-bun-dant adj. overflowing; sufficient; being well supplied **abundantly** adv.

a-buse v. to use in an improper way; to cause injury to **abuser** n.

a-but v. to border -ted, -ting v.

a-but-ment n. kind of bridge support, such as an arch

a-bys-mal adj. being immeasurably deep

a-byss n. a deep crack; a bottomless opening

a-ca-cia n. a thorny tree which is located in warmer areas or climates

ac-a-dem-ic adj. referring to or relating to liberal studies

a-cad-e-my n. a private school of learning

a-can-thus n. type of prickly plant that is found in the Mediterranean area

acap-pel-la adj. to be singing without instrumental accompaniment

a-cat-a-lec-tic adj. not stopping short; having the complete number

ac-cede v. to consent; to agree to arrive at a certain state or condition of something

ac-cel-er--ate v. to increase

-tive adj., -tor, -tion n.

ac-cent n. emphasize

ac-cept v. to take what is given **acceptor, accepter** n.

ac-cept-able adj. satisfactory proper; to be good enough for someone

ac-cep-tance n. approval; ar accepting or being accepted by someone

ac-cess n. an admission, entrance

ac-ces-sion n. in Computer Science, act of obtaining data for storage

ac-ces-si-ble adj. easy acces approach **accessibility** n.

ac-ces-sory n. contributing **accessoriness, -rily** adv.

ac-ci-dent n. an unexpected happening **accidental** adj.

ac-claim v. to greet one with approval; to hail or to cheer someone on

ac-cla-ma-tion n. applause of a group of people showing a like **acclamatory** adj.

ac-cli-mate v. to become accus tomed **acclimation** n.

ac-co-lade n. praise; award; ceremony used in conferring knighthood

ac-com-mo-date v. to make fit **accommodating** adj., -tion n.

ac-com-pa-ni-ment n. something that goes well with another

ac-com-pa-nist n. a person who plays a musical accompaniment

ac-com-pa-ny v. to go along with someone or thing

ac-com-plice n. a companion in crime

ac-com-plish v. to perform -ment n., -able adj.

ac-cord n. harmony -ant, -ing adj., -ingly adv.

ac-cor-di-on n. instrument with bellows and keys

ac-cost v. to approach

ac-count n. description **accountable** adj., -ability n.

ac-coun-tan-cy n. the profession of an accountant

ac-count-ing n. a report on how accounts have been balanced or recorded

ac-cred-it *v.* to give credit

ac-crete *v.* to grow together or to join together

ac-crue *v.* to result naturally; to increase at certain times

ac-cu-mu-late *v.* to collect -tion, -tor *n.*, -tive *adj.*

ac-cu-rate *adj.* careful and exact -ness *n.*, -ly *adv.*

ac-curs-ed *adj.* being unpleasant accursedly *adv.*

ac-cu-sa-tion *n.* charge that a person is guilty of breaking the law

ac-cuse *v.* to blame accusingly *adv.*, accuser *n.*

ac-custom *v.* to familiarize oneself by habit

ac-custom-ed *adj.* being customary or usual

ace *n.* face of a playing card

ac-e-tate *n.* type of salt

a-ce-tic acid *n.* the main ingredient of vinegar; a sour, colorless liquid that has a sharp smell

a-cet-y-lene *n.* a type of inflammable gas

ache *v.* to give pain to

a-chieve *v.* to do; to succeed -er, -ment *n.*, -able *adj.*

ac-id *n.* a chemical compound acidic *adj.*

a-cid-i-fy *v.* to turn into an acid acidifier, -fication *n.*

a-cid-u-late *v.* to make something acid acidulation *n.*

ack-ack *n.* anti-aircraft fire

ac-know-ledge *v.* to admit -er, -ment *n.*, -able *adj.*

ac-me *n.* highest point

ac-ne *n.* a skin disease

ac-o-lyte *n.* an altar boy

ac-o-nite *n.* poisonous plant

a-cous-tic *adj.* relating to sound -cally *adv.*, -cal *adj.*

a-cous-tics *n.* the scientific study of sound

ac-quaint *v.* to make familiar

ac-quaint-ance *n.* a person whom one knows -ship *n.*

ac-qui-esce *v.* to agree without arguing acquiescence *n.*

ac-quire *v.* to secure control -er, -ment *n.*, -able *adj.*

ac-qui-si-tion *n.* something which is acquired

ac-quit *v.* to discharge

acquital, acquitage *n.*

a-cre *n.* 43,560 square feet

ac-rid *adj.* being sharp and bitter acridity *n.*

ac-ro-bat *n.* one skilled in gymnastic feats -tic *adj.*

a-cross *prep.* from side to side

act *n.* a deed

ac-tion *n.* process of doing

ac-ti-vate *v.* put into action

ac-tive *adj.* full of action actively *adv.*, activeness *n.*

ac-tiv-ity *n.* being active, in motion

ac-tor *n.* a dramatic performance

ac-tu-al *adj.* existing reality actually *adv.*, actuality *n.*

ac-tu-ate *v.* put into action actuator, actuation *n.*

a-cute *adj.* being sharp acutely *adv.*, acuteness *n.*

ad-a-mant *adj.* standing firm

a-dapt *v.* to adjust adapter, adaptation *n.*

add *v.* to join together addable, addible *adj.*

ad-dict *n.* a person who has a strong habit addictive, addicted *adj.*, addiction *n.*

ad-di-tion *n.* adding of numbers -al *adj.*, -ally *adv.*

ad-dress *v.* to speak to

ad-e-noids *n.* a lymphoid tissue growth

a-dept *adj.* highly skilled adeptness *n.*, -ly *adv.*

ad-e-quate *adj.* sufficient adequately *adv.*, -ness *n.*

ad-here *v.* to stay attached adherend, adherence *n.*

ad-her-ent *n.* person who follows a leader

ad-he-sion *n.* sticking together

ad-he-sive *adj.* tenacious adhesiveness *n.*, -ly *adv.*

ad-in-ter-im *adj.* being in the meantime

ad-ja-cent *adj.* being nearby adjacently *adv.*, -ency *n.*

ad-jec-tive *n.* a word that describes a noun or pronoun adjectival *adj.*

ad-join *v.* to be next to something adjoining *adj.*

ad-journ *v.* close a meeting or session adjournment *n.*

ad-judge v. to decide by judicial procedure

ad-jure v. to ask urgently adjuratory adj., -ration n.

ad-just v. to arrange -er, -ment n., -able adj.

ad-lib v. to improvise

ad-man n. a person who works in the business of advertising

ad-min-is-ter v. to direct or to manage

ad-min-is-tra-tion n. the managers of a school

ad-mi-ra-ble adj. to be worthy of being admired

ad-mi-ral n. the highest ranking naval officer

ad-mire v. to regard with wonder -ingly, -er, -rably adv., -ration n.

ad-mis-si-ble adj. capable of being admitted -bility n.

ad-mit-tance n. the permission to enter

ad-mix-ture n. a blend; a mingling of things

a-do-be n. a building material made from clay

a-dopt v. to take legally -ion n., -ive, -able adj.

a-dor-a-ble adj. very likable

a-dore v. to love greatly

a-dorn v. to add splendor to something adornment n.

a-drift adv. floating freely

a-droit adj. skillful and clever adroitness n., adroitly adv.

a-dult n. full grown person adulthood n., adultly adv.

ad-vance v. to move ahead

ad-van-tage n. a better chance for something -geous adj., -geously adv.

ad-vent n. the four Sundays before Christmas

ad-ven-ture n. an exciting experience -er n., -ous adj.

ad-verb n. a word used to describe adverbial n.

ad-verse adj. to be opposed

ad-ver-tise v. to draw public attention to a product advertiser, advertisement n.

ad-vice n. a suggestion regarding the course of an action

ad-vis-a-ble adj. being fit to be done

ad-vise-ment n. a careful thought; deliberation

ad-vo-cate v. write or speak in favor advocation n.

aer-o-bics n. a strenuous exercise

aer-o-sol n. a liquid under pressure

a-far adv. far off

af-fa-ble adj. good natured affably adv., affability n.

af-fair n. an event

af-fect v. to move emotionally affectingly adv., -ing adj.

af-fec-tion n. a tender feeling

af-fi-da-vit n. written statement swearing something is true

af-firm-a-tive adj. asserting the fact is true -ly adv.

af-fix n. to attach; to fasten

af-flict v. to cause suffering affliction, afflicter n.

af-flu-ence n. wealth; riches affluently adv., -ent adj.

af-front v. to confront

a-fire adv. burning

a-float adv. floating on water

a-foot adj. walking on foot

a-foul adj. tangled

a-fraid adj. filled with fear

aft adv. toward the rear

af-ter-math n. consequence

a-gain adv. another time

a-gainst prep. in exchange for

age n. a length of time

age-less adj. existing forever

a-gen-cy n. the business acting for others

a-gen-da n. a list of things to be done or completed

a-gent n. one who acts as a representative agential adj.

ag-glom-er-ate v. to collect agglomerative adj., -tion n.

ag-gran-dize v. to extend aggrandizer, -ment n.

ag-gra-vate v. to annoy aggravation n., -ing adj.

ag-gres-sion n. a hostile behavior toward another

ag-i-tate v. to disturb; upset -tor, -tion n., -edly adv.

ag-o-nize v. to afflict with great anguish

ag-o-ny n. an intense mental distress

a-gree v. to consent

a-gree-ment n. concord; state

or act of agreeing

ag-ri-cul-ture n. raising of livestock -ist n., -al adj.

a-ground adv. & adj. to be stranded on the ground

a-head adv. in advance

ail v. to feel sick

ailment n., **ailing** adj.

aim v. to direct purpose

air n. a nitrogen and oxygen mixture **airless** adj.

air-craft n. machine that flies

Air Force n. an aviation branch of armed forces

air-port n. a place where air planes take off and land

air raid n. bombing attack

aisle n. a passageway

a-jar adv. & adj. to be partially opened

a-kin adj. being related

a-larm n. warning of danger **alarmingly** adv. **alarming** adj.

al-bum n. a book which is used for photographs

al-bu-men n. white of an egg

al-co-hol n. an intoxicating liquor such as whiskey

al-cove n. a partly enclosed extension of a room

a-lert adj. brisk; watchful **alertness** n., **alertly** adv.

al-ge-bra n. form of math -ically adv., -ical, -ic adj.

a-li-bi n. a form of defense

a-li-en adj. not belonging to a country or government **alienability** n., **alienable** n.

a-light v. to settle

a-lign v. to arrange in a line **aligner**, **alignment** n.

a-like adj. similar

al-i-mo-ny n. a court ordered support

a-live adj. living

all adj. a whole amount

al-lay v. to relieve **allayer** n.

al-lege v. to affirm; to assert **alleged**, **allegeable** adj.

al-le-giance n. the loyalty to one's nation

al-ler-gy n. an abnormal reaction to environmental substances

al-ley n. narrow passageway

al-li-ga-tor n. a large amphibious reptile

al-lot v. to set aside

allottable adj., **allotment** n.

al-low v. to permit **allowably** adv., **allowable** adj.

al-low-ance n. a regular amount of money or food

all-round adj. including all aspects

al-lude n. refer indirectly

al-lure v. to tempt **allurement** n., **alluring** adj.

al-lu-sion n. a hint

al-ma-ma-ter n. a school one has attended

al-ma-nac n. an annual publication

al-might-y adj. having absolute power

al-mond n. an oval and edible nut

al-most adv. not quite

alms pl., n. goods given to the poor

a-loft adv. toward the upper rigging of a ship

a-lone adj. single; solitary

a-long adv. following the path

a-loof adj. distant aloofness n.

a-loud adv. audibly

al-pha-bet n. the letters arranged in order -ically adv., -ical, -ic adj.

al-read-y adv. by this or a specified time

al-so adv. likewise; besides

al-tar n. elevated holy table

al-ter v. to make change or become different -ation, -ant, -ableness n., -ative, -able adj.

al-ter-nate v. to happen or follow in turn **alternation** n., **alternately** adv.

al-ter-na-tive n. a choice between two possibilities **alternatives** n., -ly adv.

al-though conj. even though

al-ti-tude n. height

al-to n. low female voice

al-to-geth-er adv. entirely

a-lu-mi-num n. silvery metal

al-ways adv. forever

am n. first person singular

a-mal-ga-mate v. to mix; to blend **amalgamator** n.

am-a-ranth n. weedy plants

am-a-teur n. one who lacks expertise **amateurish** adj.

a-maze v. to astound

amazement, amazely *adv.*

am-bass-a-dor *n.* representative ambassadorial *adj.*

am-ber *n.* brownish-yellow

am-bi-dex-trous *adj.* able to use both hands well

am-bi-ent *adj.* surrounding

am-big-u-ous *adj.* doubtful

am-bi-tion *n.* strong desire

am-ble *v.* to move at a leisurely pace ambler *n.*

am-bu-lance *n.* vehicle to transport injured or sick

am-bush *n.* a surprise ambushment, ambusher *n.*

a-me-lio-rate *v.* to make better -tive, -ble *adj.*, -tion *n.*

a-men *interj.* used at the end of a prayer

a-me-na-ble *adj.* responsive -ness, -bility *n.*, -bly *adv.*

a-mend *v.* to correct amender *n.*, amendable *adj.*

a-mend-ment *n.* a correction

a-men-i-ty *n.* agreeableness

a-merce *v.* to punish -er, -ment *n.*, -able *adj.*

America *n.* the United States of America

A-mer-i-ca-n *n.* a native of U.S.A.

am-e-thyst *n.* a quartz

a-mi-a-ble *adj.* being friendly -ness, -bility *n.*, -bly *adv.*

a-mi-ca-ble *adj.* harmonious -ness, -bility *n.*, -bly *adv.*

a-mid *prep.* in the middle of

a-miss *adj.* being out of order or place

am-mo-nia *n.* a pungent gas

am-mu-ni-tion *n.* the projectiles for guns

am-ne-sia *n.* loss of memory

a-mount *n.* the sum or total quantity

am-pere *n.* the unit of electric current

am-phet-a-mine *n.* a drug

am-phib-i-an *n.* animal able to live on land and in water

am-ple *adj.* sufficient

am-pu-tate *v.* to remove

a-muck *adv.* in an uncontrolled manner

am-u-let *n.* a charm worn to protect

a-muse *v.* to entertain agreeable -ment *n.*, -ing,

-able *adj.*, -ingly *adv.*

an *adj.* one sort of

an-a-con-da *n.* a large American snake that kills by crushing

an-a-gram *n.* a new word formed from another anagramatical, -matic *adj.*

a-nal *adj.* to be referring or relating to the anus

an-al-ge-sia *n.* state unable to feel pain

a-nal-o-gous *adj.* similar

a-nal-y-sis *n.* act to examine parts of something

an-a-lyst *n.* a person who analyzes others

an-a-lyze *v.* to make an analysis of -er, -ability, -ation *n.*, -able *adj.*

a-nat-o-my *n.* a structure of an organ

an-ces-tor *n.* a forefather ancestral *adj.*, ancestress *n.*

an-chor *n.* a heavy device used to keep a ship from drifting

an-cho-vy *n.* very small fish

an-cient *adj.* very old ancientness *n.*, anciently *adv.*

and *conj.* along with; added to

an-dan-te *adv.* slow in tempo

and-i-ron *n.* heavy support for wood in a fireplace

an-ec-dote *n.* a short account of a story

an-es-thet-ic *adj.* taking away pain anesthetically *adv.*

a-new *adv.* again

an-gel *n.* an immortal being angelically *adv.*, -ic *adj.*

an-ger *n.* a feeling of rage

an-gi-na *n.* disease marked by painful choking spasms

an-gle *v.* to shape that forms a corner angled *adj.*

an-go-ran *n.* the silky hair of the Angora rabbit

an-gry *adj.* feeling of anger angriness *n.*, angrily *adv.*

an-guish *n.* great suffering

an-i-mal *n.* any four-footed creature

an-i-mate *v.* to give life or spirit to animation *n.*

an-i-mos-i-ty *n.* hostility

an-kle *n.* a joint that connects the foot and leg

an-klet *n.* a short sock

an-neal v. treatment to make glass less brittle

an-nex v. to join a smaller thing to a larger thing

an-ni-ver-sa-ry n. date on which something happened

an-nounce v. to proclaim

announcer, announcement n.

an-noy v. to irritate

annoyer, -ance n., **-ing** adj.

an-nu-al adj. recurring at the same time

an-nu-i-ty n. an annual payment

an-nul v. to do away with

a-noint v. to apply oil in a religious ceremony

a-non-y-mous adj. unknown or withheld name

an-oth-er adj. additional

an-swer n. a written or spoken reply **answerable** adj.

ant n. an insect

an-tag-o-nize v. to arouse hostility

an-te-ce-dent adj. event that precedes another

an-te-lope n. a kind of swiftrunning mammal

an-ten-na n. the feelers of an insect; aerial

an-te-ri-or adj. toward front

an-te-room n. waiting room

an-them n. hymn of praise

an-ther n. part of the flower

an-thol-o-gy n. a collection of stories

an-thra-cite n. hard coal

an-thro-poid n. gorillas

an-thro-pol-o-gy n. a study and development of man

an-ti n. one who opposes policy, or proposal

an-ti-bi-ot-ic n. substance used as a germ killer

an-ti-bod-y n. proteins that counteract diseases

an-tic n. a mischievous act

an-tic-i-pate v. look forward to something **anticipation** n.

an-ti-cli-max n. decline

an-ti-freeze n. substance, mixed with water to lower the freezing point

an-ti-his-ta-mine n. a drug used to relieve symptoms of allergies

an-ti-knock n. a substance that reduces engine knock

an-ti-mo-ny n. a kind of metallic element

an-tique n. an object over 100 years old

an-tiq-ui-ty n. a quality of being old

an-ti--Sem-ite n. a person hostile toward Jews

an-tith-e-sis n. a direct contrast

ant-ler n. horns of the deer

an-to-nym n. a word with the opposite meaning

a-nus n. the lower opening of the alimentary canal

anx-i-e-ty n. a state of uncertainty

anx-ious adj. worried

any adj. no matter which

any-body pron. any person

any-thing pron. any occurrence

any-time adv. at any time

any-where adv. to any degree

a-or-ta n. the main artery of the heart

a-pace adv. rapid in pace

a-part adv. in pieces

a-part-heid n. non-white racial discrimination in South Africa

a-part-ment n. a place for individual living

ap-a-thy n. lack of emotions

ape n. large mammal

ap-er-ture n. an opening

a-pex n. a highest point

aph-o-rism n. a brief statement of truth

a-piece adv. for each one

a-pol-o-gy n. expressing regret

ap-o-plex-y n. loss of muscular control

a-pos-tle n. a person sent on a mission

a-pos-tro-phe n. a mark (') of punctuation

ap-pall v. to weaken **-ing** adj.

ap-pa-ra-tus n. instrument for a specific purpose

ap-par-el v. to adorn

ap-par-ent adj. clear to the mind **apparently** adv.

ap-pa-ri-tion n. an unusual appearance

ap-peal n. an earnest plea

ap-pear v. to come into existence **appearance** n.

ap-pease v. to pacify

ap-pend v. add an appendix

ap-petite n. desire for food

ap-pe-tiz-er n. the food which is served before a meal

ap-ple n. type of fruit

ap-pli-ance n. an equipment designed for a particular use

ap-pli-ca-ble adj. being appropriate

ap-ply v. to put something into use

ap-point-ment n. an act designating

ap-por-tion v. to divide and share

ap-praise v. estimate value

ap-pre-ci-ate v. to recognize worth appreciating, -ated v.

ap-pre-hend v. to anticipate with anxiety

ap-pren-tice n. a person learning a trade

ap-proach v. to come near

ap-pro-pri-ate v. to take possession of something

a-prove v. to give formal approval for something

ap-prox-i-mate adj. being almost accurate or exact

apri-cot n. a fruit

apron n. a garment used to protect clothing

ap-ro-pos adv. by the way

apt adj. appropriate **aptly** adv.

ap-ti-tude n. a natural talent

aquar-i-um n. artificial pond

aq-ue-ous adj. to be resembling water

ar-a-ble adj. land suitable for cultivation

ar-bi-ter n. a person chosen to decide a dispute

arc n. something curved

arch n. a structure that spans over an open area

ar-chae-ol-o-gy n. scientific study of ancient times

arch-bishop n. a bishop of the highest rank

arch-di-o-cese n. a district of an archbishop

arch-er-y n. a art of shooting with a bow and arrow

ar-chi-tect n. a person who designs and supervises construction **architect** adj.

arc-tic adj. extremely frigid

ar-dor n. extreme warmth

ar-du-ous adj. being difficult

ar-e-a n. flat piece of ground

a-re-na n. an enclosed area for entertainment

ar-gue v. to debate

ar-gu-ment n. a harsh discussion

a-right adv. correctly

a-rith-me-tic adj. math

ark n. a large ship

arm n. the upper limb of the human body

ar-ma-da n. fleet of warships

ar-ma-ment n. the military weapons

ar-ma-ture n. main moving part of an electric machine

arm-hole n. an opening in a garment

ar-mi-stice n. a truce

ar-moire n. a large wardrobe

ar-mor n. covering used to protect the body

ar-my n. the land forces of a country

a-ro-ma n. distinctive odor **aromatic** adj., **-tically** adv.

a-round adv. to or on all sides

a-rouse v. to wake up from a sleep **arousal** n.

ar-raign v. called before a court **arraignment** n.

ar-range v. to put in correct order **arrangement** n.

ar-rant adj. being extreme

ar-ray v. place or set in order

ar-rest v. to capture; to seize

ar-rive v. to reach a destination

ar-ro-gance n. an overbearing manner

ar-row n. a sign to show direction

ar-se-nal n. a collection of weapons

ar-se-nic n. a type of poisonous element

ar-son n. a fraudulent burning of property

art n. human skill

ar-ter-y n. blood vessel

art-ful adj. being performed with skill

ar-thri-tis n. an inflammation of joints

ar-ti-choke n. a plant with a thistle-like head

ar-ti-cle n. a condition or a

rule

ar-tic-u-late *adj.* able to express oneself clearly articulation *n.,* -lative *adj.*

ar-ti-fice *n.* an ingenuity

ar-ti-fi-cial *adj.* being made by man artificialness *n.*

ar-til-ler-y *n.* weapons

ar-ti-san *n.* a craftsman

art-ist *n.* a person who practices arts of painting

art-less *adj.* being lacking in knowledge artlessness *n.*

as *adv.* similar to

as-cend *v.* to rise -ant *n.,* ascendancy *n.,* -ing *adj.*

as-cent *n.* a way up

as-cer-tain *v.* to make sure

as-cribe *v.* to assign

a-shamed *adj.* feeling guilt

a-shore *adv.* to the shore

a-side *adv.* out of the way

ask *v.* to request

askance *adv.* suspicion or distrust

askew *adv. or adj.* out of line

a-sleep *adv.* being in a state of sleep

a-slope *adv.* slanting position

as-pect *n.* an appearance of something aspectual *adj.*

as-phalt *n.* a mixture of petroleum tar asphaltic *adj.*

as-phyx-i-ate *v.* to suffocate asphyxiation *n.*

as-pire *v.* to strive towards something that is higher

as-pi-rin *n.* medication

as-sail *v.* to attack violently with words

as-sas-sin *n.* a murderer -ate *v.,* -ation *n.,* -ator *n.*

as-sault *n.* a violent physical or verbal attack

as-sem-ble *v.* put together assembly *n.,* assemblage *n.*

as-sent *v.* to agree

as-sess *v.* to assign a value -ment *n.,* -or *n.,* -able *adj.*

as-set *n.* valuable quality

as-sign *v.* designate as duty assignee *n.,* assigner *n.*

as-sign-ment *n.* given task to undertake

as-sim-i-late *v.* to make similar assimilation *n.*

as-sist *v.* to give support assistance *n.,* assistant *n.*

as-so-ci-ate *v.* join together

as-sort *v.* to distribute into groups -ment *n.,* -ed *adj.*

as-sume *v.* to take responsibility for

as-sump-tion *n.* an idea believed to be true

as-sure *v.* to give confidence assurance *n.,* assured *adj.*

a-stern *adv.* toward the rear

asth-ma *n.* a respiratory disease

as-ton-ish *v.* to strike with sudden fear -ment *n.*

as-tound *v.* fill with wonder

a-stride *prep.* extending across

as-tro-dome *n.* a dome covered stadium

as-trol-o-gy *n.* study of the planets and stars

as-tro-naut *n.* space traveler

as-tute *adj.* very shrewd

asy-lum *n.* place of security

at *prep.* to indicate presence

a-the-ism *n.* the denial of God atheist *n.,* atheistic *adj.*

ath-lete *n.* person who participates in sports athletic *adj.,* -leticism *n.*

at-las *n.* collection of maps

at-mos-phere *n.* air around the earth atmospheric *adj.*

at-om *n.* smallest unit of an element atomical *adj.*

a-tone *v.* to make amends atonement *n.,* atoning *v.*

at-tach *v.* to fasten attachment *n.,* attachable *adj.*

at-tack *v.* to assault

at-tain *v.* to reach a goal attainable *adj.,* -ability *n.*

at-tempt *v.* make an effort

at-tend *v.* to look after attender, attendant *n.*

at-ten-tion *n.* mental concentration

at-ten-u-ate *v.* to weaken

at-test *v.* to give testimony

at-tire *n.* a person's clothing attirement *n.,* attiring *v.*

at-ti-tude *n.* one's manner

at-tor-ney *n.* a lawyer

at-tract *v.* to draw by appeal

at-trib-ute *v.* to explain by showing cause

au-burn *adj.* being moderately brown

auc·tion n. public sale

au·di·ble adj. capable of being heard

au·di·ence n. a group of people

au·dit n. an examination of accounts auditor n.

au·di·tion n. a trial performance

au·ri·cle n. the chambers of the heart

au·then·tic adj. being real; being genuine

au·then·ti·cate v. to prove something is true or genuine

author n. a person who writes

au·thor·i·ty n. the person with the power

au·thor·ize v. to justify

au·to·graph n. a signature autography, autographer n.

au·to·mat·ic adj. being self moving automatically adv.

au·to·mo·bile n. a car

au·top·sy n. a post-mortem examination of a body to determine cause of death

au·tumn n. season between summer and winter; the third season of a calendar year

aux·il·ia·ry adj. to be providing assistance; helping

a·vail v. to be of advantage; to profit or assist

a·vail·abil·i·ty n. the state of being available

a·vail·a·ble adj. ready or present for immediate use

av·a·lanche n. a large amount of snow, ice, earth, or rock sliding down a mountain

av·a·rice n. great desire to possess wealth

a·vast interj. the order to cease, stop, or stay

a·venge v. to take revenge; to get even with

av·e·nue n. a street; road; a means of attainment

a·verse adj. feeling of distaste averseness n., aversely adv.

a·vert v. to prevent from happening; to cause to turn away or off

a·vi·ar·y n. an enclosure for birds

a·vi·a·tion n. the operation of planes

av·id adj. greedy; enthusiastic; eager avidly adv., avidity n.

av·o·ca·do n. a pear-shaped fruit; the tree of this fruit

av·o·ca·tion n. a chosen hobby; a regular vocation

a·void v. to shun from avoidable adj., avoidance n.

a·vouch v. to guarantee

a·vow v. to state openly avower n.

a·vowed adj. acknowledged; open; declared

a·vun·cu·lar adj. pertaining to an uncle

a·wake v. to be alert

a·ware adj. being conscious

a·way adv. to another place

awe n. feeling of wonder

a·wea·ry adj. to be tired

a·weigh v. to hang just clear of a ship's anchor

awe·some adj. expressive of awe awesomely adv.

aw·ful adj. being unpleasant or dreadful in manner

a·while adv. for a short time

a·whirl adj. to spin around

awk·ward adj. not being very graceful; clumsy awkwardness n., awkwardly adv.

awl n. a type of tool used to make holes in leather

awn·ing n. structure that serves as a shelter cover a window or door

a·wry adv. in a twisted or turned position

ax or **axe** n. a type of tool used to split wood

ax·i·om n. the statement recognized as being true -matic adj., -matically adv.

ax·is n. the line around an object that rotates or may be thought to rotate

ax·le n. shaft around which a wheel revolves

a·yah n. nursemaid of India

a·zal·ea n. a shrub that is grown for its brightly colored flowers

Az·tec n. Indian people of Mexico

az·ure n. the blue color of the sky azure adj.

B, b the second letter of the English alphabet

baa *n.* the cry or the bleet of the sheep

bab-ble *v.* chatter senselessly; talk with out meaning

babe *n.* young child or infant

ba-bel *n.* babbling noise of many people talking at the same time

ba-boon *n.* species of the monkey family with a large body and big canine teeth

ba-bush-ka *n.* the headpiece that is made with a kerchief folded into a triangle

ba-by *n.* a very young child; an infant **babyish** *adj.*

ba-by car-riage *n.* a push carriage with four wheels and folding capabilities

ba-by grand *n.* a type of piano, five to six feet long

ba-by-sit *v.* to take care of young children babysitter *n.*

bac-ca-lau-re-ate *n.* a degree given by universities

bac-ca-rat *n.* a card game that involves gambling

bac-cha-nal *adj.* being noisy and riotous

bach-e-lor *n.* an unmarried male bachelorhood *n.*

bac-il-lar-y *adj.* to be rod-shaped

ba-cil-lus *n.* a rod-like microscopic organism which can cause certain diseases

back *n.* the rear part of the human body; that which is behind the front **-er, -ing** *n.*

back-ache *n.* a pain in the back

back-bite *v.* to slander in a nasty way about a person who is not present

back-board *n.* a board that gives support when placed under or behind something

back-bone *n.* spinal column; the main support

back-drop *n.* a curtain or scene behind the back of a stage set

back-er *n.* a person who gives support or aid to a cause

back-field *n.* football players who are positioned behind the line of scrimmage

back-fire *n.* premature explosion of a combustion engine; unexpected result **backfired, backfiring** *v.*

back-gam-mon *n.* a game played by two people

back-ground *n.* an area behind foreground

back-hand *n.* stroke in the game of tennis in which the hand is turned backward **backhanded** *adj.*

back-ing *n.* the support given to something or someone; endorsement

back-lash *n.* violent backward reaction or movement

back-log *n.* an accumulation of unfinished work

back-seat *n.* seat located in the rear

back-side *n.* posterior part; buttocks; rump

back-slap *v.* to express excessive goodwill **backslapper** *n.*

back-slide *v.* to lapse into a less desirable condition; to slide backwards

back-spin *n.* the reverse rotation of a ball

back-stage *adj.* referring to the area located behind a stage

back-stairs *adj.* secret; indirect

back-stitch *n.* stitch made in fabric by inserting the needle to the right and coming out in equal distance to the left

back-stop *n.* something that stops a ball, keeping it from leaving a field of play

back-stretch *n.* the opposite side of the homestretch on a racecourse

back-stroke *n.* a swimming stroke

back-swept *adj.* to be slanting backward

back-swing *n.* a movement with a racket that is the reverse of the forward swing

back-sword *n.* a sword having a single-edge blade

back-talk *n.* an insolent or disrespectful reply

back-track *v.* to retrace previous steps

back-up *n.* something that

serves as a substitute

back-ward *adv.* toward the rear or the back **backwardness** *n.*

back-wash *n.* backward movement of something as water that is produced by a propelled force

back-wa-ter *n.* the water held back as by a dam

back-woods *pl. n.* a remote unsettled backward area **backwoodsman** *n.*

back-yard *n.* the ground located in the back of a house

ba-con *n.* side and back of a pig which is salted and dried for consumption

bac-ter-i-a *n.* microscopic organisms which may produce disease or fermentation

bac-te-ri-al *adj.* caused or related to bacteria

bac-te-ri-cide *n.* substance able to destroy or kill bacteria

bac-te-ri-ol-o-gy *n.* the study of bacteria **bacteriologist** *n.*

bad *adj.* being naughty; opposite of good

badness *n.*, **badly** *adv.*

badge *n.* sign or mark worn to show rank or membership

badg-er *n.* burrowing mammal of North America

bad-min-ton *n.* court game

bad-mouth *v.* to criticize someone persistently

baf-fle *v.* to puzzle

baf-fling wind *n.* a light wind that shifts frequently from side to side

ba-gel *n.* hard, round roll

bag-gage *n.* the belongings of a traveler

bag-pipe *n.* wind instrument having pipes **bagpiper** *n.*

bail *n.* money to guarantee appearance at a trial

bai-liff *n.* an officer who guards prisoners

bait *v.* to lure

bake *v.* to cook in an oven

bal-ance *n.* amount remaining balancing, balanced *v.*

bal-co-ny *n.* platform projecting from the wall

bald *adj.* to be lacking hair on the head

balk *v.* to refuse to go on

bal-lad *n.* narrative story

bal-last *n.* a heavy material to give stability

bal-le-ri-na *n.* a female ballet dancer

bal-let *n.* an artistic dance

bal-loon *n.* a bag inflated

bal-lot *n.* a paper used in secret voting

ball-point *n.* pen with a self-inking writing point

balm *n.* ointment that heals

bal-sa *n.* light weight wood

bal-us-ter *n.* post that supports a handrail

bam-boo *n.* tall grass with hollow stems

bam-boo-zle *v.* trick or deceive

ban *v.* to prohibit; forbid

ba-nal *adj.* trite **banality** *n.*

ba-nan-a *n.* yellow, edible fruit

band *n.* group of musicians

band-age *n.* strip of cloth used to protect an injury

ban-dit *n.* a gangster

ban-dy *adv.* bent outward

bane *n.* cause of ruin

ban-gle *n.* a bracelet

ban-ish *v.* force to leave banisher, **banishment** *n.*

ban-jo *n.* an instrument similar to a guitar

bank *n.* the slope of land adjoining water

bank-er *n.* bank manager

bank-rupt *n.* a person who is insolvent **bankruptcy** *n.*

ban-quet *n.* elaborate feast

ban-yan *n.* a tree from the tropics

barb *n.* sharp projection

bar-bar-i-an *n.* a person thought to be primitive

bar-be-cue *n.* an outdoor fireplace -cued, -cuing *v.*

bar-ber *n.* a person who cuts hair **barbershop** *n.*

bare *adj.* exposed to view

bare-ly *adv.* by a little amount

bar-gain *n.* purchase of an item at a good price

barge *n.* flat-bottomed boat

bark *n.* outer surface of a tree

bar-ley *n.* grain -leys *n., pl.*

barn *n.* a farm building

bar-na-cle *n.* a type of fish with a hard shell

ba-rom-et-er *n.* an instrument

that records the weather changes

bar-rack n. the housing for soldiers

bar-ra-cu-da n. type of fish

bar-rage n. the discharge of missiles

bar-rel n. wooden container with round, flat ends and sides that bulge

bar-ren adj. to be lacking in vegetation **barrenness** n.

bar-rette n. a clasp to hold hair in place

bar-ri-er n. structure that bars or prevents entrance

bar-room n. place where drinks are sold

bar-row n. wheelbarrow

bar-tend-er n. one who serves drinks at a bar

bar-ter v. trade something

base n. fundamental part

base-ball n. game played with a ball and bat

base-board n. molding where the wall meets the floor

base-ment n. foundation of a building or home

bash v. to smash

ba-sic adj. forming the basis

bas-o-lisk n. a tropical American lizard

ba-sis n. the main part

bask v. to relax in the sun

bas-ket n. object made of woven material **basketry** n.

bass n. a fresh water fish

bas-si-net n. a basket used as a infant's crib

bas-soon n. a woodwind instrument

baste v. to sew a loose stitch

bat n. wooden stick **batted, batting** v.

bath n. act of washing the body

bat-tal-ion n. military unit

bat-ten v. to secure

bat-ter v. to beat or to strike continuously

bat-tle n. to struggle **battled, battling** v.

bawd n. a prostitute

bawl v. to cry out

bay n. inlet of a body of water

bay-berry n. evergreen shrub

bay-o-net n. spear-like weapon

ba-zaar n. a fair for charity

be v. to exist

beach n. sandy shore

bead n. small round ball for threading **beaded** adj.

beak-er n. a large cup

beam n. a large, wooden plank

bean n. an edible seed

bear n. carnivorous mammal

beard n. hair growing on the face **beardless, bearded** adj.

beast n. four-legged animal **beastliness** n., **beastly** adv.

beat v. to strike

be-a-tif-ic adj. showing joy

beau n. sweetheart; dandy

beau-ty n. pleasing to the eye

be-calm v. make quiet or calm

be-cause conj. for a reason

beck n. a summon

be-come v. to come, to be

bed n. furniture for sleeping

be-dazzle v. to confuse with bright lights

bed-fast adj. confined to a bed

bed-lam n. state of confusion

be-drag-gled adj. limp and wet

bee n. insect that makes honey

beech n. a tree with edible nuts

beef n. cow, steer, or bull

beer n. alcoholic beverage

beet n. red root vegetable

bee-tle n. an insect

be-fore adv. previously

beg v. to ask for charity

be-get v. to cause or produce

be-gin v. to start

be-grudge v. to envy someone

be-guile v. to deceive

be-half n. a support of another person

be-have v. to function in a certain manner

be-head v. to remove the head

be-hind adv. to or at the back

be-hold v. to look at

be-hoove v. to benefit

beige n. or adj. being light brown color

being n. one's existence

be-la-bor v. to discuss beyond the point that is necessary

be-lat-ed adj. late -ly adv.

belch v. to expel gas through the mouth

be-lief n. something that is trusted

bell n. instrument that rings

bel-lows *n.* instrument that produces air

bel-ly *n.* the abdomen

be-long *v.* to be a part of belongings *n., pl.*

be-loved *adj.* dearly loved

be-low *adv.* at a lower level or place

belt *n.* a band worn around the waist belted *adj.*

be-muse *v.* to bewilder

bench *n.* a long seat

bend *v.* to arch

be-neath *adv.* to be below; underneath

ben-e-dict *n.* bachelor who is recently married

ben-e-dic-tion *n.* blessing

ben-e-fit *n.* aid -ed, -ing *v.*

be-nev-o-lence *n.* inclination to be charitable

be-nign *adj.* having a kind disposition benignly *adv.*

ben-i-son *n.* a blessing

bent *adj.* being curved

be-numb *v.* to dull

be-queath *v.* to give or leave to someone by will

be-reave *v.* to suffer the loss of a loved one

berg *n.* large mass of ice

ber-i-ber-i *n.* nervous disorder

berry *n.* edible fruit

berth *n.* space to dock a ship

be-ryl-li-um *n.* a type of metallic element

be-seech *v.* to ask earnestly

be-side *prep.* next to

be-siege *v.* to surround with troops

be-spat-ter *v.* to soil

be-speak *v.* to foretell

best *adj.* exceeding all others

be-stir *v.* to rouse into action

be-stow *v.* to present

be-stride *v.* to step over

bet *n.* the amount which is risked on a wager

be-take *v.* to move or to go

be-think *v.* to remember

be-tide *v.* to happen to

be-to-ken *v.* to show by a sign

be-tray *v.* to be disloyal

be-troth *v.* to promise to marry

bet-ter *adj.* more suitable

be-tween *prep.* in the middle

bev-er-age *n.* refreshing liquid

bev-y *n.* collection or group

be-ware *v.* to be cautious

be-wilder *v.* to confuse

be-witch *v.* to captivate someone completely

be-yn *n.* turkish title

be-yond *prep.* outside the reach

be-zique *n.* a card game

bi-an-nu-al *adj.* twice a year

bi-as *n.* line cut diagonally

bib *n.* cloth tied under the chin to protect from spilling food

Bi-ble *n.* holy book of the Old and New Testaments

bib-li-og-ra-phy *n.* a list of work by a writer

bib-u-lous *adj.* being inclined to drink bibulously *adv.*

bi-cen-ten-ni-al *adj.* happening every 200 years

bi-ceps *n.* an upper arm muscle

bick-er *v.* to quarrel or argue

bi-cus-pid *n.* a tooth having two roots

bi-cy-cle *n.* vehicle propelled by pedals

bid *v.* to offer a price

bi-det *n.* a basin for bathing the private parts

bi-en-ni-al *adj.* happening every two years -ly *adv.*

bier *n.* a stand for a coffin

bi-fo-cal *adj.* having two different focal lengths

bi-fur-cate *v.* to divide into two parts bifurcation *n.*

big *adj.* being very large bigger, biggest *adj.*

big-a-my *n.* married to two people at the same time

big-wig *n.* person of authority

bike *n.* a bicycle

bi-ki-ni *n.* a two-piece bathing suit

bi-lat-er-al *adj.* to be having two sides bilateralness *n.*

bile *n.* a liquid secreted by the liver

bilge *n.* the hull of a ship

bi-lin-gual *adj.* being able to speak two languages

bil-ious *adj.* gastric distress

bill *n.* money owed -able *adj.*

bill-fold *n.* pocket-sized wallet

bil-liards *n.* a game played at a table

bil-lion *n.* thousand million

bill of lading *n.* list of merchandise

bil-low n. a large wave

billy goat n. a male goat

bi-month-ly adj. to be happening every two months

bin n. enclosed place for storage

bi-na-ry adj. made of two parts

bind v. to hold with rope

bind-er n. a notebook

bind-er-y n. place where books are bound

bin-go n. game of chance

bin-oc-u-lar n. device to bring objects far away into focus

bi-o-chem-is-try n. chemistry of substances **biochemist** n.

bi-ol-o-gy n. science of living organisms **biologist** n.

bi-o-phys-ics n. physics of living organisms

bi-par-ti-san adj. support by two political parties

bi-plane n. airplane with wings on two levels

bi-po-lar adj. referring to two poles **bipolarity** n.

birch n. large tree with little leaves **birchen** adj.

bird n. egg-laying flying animal.

bird-bath n. basin where birds can get wet

bird-brain n. person who does not have much sense

bird-call n. a sound a bird makes

bird dog n. dog used for hunting birds

bi-ret-ta n. cap worn by Roman Catholic clergy

birl v. act of pouring

birth n. beginning of existence

birth cer-ti-fi-cate n. one's record of their birth

birth-day n. the day a person is born

birth-mark n. mark on the skin present at birth

birth-place n. place where one is born

birth-rate n. ratio of the number of births to a given population

birth-stone n. the stone associated with a month of the year

bis-cuit n. small piece of bread

bi-sect v. divide into two parts

bisector, bisection n.

bi-sex-u-al adj. sexually attracted to both sexes

bish-op n. a Christian clergyman **bishopric** n.

bis-muth n. metallic element

bi-son n. a large buffalo

bis-que n. a creamy soup

bis-ter n. brown color used for drawing **bistered** adj.

bis-tro n. a small club or restaurant

bit n. a tiny amount

bitch n. a female dog

bite v. cut with the teeth

biting adj., **bitingly** adv.

bit-ter adj. sharp taste

bitterish adj., **bitterly** adv.

bit-ter-sweet n. a poisonous woody vine

bi-valve n. a mollusk that has a hinged two-part shell

biv-ou-ac n. the temporary military camp

bi-week-ly n. every two weeks

bi-year-ly n. every two years

bi-zarre adj. extremely strange

bizarreness n., **bizzarely** adv.

blab v. to reveal a secret

blab-ber n. to chatter

black adj. very dark in color

black-ball n. vote to prevent admission to a club

black-board n. slate board written on with chalk

black eye n. bruise forming around the eye

black-head n. small mass of dirt that clogs skin pores

black-out n. temporary loss of electrical power

black-snake n. dark colored snake of the U.S.

black-top n. asphalt

black wal-nut n. nut of tree grown in North America

black wid-ow n. extremely poisonous spider

blad-der n. sac that holds urine **bladderlike** adj.

blade n. the part of a knife which cuts

blame v. to find fault in something that is done

blameful, -able, -less adj.

blanch v. remove the color

blan-dish v. coax by flattery

blandishment, blandisher n.

blank adj. being empty

blankness n., **blankly** adv.

blan-ket n. covering on a bed

blare v. make a loud sound

blar-ney n. the talk that is deceptive

blas-pheme v. to talk badly about someone

blasphemeous adj., **-y**, **-er** n.

blast n. strong gust of air

blast-off n. launching of a spaceship

bla-tant adj. unpleasant

blatancy n., **blatantly** adv.

blaze n. bright burst of fire

bla-zon v. to make known

bleach v. to remove the color from something

bleach-ers pl., n. the seating for spectators

bleak adj. being depressing

bleakness n., **bleakly** adv.

bleat n. cry of a sheep or goat

bleed v. to lose blood

bleep n. a signal with a loud sound

blem-ish n. flaw; defect

blend v. to mix together smoothly **blender** n.

bless v. to honor or praise

bless-ed adj. with blessings

blessedness n., **blessedly** adv.

bless-ing n. short prayer

blight n. disease of plants

blimp n. large aircraft

blind adj. not having eyesight; window shade **blindness** n., **blinding** adj., **blindly** adv.

blind-fold v. cover the eyes

blink v. to open and close the eyes quickly

blintz n. very thin pancake

bliss n. have great happiness

blissful adj., **blissfulness** n.

blis-ter n. swelling of a thin layer of skin **blistery** adj.

blithe adj. carefree **-ly** adv.

blitz n. sudden attack

bliz-zard n. a severe winter storm

bloat v. swell or puff out

blob n. small shapeless mass

block n. solid piece of matter

block-ade n. the closure of an area **blockader** n.

blond adj. golden color

blood n. red fluid in the veins circulated by the heart

blood-shot adj. redness of the eyes

blood-stream n. blood in the vascular system

blood ves-sel n. canal which circulates blood

bloom v. to bear flowers

bloom-ers n., pl. loose trousers

bloom-ing adj. to grow; to blossom **bloomingly** adv.

blos-som n. flower of a plant

blot n. an area that is stained

blotch n. area of a person's skin that is discolored

blouse n. a shirt

blow v. current of air **-er** n.

blow-out n. sudden deflation of a tire

blow-torch n. tool that melts soft metals

blow-up n. enlargement

blue n. the color of the sky

blue-berry n. edible berry

blue jay n. bird having blue colored feathers

blue-print n. reproduction of drawings or plans

blues pl., n. style of jazz

bluff v. to deceive

blun-der n. error or mistake **blunderingly** adv., **-er** n.

blunt adj. frank and abrupt **bluntness** n., **bluntly** adv.

blur v. to smear **blurry** adj.

blurt v. speak impulsively

blush v. to become red in the face **blushful** adj.

blus-ter n. violent storm **blusterous** adj., **blusterer** n.

bo-a n. a nonvenomous snake

boar n. the male pig

board n. a flat piece of lumber; get on a train, plane etc.

board-walk n. a walkway at the beach

boast v. to brag **boastful** adj., **boastfulness**, **boaster** n.

boat n. small ship

boat-swain n. officer in charge of rigging

bob v. to cause to move up and down

bob-bin n. a spool that holds thread

bob-cat n. wild-cat

bob-sled n. a sled with steering controls

bod-ice n. the upper section of a dress

bod-y *n.* the physical part of a person **bodied** *adj.*

body-guard *n.* person hired to protect another

bo-gus *adj.* something not real

boil *v.* to raise the temperature of liquid until it bubbles

boil-er *n.* vessel for heating water for power

bois-ter-ous *adj.* undisciplined **boisterousness** *n.*, **-ly** *adv.*

bold *adj.* courageous **boldness** *n.*, **boldly** *adv.*

bold-face *n.* style of printing

bo-le-ro *n.* short jacket

bo-lo-gna *n.* smoked sausage

bol-ster *n.* round pillow

bolt *n.* a threaded metal pin

bomb *n.* weapon detonated upon impact

bom-bard *v.* to attack repeatedly **bombardment** *n.*

bom-bast *n.* very ornate speech **bombastically** *adv.*, **-ic** *adj.*

bomber *n.* military aircraft

bo-na fide *adj.* genuine; authentic

bond *n.* something that binds together **bonded** *adj.*

bone *n.* connecting tissue of the skeleton

bon-fire *n.* open outdoor fire

bon-net *n.* woman's hat

bon-sai *n.* a small ornamental shrub

bo-nus *n.* over and above what is expected

bon voy-age *n.* farewell wish

boo *n.* disapproval or contempt

book *n.* literary work that is written or printed

book-keep-ing *n.* the person who records transactions of a business

boom *n.* deep, resonant sound

boo-mer-ang *n.* curved, flat missile

boon *n.* something that is pleasant

boor *n.* person with little refinement **boorish** *adj.*

boost *v.* to lift by pushing up

boost-er *n.* a promoter

boot *n.* covering for the foot

booth *n.* small compartment

bo-rax *n.* cleaning compound

bor-der *n.* the margin or the edge **borderline** *n.*

bore *v.* to make a hole

born *adj.* brought into life

bor-ough *n.* a self-governing town

bor-row *v.* receive money with the intentions of returning it

bos-om *n.* female's breasts

boss *n.* supervisor

bot-a-ny *n.* science of plants

botch *v.* to ruin something

both *adj.* two in conjunction

both-er *v.* pester or to harass someone **bothersome** *n.*

bot-tle *n.* a receptacle, made of glass

bot-tom *n.* lowest part

bot-u-lism *n.* food poisoning

bouil-lon *n.* clear broth

boul-der *n.* large round rock

boul-e-vard *n.* broad city street

bounce *v.* to leap suddenly

bound-a-ry *n.* limit or border

boun-te-ous *adj.* being plentiful

boun-ti-ful *adj.* being abundant

bounty *n.* generosity

bou-quet *n.* a group of cut flowers

bour-geois *pl.*, *n.* a member of the middle class

bout *n.* a contest

bou-tique *n.* small retail shop

bow *n.* front section of a boat

bow-el *n.* digestive tract

bowl *n.* container for food

bow-leg *n.* outward curve of the knee

box *n.* a small container

box-car *n.* enclosed railway car

box-er *n.* person who boxes professionally

box-office *n.* place for selling tickets

boy *n.* a male child

boy-cott *v.* means of protest

brace *n.* device that supports something

brace-let *n.* band for the wrist

brack-et *n.* support to hold a shelf

brad *n.* small nail

brag *v.* talk boastfully

braid *v.* to interweave

braille *n.* printing for the blind

brain *n.* nerve tissue enclosed in the cranium **-less** *adj.*

brake *n.* device to stop motion

bran *n.* husk of cereal grains

branch *n.* extension from the

trunk of a tree

bras-siere n. a woman's undergarment

brat-wurst n. fresh pork sausage

brave adj. having courage

bra-vo Interj. expressing approval

brawl n. noisy argument or fight

bray v. to make a loud cry

bra-zen adj. made of brass

breach n. ruptured, or broken

bread n. leavened food made from a flour and yeast

breadth n. measurement from side to side

break v. to separate something into parts -able adj.

break-down n. failure to function

breast n. milk-producing glandular organs

breath n. air inhaled and exhaled breathless adj.

breech n. buttocks

breed n. genetic strain of domestic animals -ing v.

breeze n. slight gentle wind

brev-i-ty n. a brief duration

brew v. to make beer

brew-er-y n. plant where beer is brewed

bribe v. to influence

brick n. a block of baked clay

bri-dal adj. to be relating to nuptial ceremony

bride n. woman just married

bride-groom n. man just married

brides-maid n. woman who attends a bride at her wedding

bridge n. structure over water

bri-dle n. harness used to guide a horse

brief n. concise, formal statement briefness n.

brief-case n. case for carrying papers or book

brig n. prison on a ship

bri-gade n. a military unit

brig-and n. a bandit

bright adj. being brilliant in color brightness n.

bril-liant adj. being very bright color brilliantly adj.

brim n. an edge or a rim of a cup brimming v.

brine n. salt water

bring v. carry with oneself

brink n. upper edge or margin

bri-oche n. a sweet roll

brisk adj. moving or acting quickly briskly adv.

bris-tle n. stiff and coarse

brit-tle adj. being very easy to break brittleness n.

broach n. tool used for enlarging hole

broad adj. to be covering a wide area broaden v.

broad-cast v. to make widely known; to transmit a program by television

broad-cloth n. a textured woolen cloth with a lustrous finish to it

broad-en v. to become or make wider or broader

broad-loom n. carpet woven on a wide loom

broad-mind-ed adj. fair; tolerant of varied views

broad-side n. side of a ship

bro-cade n. silk fabric having raised patterns

broc-co-li n. green vegetable which is from the cauliflower family

bro-chure n. a booklet

brogue n. a kind of strong regional accent

broil v. cook by direct heat

broil-er n. part of a stove that is used to broil meat

broke adj. being penniless

bro-ken adj. being separated into parts

bro-ken-hearted adj. overcome by grief or despair

bro-mide n. a sedative

bron-chi-al adj. pertaining to the bronchi -ly adv.

bronze n. an alloy of tin and copper

brooch n. a decorative pin

brood n. the young of an animal brooder n.

brook n. a small stream

broom n. an implement used for sweeping

broth n. juices from meat

broth-er n. male with the same parents

brow n. the ridge above the eye

brow-beat v. to bully

brown *n.* a dark yellowish red color

brown-ie *n.* chewy piece of chocolate cake

bruise *n.* an injury that ruptures small blood vessels

bru-net person with brown hair

brush *n.* device used for grooming hair

bru-tal *adj.* cruel treatment

bub-ble *n.* round hollow object

bub-ble gum *n.* chewing gum used to with make large bubbles

bu-bon-ic plague *n.* highly infectious disease causing death

buck *n.* adult male deer

buck-et *n.* a pail which is used to carry liquids or solids

buck-et seat *n.* a separate seat with a rounded back

buck-eye *n.* type of shrub having flower clusters and glossy brown nuts

buckle *v.* to warp

buck-ram *n.* fabric stiffened with a glue for the making of book covers

buck-shot *n.* a coarse lead shot for shotgun shells

buck-skin *n.* hide of a deer or buck, used as clothing

buck-tooth *n.* a large, prominently projecting front tooth, such as a rabbit's

buck-wheat *n.* grain used for pancakes, dark in color

bud *n.* something that is not developed completely

bud-dy *n.* a good companion, partner, or friend

budge *v.* to move slightly

budg-et *n.* total amount of money allocated **-ary** *adj.*

buff *v.* to polish

buf-fa-lo *n.* wild ox; bison

buff-er *n.* a tool used to polish or shine

buf-foon *n.* a clown **buffoonish** *adj.*, **buffoonery** *n.*

bug *n.* an insect **buggy** *adj.*

bug-gy *n.* small carriage

bu-gle *n.* a brass instrument

build *v.* to erect **builder** *n.*

build-ing *n.* roofed and walled structure which is used as a permanent dwelling

built--in *adj.* containing something within a structure

bulb *n.* electricity for lamps

bulge *n.* the swelling of the surface **bulgy** *adj.*

bulk *n.* large mass; anything **bulkiness** *n.*, **bulky** *adj.*

bulk-age *n.* a substance that increases the bulk of material in the intestine

bulk-head *n.* a retaining wall

bull *n.* adult male in cattle

bull-dog *n.* small, rough dog

bull-doze *v.* to dig up land

bull-dozer *n.* machine for moving earth

bul-let *n.* cylindrical projectile fired from a gun

bul-le-tin *n.* a public notice

bul-let-proof *adj.* condition which doesn't allow a bullet to pass through something

bull-fight *n.* fight between a bull and a man; Spanish tradition **-ing**, **-er** *n.*

bull-finch *n.* bird of Europe, kept as a pet

bull-frog *n.* type of a frog, large in size

bull-head-ed *adj.* headstrong and stubborn in character

bul-lion *n.* refined gold; gold bars, in the uncoined state

bull-ish *adj.* tending to cause or hopeful of rising prices, as in the stock market

bull-pen *n.* place where the pitcher of a baseball game warms up

bull ring *n.* area where a bullfight takes place

bull's eye *n.* the center of a target, as in shooting arrows

bul-ly *n.* a person who is mean and cruel to others

bul-rush *n.* tall grass as is found in a marsh

bul-wark *n.* defense; strong protection or support

bum *n.* one who begs from others **bummer** *adj.*

bum-ble-bee *n.* large hairy bee

bump *v.* to collide with **bumpy** *adj.*, **bumpiness** *n.*

bump-er *n.* device on the front of vehicles

bump-er--to--bump-er *adj.* a

long line of cars that is moving very slowly

bump-kin *n.* awkward person

bump-tious *adj.* forward; pushy **bumptiousness** *n.*

bunch *n.* group of items

bun-dle *n.* anything wrapped or held together **bundled, bundling** *v.*

bun-dle up *v.* to dress warmly, usually using many layers of clothing to stay warm

bung *n.* barrel stopper

bun-ga-low *n.* a small one-story cottage

bun-gle *v.* act clumsily

bun-ion *n.* the swelling of the big toe

bunk *n.* a small bed used for sleeping

bun-ker *n.* a tank for storing fuel on a ship

bun-kum *n.* meaningless talk

bun-ny *n.* small rabbit

bunt *v.* to tap a pitched ball

bunt-ing *n.* the hooded blanket for babies

buoy *n.* floating object to mark a channel

buoy-an-cy *n.* tendency to remain afloat

bur-den *n.* something hard to bear **burdensome** *adj.*

bur-dock *n.* coarse plant with purplish flowers

bu-reau *n.* a low chest for storing clothes

bu-reauc-ra-cy *n.* body of non-elected officials in a government

burg *n.* a town or city

bur-geon *v.* to put forth new life as in leaves or buds

bur-glar *n.* person who steals from others

bur-glar-ize *v.* to commit a burglary or intending to steal something

bur-glar-proof *adj.* being protected and secure against burglary

bur-gla-ry *n.* the breaking into and entering of a private home with the intent to steal

bur-i-al *n.* act of burying

burl *n.* a woody, often flat and hard, hemispherical growth on a tree

bur-lap *n.* coarse cloth

bur-lesque *n.* theatrical entertainment having comedy and imitations **-er** *n.*

bur-ly *adj.* very heavy and strong **-iness** *n.*, **-ily** *adv.*

burn *v.* be destroyed by fire **bruned** *v.*, **burning** *adj.*

bur-nish *v.* polish **burnisher** *n.*

burr *n.* rough edge

bur-ro *n.* a small donkey

bur-row *n.* tunnel dug by an animal **burrower** *n.*

burst *v.* to explode **-ing** *v.*

bury *v.* cover; hide

bus *n.* large passenger vehicle

bush *n.* dense tuft **bushy** *adj.*

bush-el *n.* unit of dry measurement which equals four pecks

bush-mas-ter *n.* a large venomous snake

bush-rang-er *n.* person who resides in the woods

bush-whack *v.* to ambush someone **-ing**, **-er** *n.*

busi-ness *n.* a person's occupation or job

bus-kin *n.* a boot which only extends halfway up the leg

bust *n.* female breast

bus-tle *n.* to busy oneself **bustling** *adj.*, **bustler** *n.*

bus-y *adj.* full of activity; occupied **busyness** *n.*

bus-y bod-y *n.* person concerned with others affairs

but *conj.* on the contrary to

butch-er *n.* one who slaughters animals

but-ler *n.* a male servant

butt *n.* the object of ridicule

but-ter-fat *n.* fat from milk

but-ter-fin-gers *n.* a clumsy person

but-ter-milk *n.* liquid that comes from churned milk

but-tocks *pl.*, *n.* two round fleshy parts of the rump

but-ton *n.* a small disk used to close a piece of garment

buy *v.* to purchase in exchange for money **buyable** *adj.*

buzz *v.* low vibrating sound

by *prep.* up to and beyond

by-gone *adj.* past

byte *n.* the binary digits in computers

C, c the third letter of the English alphabet

cab *n.* the car used to carry people for money

ca-bal *n.* group of people united in intrigue

ca-bal-le-ro *n.* horseman; Spanish gentleman

ca-ban-a *n.* beach house

cab-a-ret *n.* restaurant with entertainment

cab-bage *n.* type of vegetable with leaves making a head cabbaging, cabbaged *v.*

cab-bage palm *n.* type of palm with an edible bud

cab-by *n.* one drives a cab

ca-ber *n.* pole used for throwing to show one's strength

cab-in *n.* small house or hut; a room on a ship

ca-bin boy *n.* boy hired to wait on the passengers of a ship

cab-i-net *n.* storage unit

cab-i-net-mak-er *n.* one who makes cabinets

ca-ble *n.* thick rope or wire -bling, bled *v.*

ca-ble car *n.* vehicle used for transporting on a cable

ca-boose *n.* last train car

ca-chet *n.* seal on an envelope

cack-le *v.* to give off a noisy yell cackler *n.*

cac-tus *n.* plant with thorns which grows in the desert

ca-det *n.* military student

Cae-sar *n.* Roman leader

ca-fe *n.* small diner

caf-e-te-ri-a *n.* restaurant

caf-feine *n.* stimulant

cage *n.* enclosure to hold something caging, caged *v.*

cai-man *n.* type of crocodile

ca-jole *v.* to coax wrongfully cajolingly *adv.*, cajolery *n.*

cake *n.* sweet dessert caking, caked *v.*

cal-a-mine *n.* lotion for skin

ca-lam-i-ty *n.* a misfortune -tous *adj.*, -tousness *n.*

cal-ci-fy *v.* become like bone calcification *n.*, -fying *v.*

cal-ci-um *n.* element found in teeth and bones

cal-cu-late *v.* to find a sum calculation *n.*, calculated *adj.*

cal-cu-la-tor *n.* machine for

math operation

calf *n.* young animal offspring

calf-skin *n.* leather

call *v.* to call out; to telephone

call-ing *n.* a job

call num-ber *n.* numbers used for finding books at a library

cal-lous *adj.* tough as with skin calloused *adj.*

cal-low *adj.* being without experience

cal-lus *n.* the thickening of the skin

calm *adj.* absence of motion

cal-o-rie *n.* measurement of food energy

cam-er-a *n.* apparatus for taking pictures

cam-er-a-man *n.* one who uses a camera

cam-i-sole *n.* woman's dressing gown

cam-o-mile *n.* an herb

cam-ou-flage *n.* disguise to deceive enemy -ing, -ed *v.*

camp *n.* temporary lodging

cam-paign *n.* the actions taken before a political election campaigner *n.*

cam-pus *n.* the buildings of a school

cam-paign *n.* a political competition

ca-nal *n.* man-made water-way

ca-nard *n.* untrue story

ca-nar-y *n.* type of pet bird

ca-nas-ta *n.* card game

can-can *n.* dance having high kicks

can-cel *v.* to invalidate cancellation *n.*, -lable *adj.*

can-cer *n.* malignant tumor cancerous *adj.*, -ously *adv.*

can-de-la-brum *n.* type of candlestick

can-did *adj.* being very outspoken candidness *n.*

can-di-date *n.* person seeking an office candidacy *n.*

can-died *adj.* cook with sugar; to make sweet

can-dle *n.* wax lighting device candling, candled *v.*

can-dle-stick *n.* a candle holder

can-dy *n.* sweet treat made with sugar -dying, -died *v.*

can-dy strip-er *n.* a hospital volunteer

cane n. a walking stick
-**canng, caned** v.

ca-nine n. pertaining to dogs

can-is-ter n. container

can-ker n. type of blister on lips or in the mouth
cankerous adj., **cankering** v.

canned adj. saved for later use in a jar or can

can-nel coal n. a coal which burns a bright light

can-ner n. person who engages in canning of foods

can-ner-y n. place where canning is done

can-ni-bal n. person who eats the flesh of humans

can-non n. heavy war weapon

can-non ball n. object shot from a cannon, usually at a target

can-ny adj. careful; cautious
canniness n., **cannily** adv.

ca-noe n. lightweight boat
-**ist** n., -**ing**, -**ed** v.

can-o-py n. an overhang

can-ta-loupe n. an orange muskmelon

can-ter n. slow gallop

can-vas n. a heavy woven fabric

can-vass v. seek **canvasser** n.

can-yon n. deep gorge

cap n. covering for the head

ca-pa-ble adj. having ability

ca-pa-cious adj. to be holding much

ca-pac-i-ty n. volume

ca-par-i-son n. a type of horse covering

cape n. covering for the shoulders

cap-il-lary n. small vessels that connect **capillarity** n.

cap-i-tal n. seat of government

Cap-i-tol n. U.S. Congress meeting place

ca-pit-u-late v. surrender **capitulator** n. **capitulation** n.

ca-pon n. a rooster

ca-pote n. a hooded cloak

ca-price n. change of mind on a whim **capriciously** adv.

cap-ri-ole n. type of a jump **caprioling, caprioled** v.

cap-size v. to overturn a boat **capsizing, capsized** v.

cap-sule n. small type of container **capsular** adj.

cap-tain n. a chief leader

cap-ti-vate v. to charm; to attract by beauty

cap-tive n. a prisoner **captivity** n.

cap-ture v. take by force

car-at n. unit weight for precious gems

car-cass n. the dead body of an animal

car-di-ol-o-gy n. the study of the heart

care n. concern

ca-reer n. profession life

care-free adj. free from worries

care-ful adj. exercising care

ca-ress v. to touch

car-go n. freight

car-na-tion n. fragrant flower

car-ni-val n. an amusement show

car-ol n. joyous song of praise

car-pen-ter n. one who works with lumber

car-pet n. floor covering

car-rot n. orange vegetable

car-rou-sel n. a merry-go-round

car-ry v. to transport

cart n. two-wheeled vehicle

car-ti-lage n. elastic bone-like tissue **cartilaginous** adj.

car-toon n. funny caricature

carve v. slice; cut

case n. particular occurrence

cash-ier n. person who handles cash in a store

ca-si-no n. the public place used for gambling

cas-ket n. a coffin

cas-se-role n. a baking dish

cas-sette n. magnetic tape

cast v. to throw something with force **castaway** adj.

cast-er n. the wheels which are under furniture

cas-tle n. large, stone dwelling

cast-off adj. discarded

cas-trate v. remove testicles

ca-su-al adj. informal

ca-su-al-ty n. injured person

cat-a-log n. publication of a list of names **cataloging, -loged** v., **-logist, -loger** n.

ca-tal-pa n. tree with leaves shaped like hearts

ca-tal-y-sis n. an agent introduced to bring about desired chemical change in something **catalytic** *adj*.

cat-a-ma-ran *n*. flat boat made of logs

cat-a-mount *n*. member of the wildcat family

cat-a-pult *n*. the weapon used to launch large objects at the enemy

cat-a-ract *n*. an eye disease

ca-tarrh *n*. mucous membrane inflammation

ca-tas-tro-phe *n*. sudden disaster **catastrophic** *adj*.

cat-bird *n*. bird that makes a cry like a cat

cat-boat *n*. type of a sailboat

cat-call *n*. yell which is very shrill in sound

catch *v*. to capture

cat-e-go-ry *n*. grouping **categorical** *adj*., **categorize** *v*.

ca-ter *v*. to provide a food service **caterer** *n*.

cat-er-pil-lar *n*. larva of a moth

cat-er-waul *v*. making a sound that a cat makes

cat-fish *n*. scaleless, freshwater fish

cat-gut *n*. rope made from sheep intestines

ca-the-dral *n*. large church

cath-e-ter *n*. tube put into body to drain cavities

cath-ode *n*. a negative electrode

cat-tle *n*. farm animals

cau-li-flow-er *n*. vegetable

caulk *v*. to seal against leakage

cause *v*. produce a result

cau-ter-ize *v*. to sear with a hot instrument

cau-tion *n*. a warning

cau-tious *adj*. very careful

cav-al-ry *n*. army troops

cave *n*. underground tomb

ca-vern *n*. a large underground cave **cavernous** *adj*.

cav-i-ty *n*. decayed place

cease *v*. to put an end to something **ceaseless** *adj*.

cease-fire *n*. to stop fighting

ce-cum *n*. sac of the large intestine **cecal** *adj*.

ce-dar *n*. an evergreen tree

ce-dar wax-wing *n*. bird of North America

cede *v*. to surrender

ceil-ing *n*. an overhead covering

cel-an-dine *n*. herb of the poppy family

cel-e-brant *n*. the person which celebrates

cel-e-brate *v*. to observe an event with ceremonies **celebrator**, **celebration** *n*.

cel-e-brat-ed *adj*. state of being well-known

ce-leb-ri-ty *n*. a famous person; well-known

ce-ler-i-ty *n*. quickness

ce-les-tial *adj*. heavenly

cell *n*. a small room

cel-lar *n*. underground area

cel-lo *n*. stringed instrument large in size **cellist** *n*.

ce-ment *v*. to bond

cem-e-ter-y *n*. a place for burying

cen-sor *n*. one who examines **censorial**, **censorship** *n*.

cen-so-ri-ous *adj*. being very picky

cen-sus *n*. official count **censusing**, **censused** *v*.

cen-taur *n*. being believed to be half horse and half man

cen-te-na-ry *n*. a period of one hundred years

cen-ter *n*. equal distance from all sides

cen-tral *adj*. center; main

cen-tu-ry *n*. 100 years

cer-e-bel-lum *n*. lower part of the brain

cer-e-brum *n*. the upper part of the brain

cer-e-mo-ny *n*. a ritual

cer-tain *adj*. being without any doubt

cer-tif-i-cate *n*. a document of truth

cer-ti-fy *v*. to declare in writing to be true

chafe *v*. to irritate

chain *v*. to fasten

chal-ice *n*. drinking goblet

chalk *n*. soft limestone used for writing

chalk-board *n*. blackboard

chal-lenge *n*. contest demand

cham-ber *n*. bedroom; hall

champ *n*. champion

chance *v*. to risk

chan-cel-lor n. chief director

chan-de-lier n. light fixture

change v. to become different; to alter **changeable** adj.

chan-nel n. deepest part of a river or harbor -led v.

chant n. type of song

cha-os n. total disorder

chap n. a fellow

chap-el n. a place to worship

chap-er-on n. supervisor

chap-lain n. a religious clergyman **chaplaincy** n.

chap-ter n. one division of a book

char-ac-ter n. a persons quality

char-coal n. a carbonaceous material

charge v. give responsibility

char-i-ot n. ancient horse-drawn vehicle

char-i-ty n. money for the needy; helpfulness

charm n. ability to delight

chart n. map, or graph

char-ter n. document granting privileges **charterer** n.

chase v. to pursue

chas-tise v. to reprimand

chat v. to talk friendly

chat-tel n. movable property

chauf-feur n. person who drives someone

cheap adj. being inexpensive **cheapen** v., **cheapness** n.

check v. restrain; stop

check-ers n. board game

ched-dar n. a yellow cheese

cheek n. face below the eye

cheese n. milk product

chef n. male cook

chem-ist n. person versed in chemistry **chemistry** n.

che-mo-ther-a-py n. treatment for a disease

cher-ish v. to hold dear

chess n. a board game

chest n. the upper part of one's body; trunk

chest-nut n. tree with edible nuts

chew v. grind with the teeth

chick n. young bird **chicken** n.

chief n. the person of highest rank; head of a group

chif-fon n. sheer fabric

chif-fo-nier n. the chest of drawers

chig-ger n. a mite; insect

child n. young person

chill v. to be cold **chilly** adj.

chim-ney n. flue for smoke

chim-pan-zee n. an anthropoid ape and small in size

chin n. lower part of the face

chintz-y adj. being cheap

chip n. a small broken off piece of something

chi-ro-prac-tic n. a method of therapy for bones

chis-el n. a tool having a sharp edge **chiseler** n.

choc-o-late n. preparation from cocoa beans

choir n. organized group of singers

chop v. cut into small pieces

chop-py adj. rough

chop--sticks pl., n. slender sticks used for eating

chore n. a daily task

cho-re-a n. an acute nervous disease

cho-rus n. people who sing together as a group

cho-sen adj. being selected

Christ n. Jesus

chris-ten v. to baptize

chron-ic adj. frequently recurring **chronically** adv.

chron-i-cle n. the record of events taking place

chum n. close friend or pal

ci-gar n. rolled tobacco leaves used for smoking

cig-a-rette n. tobacco rolled in thin paper saddle

cin-e-ma n. motion picture

cin-na-mon n. a spice

cir-cle n. a process that ends at its beginning

cir-cu-late v. to pass from place to place

cir-cum-stance n. a condition

cir-cum-vent v. to outwit

cir-cus n. traveling entertainment featuring clowns

cir-rho-sis n. liver disease

cit-i-zen n. resident of a town or city **citizenship** n.

cit-y n. large community

civ-il adj. to be relating to citizens **civilian** n.

civ-i-li-za-tion n. high level of cultural

claim v. ask for one's due

clair-voy-ance n. a sharp insight clairvoyant adj.
clam n. bivalve mollusks
clam-my adj. damp and cold
clam-or n. a loud noise
clamp n. device for holding
clap v. to applaud
clap-board n. board covering for a house
clar-i-fy v. make clearer
clar-i-ty n. clearness
clash v. to collide
clasp v. to hold
class n. a group of people
clas-sic adj. belonging in a certain category
clas-si-fy v. arrange in order
clat-ter n. rattling sound
clav-i-cle n. the collarbone
claw v. to scratch
clay n. an earth substance
clean adj. being free from impurities
cleanse v. to make clean cleanser n.
clear adj. to be free from doubt clearance n.
cleat n. metal shoe spike
cleav-age n. division
cleav-er n. type of large knife
clef n. musical staff symbol
cler-gy n. religious leaders
cler-i-cal adj. relating to office duties clerically adv.
clerk n. store or office worker
clev-er adj. mentally quick
cli-ent n. the person who receives
cliff n. steep edge
cli-mate n. weather conditions
cli-max n. the peak of greatest intensity
climb v. to move up
clinch v. to secure; to fasten
cling v. to hold fast to
clin-ic n. a medical establishment clinical adj.
clink v. to cause a ringing sound
clip v. to cut off
clip-per n. a sailing vessel
clique n. an exclusive group
clob-ber v. to hit repeatedly
clock n. an instrument that measures time
clod n. large piece earth
clog v. to choke up
clone n. an identical reproduc-

tion of something
close adj. near, as in time
clos-et n. a small cabinet
clot n. a thick or solid mass
clothe v. provide clothes
clout n. a heavy blow
clove n. type of spice
clo-ver n. herb with trifoliolate leaves
club n. heavy stick
clump n. mass clumpy adj.
clus-ter n. bunch; a group
clutch v. seize and hold tightly
clut-ter n. disorder
coach n. director of athletics
coal n. carbon mineral
coarse adj. to be lacking refinement coarsely adv.
coast n. shoreline
coat n. outer garment
coax v. to persuade by tact
cob n. male swan
cob-ble v. to make or to repair shoes cobbler n.
co-bra n. venomous snake
cob-web n. a spider's web
co-caine n. narcotic drug
coch-le-a n. inner ear tube
cock-ade n. a hat badge
cock-a-too n. crested parrot
cock-pit n. pilot area
cock-roach n. a black, nocturnal insect
co-coa n. ground cocoa seeds
co-coon n. silky, protective covering of insects
cod n. fish of North Atlantic
code n. system of secret writing
co-ed-u-ca-tion n. educating of both men and women
co-erce v. dominate force
co-ex-ist v. exist at the same
cof-fee n. beverage
cof-fin n. casket for burying a corpse
cog n. projection in a gear wheel
co-gent adj. to be compelling
cog-i-tate v. think carefully
co-gnac n. a brandy
cog-nate adj. from a common ancestor cognately adv.
co-hab-it v. to live as husband and wife cohabitation n.
co-here v. hold together
co-hort n. a partner
coil n. a series of connecting rings coilability n.

coin n. flat, metal money

co-in-cide v. to agree exactly

co-in-ci-dence n. two events happening at the same time

cold adj. to be of a low temperature **coldness** n.

cold--blood-ed adj. done without feeling

col-ic n. sharp pain **-icky** adj.

col-i-se-um n. large building

col-lab-o-rate v. work together

col-lapse v. to fall

col-lar n. something encircling the neck **collarless** adj.

col-late v. in sequence; arrange

col-lect v. to gather

col-lege n. institution of higher education **collegian** n.

col-lide v. to come together

col-lu-sion n. a secret agreement **collisional** adj.

co-lon n. punctuation mark (:)

colo-nel n. army officer

col-o-ny n. group living in a new land

col-or n. a hue or tint **colorful** adj.

col-or--blind adj. unable to distinguish colors

co-los-sal adj. enormous

colt n. young horse

col-umn n. supporting pillar

col-um-nist n. person who writes an article

co-ma n. deep sleep

comb n. instrument to keep hair neat

com-bat v. to oppose

com-bi-na-tion n. process of combining **-al** adj.

com-bine v. to unite

com-bus-tion n. burning

come v. to arrive

com-e-dy n. humorous actor

com-et n. celestial body

com-fort v. to relieve comfortable **adj.**

com-fort-er n. heavy blanket

com-ic adj. characteristic of comedy **comical** adj.

com-ma n. the punctuation mark (,)

com-mand v. to rule over

com-mence v. to begin

com-mence-ment n. graduation from a school

com-mend v. to give praise

com-men-su-rate adj. to be equal to something

com-ment n. statement **-ary** n.

com-merce n., v. trade

com-mer-cial adj. relating to a product **commercially** adv.

com-mis-sion n. money paid for selling **commissioner** n.

com-mit-tee n. group of persons working together

com-mode n. movable toilet

com-mo-di-ous adj. roomy

com-mo-dore n. a naval officer

com-mon adj. being general; ordinary **commonness** n.

com-mu-ni-cate v. to make known **communicative** adj.

com-mu-ni-ca-tion n. act of transmitting ideas

com-mun-ion n. the sharing of things

com-mu-ni-ty n. people living in the same area

com-pact adj. being packed together **compactible** adj.

com-pan-ion n. an associate

com-pa-ny n. guests; business organization

com-pa-ra-ble adj. capable of comparison **-ness** n.

com-pare v. to note the similarities of things

com-part-ment n. an enclosed area **compartmental** adj.

com-pass n. an instrument used to determine direction

com-pas-sion n. sympathy

com-pat-i-ble adj. able to get along together **-ness** n.

com-pel v. to urge or to force action **-ler** n., **-lable** adj.

com-pen-sate v. make up for

com-pete v. to contend with

com-pe-tent adj. being capable, skillful **-ly** adv.

com-pe-ti-tion n. a rivalry

com-pet-i-tor n. one who competes

com-pile v. to put together information **compiler** n.

com-plain-ant n. person filing a formal charge

com-plaint n. the expression of an objection

com-plai-sance n. the willingness to please another

com-ple-ment n. something that adds to another

com-plete adj. being whole

com-plex *adj.* difficult **-ity** *n.*

com-plex-ion *n.* the natural skin color **complexional** *adj.*

com-pli-ance *n.* an agreement

com-pli-cate *v.* make something complex **-ed** *v.*

com-pli-ment *n.* praise

com-ply *v.* to agree, to consent

com-po-nent *n.* a constituent part **componential** *adj.*

com-port *v.* to agree; to behave **comportment** *n.*

com-pose *v.* to create something **composed** *v.*

com-pos-ite *adj.* made of separate elements or parts

com-post *n.* fertilizing mixture

com-po-sure *n.* tranquillity

com-pote *n.* fruit preserved syrup

com-pound *n.* combination of two or more parts

com-pre-hend *v.* to understand something **-ible** *adj.*

com-pro-mise *v.* to settle by yielding **compromiser** *n.*

comp-trol-ler *n.* person that examines accounts

com-pute *v.* to determine sum through math

com-puter *n.* speed machine

com-rade *n.* an associate or a friend **comradeship** *n.*

con-cat-e-nate *v.* to join, connect **concatenation** *n.*

con-cave *adj.* curved inward

con-ceal *v.* to hide **-ment** *n.*

con-cede *v.* to yield

con-ceive *v.* to understand

con-cen-trate *v.* to give intense thought **concentrative** *adj.*

con-cept *n.* idea, thought

con-cep-tion *n.* a beginning

con-cern *v.* to care about

con-cert *n.* musical performance **concerted** *adj.*

con-cise *adj.* short **-ly** *adj.*

con-clave *n.* private meeting

con-clude *v.* bring to an end

con-cord *n.* accord **-dance** *n.*

con-crete *adj.* actual **-ness** *n.*

con-cur *v.* to agree or express approval of **concurrence** *n.*

con-cus-sion *n.* a sudden brain injury **concussive** *adj.*

con-demn *v.* to find to be wrong **condemner** *n.*

con-di-ment *n.* a spice

con-di-tion *n.* a state of existence **conditionable** *adj.*

con-di-tioned *adj.* accustomed

con-done *v.* to overlook

con-duct *v.* to direct

con-duc-tor *n.* a person who leads **conductional** *adj.*

cone *n.* tapered form

con-fec-tion-er-y *n.* candy and sweets as a whole

con-fed-er-a-cy *n.* union of states **confederalist** *n.*

con-fed-er-ate *n.* ally or friend

con-fer *v.* consult with

con-fess *v.* to admit **-ional** *n.*

con-fet-ti *pl., n.* small pieces of colored paper for tossing

con-fide *v.* to entrust a secret

con-fi-dence *n.* self-assurance

con-fi-den-tial *adj.* being secret

con-fine *v.* to keep within a boundary **confinement** *n.*

con-firm *v.* to verify

con-fis-cate *v.* to seize

con-flict *n.* a battle

con-found *v.* to confuse **-er** *n.*

con-front *v.* to oppose **-er** *n.*

con-fuse *v.* mislead **-ingly** *adv.*

con-fute *v.* prove to be invalid

con-geal *v.* to jell **-ment** *n.*

con-gen-i-tal *adj.* inherited

con-grat-u-late *v.* to acknowledge efforts **-lation** *n.*

con-gre-gate *v.* to assemble together **congregation** *n.*

con-jec-ture *n.* an uncertain opinion **conjecturer** *n.*

con-ju-gate *adj.* join in pairs

con-junct *adj.* being combined

con-junc-ti-va *n.* membrane part of eyelids

con-jure *v.* to bring into the mind **conjurer** *n.*

con-nect *v.* to join **-ion** *n.*

con-nive *v.* to plot secretly

con-quer *v.* to subdue; to win

con-scious *adj.* aware; alert

con-sec-u-tive *adj.* following uninterrupted

con-sent *v.* to agree

con-serve *v.* to save

con-sid-er *v.* regard **considerable** *adj.*

con-sign *v.* to deliver

con-sist *v.* to be made up of

con-sis-ten-cy *n.* degree of texture

con-sole *v.* to comfort

con-sol-i-date v. to combine in one consolidator n.

con-sort n. a companion

con-spir-a-cy n. a plan

con-spire v. to plan in secret

con-sta-ble n. peace officer

con-stant adj. faithful

con-sti-pa-tion n. unable to empty bowels

con-sti-tu-tion n. fundamental laws, governing a nation constitutional adj.

con-strain v. to restrain by force constrainedly adv.

con-straint n. force; confinement

con-struct v. to build -tion n.

con-strue v. to interpret

con-sul n. government official living foreign country

con-sult v. to compare views

con-sume v. to absorb -er n.

con-sum-mate v. to conclude something consummator n.

con-tact n. to touch

con-ta-gion n. to spread

con-tain v. to include -er v.

con-tam-i-nate v. to pollute

con-tempt n. hate -ibleness n.

con-tend v. to dispute

con-tent n. main substance

con-ten-tion n. strife

con-test n. strife; rivalry

con-ti-nent n. land mass

con-tin-ue v. to happen without interruption continuer n.

con-tort v. twist out of shape

con-tract n. a formal agreement contractible adj.

con-tra-dict v. to oppose

con-trast v. to note the differences contrastable adj.

con-trib-ute v. to give

con-trol v. to have direct authority controllable adj.

con-tro-ver-sy n. a dispute

con-vent n. a home for nuns

con-ven-tion n. a formal meeting -alism n., -ally adv.

con-verge v. come together

con-ver-sa-tion n. an informal talk or discussion

con-vert-i-ble adj. car with a removable top

con-vex adj. curved outward

con-vey v. to transport something conveyance n.

con-vict v. to prove guilty

con-voy n. vehicles traveling together

con-vulse v. shake violently

cook v. to prepare food

cook-ie n. sweet, flat cake

cool adj. without warmth

co-op-er-ate v. work together

co-or-di-nate n. put together

cope v. to strive for

co-pi-lot n. an assistant pilot

cop-per n. a metallic element

copy v. to reproduce an original copyright n.

cord n. a string

cor-dial adj. warm-hearted

cor-du-roy n. durable fabric

core n. center of soemthing

cork n. the outside surface of a tree

cork-screw n. a device used to remove corks

corn n. yellow vegetable

cor-ne-a n. the eyeball covering

cor-ner n. the outer edge of an angle

cor-o-nar-y adj. of the heart

cor-po-rate adj. joint -ly adv.

cor-po-ra-tion n. a united merchants

corpse n. dead body

cor-ral n. animal enclosure

cor-rect v. to make right

cor-re-spond v. to communicate by written words

cor-ri-dor n. long hall

cor-ri-gi-ble adj. able to correct

cor-rob-o-rate v. to support

cor-rupt adj. dishonest; evil

cor-sage n. flower worn by a women on her lapel

cos-met-ic n. preparation for the face

cos-mos n. the universe

cost n. the price

cos-tume n. a disguise; clothing costumey adj.

cot n. a small, bed

cot-tage n. a small house

cot-ton n. the fabric

couch n. the sofa

cough v. to expel air from the lungs

coun-cil n. the people assembled for consultation

coun-sel n. advice, guide

count v. to find the total amount

count-down n. a descending

order of counting

coun-te-nance n. face

counter-act v. oppose **-ion** n.

counter-attack n. attack against an enemy attack

counter-feit v. to forge

coun-try n. given area

coun-ty n. division of state

cou-ple n. a pair

cou-pon n. certificate

cour-age n. mental or moral strength **courageous** adj.

course n. a path

court n. where trials are conducted

cour-te-ous adj. kind, polite

cour-te-sy n. polite behavior

cous-in n. the child of uncle or aunt

cove n. inlet of water

cov-e-nant n. a binding agreement

cov-er v. to place something over something

cov-ert adj. hidden; secret

cow n. mature female of cattle

cow-ard n. one with great fear

cow-boy n. cattle herder

coy adj. quiet or shy

coy-ote n. prairie wolf

co-zy adj. being comfortable

crab n. shellfish

crab-by adj. ill tempered

crack v. to break without separating

cra-dle n. a small bed used for infants

craft n. special skill or ability

cram v. pack tightly or stuff

cramp n. a muscle contraction causing pain

cran-ber-ry n. a sour red berry

crane n. bird

cra-ni-um n. skull

crank n. the machine arm for turning

crank-y adj. grouchy

crash v. to break violently

cra-ter n. volcano opening

crave v. to desire

crawl v. to move slowly

cray-on n. wax for drawing

craze v. to make insane

cream n. fatty part of milk

crease n. fold in a material

cre-ate v. to make

cre-a-tion n. the universe

cred-it n. trust; amount allowed to spend

creep v. to advance at a slow pace **creeper** n.

cre-mate v. to reduce something to ashes

cre-scen-do adv. loudness increase

cres-cent n. the first quarter of the moon

crest n. top of a mountain

cre-vasse n. deep crack

crew n. group

crib n. the small bed for an infant

crick-et n. insect

crime n. an act forbidden by law **criminal** n.

crimp v. to cause to become bent or wavy

cringe v. to recoil in fear

crip-ple v. to disabled

cri-sis n. an unstable time

crisp adj. easily broken

crit-ic n. a person who is critical about something

crit-i-cal adj. very important

crit-i-cism n. act of criticizing

crit-i-cize v. to find fault with

croc-o-dile n. large reptile

cro-ny n. close friend; buddy

crook n. bend; a dishonest, fraudulent person

croon v. to sing

crop n. a food plant

cross n. an upright post and crossbar

crouch v. bend at the knees

croup n. a throat disease

crow n. large, black bird

crowd n. large group

crown n. top of something

cru-cial adj. extremely important **crucially** adv.

cru-ci-fy v. to put to death by nailing to a cross

crude adj. unrefined; rough

crumb n. small piece of bread

crum-ble v. break into small pieces; collapse

crunch v. to chew with a crackling noise

cru-sade n. religious journey

crush v. to squeeze with pressure

crust n. hardened covering

crux n. an essential point

cry v. to shed tears

crypt n. an underground burial place for the dead

cry-stal n. mineral; glass

cub n. a young animal

cube n. solid with six sides

cud-dle v. caress fondly

cue n. a signal given

cuff n. lower part of pants

cui-sine n. style

cull v. to select the best

cul-prit n. a person who is guilty of a crime

cul-ti-vate v. to improve land

cul-ture n. developing intellectual cultured adj.

cum-ber-some adj. clumsy

cum-mer-bund n. wide piece of material worn around the waist

cu-mu-late v. collect -tion n.

cu-mu-la-tive adj. to become larger in amount

cu-mu-lo-nim-bus n. type of cloud; thundercloud

cup n. drinking container holding eight ounces of liquid or dry material

cup-board n. closet for storing dishes

cup-cake n. small cake, baked in individual cups

cup-ful n. the amount that one cup holds

curb n. something that restrains curbable adj.

cur-dle v. to coagulate; to go bad or spoil

cure n. the recovery from a sickness cureless adj.

cur-few n. a signal used to clear the streets

cu-ri-os-i-ty n. one's inquisitiveness

cu-ri-ous adj. questioning

curl v. twist into curves

cur-rant n. small, edible, round fruit

cur-ren-cy n. money; coins

cur-rent adj. present time

cur-ric-u-lum n. the school courses one's takes

cur-ry v. groom a horse

cur-ry-comb n. comb used to brush and clean horses

cursor n. a computer screen indicator

cur-sive n. method of writing

cur-so-ry adj. done rapidly

without paying attention to details -ly adv., -ness n.

curt adj. being abrupt

curtly adj., curtness n.

cur-tail v. to shorten

curtailment n.

cur-tain n. window covering

cush-ion n. pillow

cus-tard n. dessert

cus-to-di-an n. caretaker

cus-tom n. an accepted practice of someone

cus-tom-ar-y adj. according to established usage

customarly adv., -ness n.

cus-tom-ize v. to design to individual specifications

cus-tom--made adj. something made to order

cut back v. to prune; to reduce

cute adj. attractive in a manner that is delightful

cut glass n. glass shaped and decorated by using a cutting instrument or tool

cu-ti-cle n. the non-living skin which is located around one's nails

cut-less n. short, heavy sword

cut-lery n. eating and cooking instruments

cut-let n. thin piece of meat

cut-ter n. fast-sailing vessel

cy-a-nide n. type of poison

cy-a-no-sis n. the blueness of the skin

cy-cle v. ride bikes cyclist n.

cy-clic adj. referring or pertaining to a cycle

cy-clone n. a storm with strong winds

cyl-in-der n. a long, round body or shape cylindric n.

cyn-i-cal adj. sarcastic; sneering cynically adv.

cy-press n. an evergreen tree of the pine family

cyst n. an abnormal sac that contains fluid

cys-tic fi-bro-sis n. a hereditary childhood disease the involves the lungs and pancreas

cy-tol-o-gy n. scientific study of the functions, structure, and life cycle of cells

cytologist n.

czar n. emperor or king

D, d the fourth letter of the English alphabet

dab *v.* to touch quickly with light, short strokes **dabbing, dabbed** *v.*

dab-ber *n.* a brush used to ink engraving plates

dab-ble *v.* to play in water or other liquid with the hands **dabbling, dabbled** *v.*

dab-bler *n.* one who is not deeply concerned with something

dab-chick *n.* a small grebes

da ca-po *adv.* direction in music meaning from the beginning

dace *n.* a freshwater cyprinid fish found in Europe

dachs-hund *n.* small dog having very short legs and a long body of German origin

da-cron *n.* synthetic fiber

dac-ty-lol-o-gy *n.* communicating thoughts and ideas with the fingers

dad *n.* Father

da-da *n.* type of art where traditional artistic values are negated

dad-dy--long-legs *n.* a long-legged spider having a rounded body

da-do *n.* part of a column between a base and surbase

daff *v.* to put something off

daf-fo-dil *n.* bulbous plant with solitary yellow flowers

daf-fy *adj.* being foolish

daft *adj.* to be weird or silly **daftly** *adv.*, **daftness** *n.*

dag-ger *n.* a pointed short-edged weapon

da-guerre-o-type *n.* type of photographic method

dah *n.* the dash in a telegraphic code

dahl-ia *n.* perennial plant with tuberous roots

dai-ly *adj.* to be occurring or happening every day of the week, month, and year

dai-ly dou-ble *n.* a bet that is won by picking the winners of two races on the same day

dain-ty *adj.* delicately beautiful; having refined taste; pleasing

daintiness *n.*, **daintily** *adv.*

dai-qui-ri *n.* cold, slushy alcoholic drink

dair-y *n.* the place which processes milk for resale

dairying *v.*, **dairymaid** *n.*

dair-y cat-tle *n.* the cattle used for dairy products

dair-y-ing *n.* the business a producing dairy products

dair-y-man *n.* person who works at a dairy

da-is *n.* raised platform

dai-sy *n.* kind of yellow flower having yellow disks and white rays

dal-a-pon *n.* type of herbicide used for unwanted grasses

dale *n.* kind of valley which is small in size

dales-man *n.* a person born or living in a dale

dal-ly *v.* waste time; to dawdle; to flirt **dalliance, dallies** *n.*, **dallying, -lied** *v.*

dam *n.* type of barrier which is used for raising water

damming, dammed *v.*

dam-age *n.* an injury occurring to something or someone **damageable** *adj.*, **damaging, damaged** *v.*

dam-a-scene *v.* to be etching designs into something **damascening, damascened** *v.*

dam-ask *n.* a kind of reversible fabric

dam-ask steel *n.* the metal used for swords

dame *n.* mature woman

damp *adj.* between dry and wet

damp-en *v.* to make wet

damp-er *v.* to depress something

dam-sel *n.* a maiden

dam-son *n.* a type of small purple plum

dance *v.* move rhythmically to music **dancing, danced** *v.*

dan-de-lion *n.* a kind of weed, usually having yellow flowers and a leafy base

dan-der *n.* ones temper

dan-dle *v.* act of moving slowly on a person's arms

dan-druff *n.* scaly material on the scalp

dan-dy *n.* person who dresses

very nicely

dandiest, dandier adj., **-ism** n.

dan-ger n. exposure to injury

dangerous adj., **-ousness** n.

dan-gle v. to hang loose; swing to and fro **-gling** adj., **-er** n.

dank adj. wet and cold

dankness n., **dankly** adv.

dan-seuse n. ballet dancer

dap-per adj. stylishly dressed

dap-ple n. colored spots

dappled adj., **-pling**, **-pled** v.

dare v. risk; challenge

dare-devil n. person who is foolhardy

dar-ing n. braveness **-ly** adv.

dark adj. lacking light

-ness n., **-ish** adj., **-ly** adv.

Dark Ag-es n. period in time of the Middle Ages

dark-en v. to cause something to become dark

dark lan-tern n. lantern held in the hand with a slide which covers the light hole

dark room n. place used to develop pictures

dar-ling n. someone very dear

darlingness n., **darlingly** adv.

darn v. to mend a hole **-er** n.

dart n. pointed missile

dart-er n. fish of the perch family which moves quickly

dash v. to move quickly

dash-board n. panel of instruments in a car

dash-ing adj. to be showy

das-tard n. a frightful person

dastardly adj., **-liness** n.

da-ta pl., n. facts from which conclusions may be drawn

da-ta proc-ess-ing n. using computers to process material or data

date n. particular point in time

dateable adj., **dating** n.

date-less adj. to be undated or without a date

date line n. imaginary line; date of newspaper

da-tive adj. referring to indirect object of a sentence

da-tum n. something that is used for research

daub v. to cover up **dauber** n.

daugh-ter n. female child of a man or woman

daunt v. discourage

dauntless adj., **-lessly** adv.

dav-en-port n. sofa

dav-it n. tool used in boats to lower boats to the water, such a lifeboat

daw-dle v. to waste

dawdler n., **-ing**, **-ed** v.

dawn n. beginning of a new day

day n. time that falls between dawn and nightfall

day-break n. the beginning of daylight

day-care n. child care service for working parents

day-dream n. a dream dreamt while one is awake **-er** n.

daze v. to bewilder

-edly adv., **-ing**, **-ed** v.

daz-zle v. to overcome with brightness **-zling** adj., **-er** n.

dea-con n. a clergyman

deaconship, deaconry n.

dead adj. without life; dormant

dead-beat n. the person who does not want to pay for things they get

dead-en v. to dull the pain of something **deadener** n.

dead-end n. cannot progress

dead let-ter n. mail unable to be delivered by the post office

dead-line n. time limit when something must be finished

dead-lock n. a stopping due to different ideas

dead-ly adj. fatal

dead-pan adj. without facial expression

dead reck-on-ing n. figuring out the local of a ship

dead-wood n. of a tree, the dead branches

deaf adj. unable to hear

deafness n., **deafly** adv.

deaf-en v. use of a loud noise to stun one for a while

deal v. to distribute playing cards **dealer** n.

deal-er-ship n. franchise to sell certain items

deal-ing n. involved in the traffic of illegal drugs

dean n. the head of a school or college

dear adj. greatly cherished

dearly adv., **dearness** n.

death n. termination

deathly *adv.*, **deathless** *adj.*

death-bed *n.* a bed on which a person dies

death-blow *n.* a hard hit which causes the death of something or someone

death-ly *adj.* being fatal; causing death

death rate *n.* ratio of deaths to the population of an area

death-trap *n.* unsafe structure

death-war-rant *n.* a document stating the execution of someone

death-watch *n.* the vigil kept on a dying person

deb *n.* debutante

de-ba-cle *n.* sudden downfall

de-bar *v.* to prohibit something **debarment** *n.*

de-bark *v.* disembark **-ation** *n.*

de-base *v.* demean **-ment** *n.*

de-bate *v.* to consider something **debater** *n.*, **-able** *adj.*

de-bauch *v.* to corrupt **debauchment**, **-ery**, **-er** *n.*

de-ben-ture *n.* voucher given as acknowledgment of a debt

de-bil-i-tate *v.* to make something feeble **-tation** *n.*

de-bil-i-ty *n.* weakness

deb-it *n.* an item that is recorded in an account

de-brief *v.* interrogate in order to obtain information

de-bris *n.* discarded waste

debt *n.* that which someone owes

debt-or *n.* one who owes money or something else

de-bug *v.* to remove concealed listening devices

de-bunk *v.* to expose false pretensions **debunker** *n.*

de-but *n.* first appearance

deb-u-tante *n.* young woman making her debut in society

de-cade *n.* period of ten years

dec-a-logue *or* **dec-a-log** *n.* The Ten Commandments

de-cant-er *n.* decorative bottle

de-cap-i-tate *v.* to behead the head of something **-tion** *n.*

dec-a-pod *n.* crustacean that has ten feet

de-cath-lon *n.* athletic contest with ten events

de-cay *v.* to rot

de-cease *v.* to die **deceased** *adj.*

de-ceit *n.* deception

deceitful *adj.*, **-fully** *adv.*

de-ceive *v.* to mislead by falsehood **deceivingly** *adv.*, **deceiver** *n.*, **deceivable** *adj.*

de-cel-er-ate *v.* to decrease the speed of something

de-cen-cy *n.* the state of being proper

de-cen-ni-al *adj.* every ten years **decennially** *adv.*

de-cent *adj.* being in good taste

de-cep-tion *n.* act of deceiving **-tively** *adv.*, **-tiveness** *n.*

de-cide *v.* to settle an issue or idea **decidable** *adj.*

de-cid-ed *adj.* unquestionable **decidedness** *n.*, **-ly** *adv.*

de-cid-u-ous *adj.* shedding at maturity **deciduously** *adv.*

dec-i-mal *n.* proper fraction

de-ci-pher *v.* to determine the meaning **decipherable** *adj.*

de-ci-sion *n.* act of deciding

de-ci-sive *adj.* firm mind; unquestionable **decisively** *adv.*

deck *n.* floor of a ship; pack of cards

deck hand *n.* person who works on the ship

de-claim *v.* to speak loudly **declamatory** *adj.*, **-ation** *n.*

de-clare *v.* make known **-ration**, **-er** *n.*, **-ative** *adj.*

de-clas-si-fy *v.* make public **declassifying**, **declassified** *v.*

de-cline *v.* refuse something **-able** *adj.*, **-ing**, **-ed** *v.*

de-com-pose *v.* decay

de-com-press *v.* releasing of pressure **decompression** *n.*

de-con-tam-i-nate *v.* make free of contamination **decontamination** *n.*

de-con-trol *v.* to remove all controls

de-cor *n.* decoration

dec-o-rate *v.* furnish with fashionable things **-tor**, **decoration** *n.*, **decorative** *adj.*

de-co-rum *n.* polite behavior

de-coy *v.* lure into trap

de-crease *v.* to grow smaller in amount or size

de-cree *n.* formal order **decreeing**, **decreed** *v.*

de-crep-it *adj.* worn out by old

age **decrepitly** adv.

de-cry v. to denounce

ded-i-cate v. commit oneself to a serious purpose
dedication n., **dedicative** adj.

de-duct v. take away from

deed n. anything done

deem v. to judge

deep adj. extending far below a surface -ness n., -ly adv.

deep freeze n. frozen food box

deep seat-ed adj. fixed strongly within

deer n. a hoofed ruminant mammal

de-face v. spoil the appearance of **defacer**, **defacement** n.

de-fal-cate v. to embezzle

de-fame v. slander or libel -famation n., -ing, -ed v.

de-feat v. to win -ist, -ism n.

def-e-cate v. to discharge feces from the bowels -tion n.

de-fect n. lack of perfection

de-fend v. to protect -er n.

de-fend-ant n. person charged in a lawsuit

de-fense n. protection **defenseless**, **defensible** adj.

de-fer v. to delay -ring v.

de-fi-ance n. a challenge

de-fi-cient adj. lacking a necessary element

def-i-cit n. deficiency in amount

de-flate v. cause to collapse by removing air **deflation** n.

de-flect v. to turn aside

de-form v. to distort the form of something **deformed** adj.

de-fraud v. to cheat; to swindle

de-fray v. to provide for

de-frost v. to cause to thaw out **defroster** n.

deft adj. neat in one's actions

de-funct adj. deceased

de-fy v. to resist boldly

de-gen-er-ate v. to decline in value **degeneration** n.

de-grade v. to reduce in rank

de-gree n. academic title

de-hy-drate v. to lose water

de-i-fy v. to glorify

deign v. to condescend

de-lay v. to put off

del-e-gate n. deputy or agent

de-lete v. to take out

del-e-teri-ous adj. dangerous

de-lib-er-ate v. plan in advance

del-i-ca-cy n. select food

del-i-cate adj. being of fine workmanship

de-li-cious adj. pleasant to the taste **deliciousness** n.

de-light n. great joy or pleasure

de-lim-it v. to prescribe the limits **delimitation** n.

de-lin-quent n. neglecting to do what is required

de-liv-er v. to hand over

de-lude v. to deceive

del-uge v. to flood with water

de-lu-sion n. false, fixed belief

de-mand v. to ask for in a firm tone or manner

de-mer-it n. fault; a defect

de-mise n. death

de-mo-bi-lize v. to disband

de-moc-ra-cy n. the form of government exercised by the people

dem-o-crat n. one who prefers a democracy

de-mol-ish v. to tear down

de-mon n. evil spirit

dem-on-strate v. show by reasoning **demonstrable** adj.

de-mor-al-ize v. to undermine confidence

de-mote v. to reduce in rank

de-mur v. to object

den n. shelter for a wild animal

de-ni-al n. refusal to comply with a request

den-im n. jeans

de-note v. to make known

de-nounce v. to accuse formally

dense adj. compact

den-si-ty n. close in parts

dent n. small depression

den-tal adj. to be pertaining to the teeth

den-tist n. dental doctor

den-ti-tion n. an arrangement of teeth

den-ture n. artificial teeth

de-ny v. to declare untrue

de-o-dor-ant n. product to prevent odors

de-part v. to leave

de-part-ment n. the part of something

de-pend v. to rely on

de-pend-ence n. the trust or the reliance

de-pend-ent adj. help support

another

de-pict v. represent in a picture

de-plete v. to exhaust

de-plor-a-ble adj. grievous

de-plore v. to feel disapproval of something

de-ploy v. to spread out

de-pose v. to remove from a powerful position

de-pos-it v. to entrust money to a bank

dep-o-si-tion n. a sworn testimony by someone

de-pot n. railroad station

de-pre-ci-ate v. lessen in price

de-press v. to make gloomy

de-prive v. to take something away from another

depth n. state of being deep

dep-u-ty n. sheriff's assistant

de-rail v. to run off the rails

de-range v. to disturb the normal order

der-i-va-tion n. the process of deriving soemthing

de-rive v. obtain from a source

der-mal adj. relating to the skin

der-rick n. machine to lift heavy loads

der-ri-ere n. the buttocks

de-scend v. to move from a higher level to a lower level

de-scen-dent adj. to be proceeding downward

de-scribe v. to explain

de-scry v. catch sight of

des-e-crate v. violate something sacred

de-seg-re-gate v. eliminate racial segregation -gation n.

de-sert v. to abandon

de-serve v. to be entitled to

de-sign v. to create in the mind

des-ig-nate v. to point out

de-sir-a-ble adj. attractive

de-sir-ous adj. strong desire

de-sist v. stop doing something

desk n. piece of furniture

des-o-late adj. to be foresaken

de-spair v. give up hope

des-per-a-do n. a violent criminal

des-per-ate adj. intense

des-pi-ca-ble adj. to be deserving scorn

de-spise v. to regard another with contempt

de-spite prep. not withstanding

des-pot n. absolute ruler

des-sert n. a serving of sweet food such as cake

des-ti-na-tion n. point or place

des-ti-ny n. one's fate

de-stroy v. to ruin

de-struct n. an act of being destroyed

des-ul-to-ry adj. occurs by chance

de-tach v. to disconnect

de-tail n. item that is separate

de-tain v. to keep from proceeding

de-tect v. to find out or perceive detectable adj.

de-tec-tive n. a person who investigates crimes

de-ter v. intimidation -rent n.

de-ter-gent n. cleansing agent

de-ter-mine v. to decide conclusively

de-test v. dislike strongly

de-tract v. take away from

deuce n. two; tennis score

de-val-u-ate v. lessen the value

dev-as-tate v. to destroy something devastation n.

de-vel-op v. to expand potentialities development n.

de-vi-ate v. turn away from

dev-il n. spirit of evil

de-void adj. being empty

de-volve v. to pass on to

de-vote v. to apply time to

de-vour v. to destroy or waste

de-vout adj. extremely religious

dew n. moisture

dex-ter-i-ty n. skill of the hands

di-a-be-tes n. a metabolic disorder

di-a-bol-ic adj. wicked -al adv.

di-a-dem n. crown

di-ag-no-sis n. identify a disease

di-a-gram n. illustrate how something works

di-al n. the circular plate with clock

di-a-lect n. the usage of local language

di-a-logue n. a conversation involving two

di-am-e-ter n. width of a circle

dia-mond n. a precious gem

di-ar-rhe-a n. the loose bowel movements

di-a-ry n. daily record -rist n.

di-a-ther-my n. heat in the body **diathermize** v.

dice pl., n. cubes used in a game

dic-tate v. to record **-tation** n.

dic-tion-ar-y n. definitions of words in a book

dic-tum n. an authoritative utterance

di-dac-tic adj. teach or moralize

die v. to expire

di-et n. selection of foods

dif-fer v. to disagree

dif-fer-ence n. unlike

dif-fi-cult adj. hard to do

dif-fi-dent adj. to be timid

dif-frac-tion n. light rays

dif-fuse v. to scatter

dig v. break up the earth

di-gest v. to endure

di-ges-tion n. the dissolving food in the stomach

dig-it n. a finger or toe

dig-ni-tary n. the person of high rank

dig-ni-ty n. being excellent

di-gress v. to wander

dike n. a flood wall

di-late v. to become larger

di-lem-ma n. a perplexing situation

dil-et-tante n. superficial interest in something

dil-i-gent adj. industrious

dill n. aromatic herb

di-lute v. to reduce concentration

dim adj. to be dull

dime n. a ten cent coin

di-men-sion n. the measurable extent of something

di-min-ish v. make smaller

di-min-u-tive adj. very small

dim-ple n. the depression of the skin

din n. a loud noise

dine v. to eat dinner

din-ner n. last meal of the day

di-no-saur n. extinct reptiles

dip v. to put something into a liquid momentarily

diph-the-ri-a n. an acute infectious disease

di-plo-ma n. the document from school

dip-per n. one that dips

dire adj. being dreadful

di-rect v. to give orders

di-rec-to-ry n. book listing data

dir-i-gi-ble n. very light plane

dirt n. soil; ground

dis-a-ble v. to incapacitate someone or thing **-bility** n.

dis-ad-van-tage n. detriment

dis-a-gree v. vary in opinion **disagreeable** adj.

dis-al-low v. refuse to allow

dis-ap-pear v. to vanish

dis-ap-point v. to fail to satisfy someone **-ment** n.

dis-ap-prove v. refuse approval

dis-arm v. to make harmless

dis-ar-range v. to disturb the order of something

dis-as-sem-ble v. to take apart

dis-as-ter n. an event that causes distress

dis-a-vow v. disclaim or deny

dis-band v. to disperse

dis-be-lieve v. refuse to believe

dis-burse v. to pay out

disc n. phonograph record

dis-card v. to throw out

dis-cern v. detect something visually **discernment** n.

dis-charge v. to release

dis-ci-ple n. Christ's followers

dis-ci-pline n. punishment

dis-claim v. speak formally in public **disclaimer** n.

dis-close v. make known

dis-con-cert v. to upset

dis-con-tent n. dissatisfaction **discontentedness** n.

dis-cord n. lacking accord; dis agreement

dis-co-theque n. type of nightclub for dancing

dis-count v. lower the price

dis-cour-age v. deprived of courage **discouragement** n.

dis-course n. a conversation

dis-cov-er v. to learn for the first time

dis-cred-it n. disbelief

dis-creet adj. being tactful

dis-crete adj. separate

dis-crim-i-nate v. choose between **discrimination** adj.

dis-cuss v. to talk

dis-dain v. ignore; scorn

dis-ease n. sickness

dis-em-bark v. unload

dis-en-chant v. free from false beliefs **disenchantment** n.

dis-en-gage v. to set free

dis-en-tan-gle v. relieve of en

tanglement -ment n.

dis-es-teem n. lack of esteem

dis-fa-vor n. disapproval

dis-fig-ure v. to deform appearance disfiguration n.

dis-fran-chise v. deprive the legal right

dis-grace n. loss of honor

dis-guise v. change appearance

dis-gust v. aversion

dish n. eating utensil

dis-har-mo-ny n. discord

dis-heart-en v. to lose spirit in something -ing adj.

dis-shev-el v. to mess up

dis-hon-or n. disgrace

dis-il-lu-sion v. to disenchant

dis-in-fect v. to sterilize something disinfectant adj.

dis-in-her-it v. to deprive of inheritance

dis-in-te-grate v. break into small particles -gration n.

dis-lo-cate v. put out of place

dis-lodge v. move from

dis-loy-al adj. being not true to something or someone

dis-man-tle v. to take apart

dis-may v. to deprive or be deprived of courage or resolution

dis-mem-ber v. cut into pieces

dis-miss v. to discharge

dis-mount v. to get down from

dis-o-bey v. refuse or fail to obey someone or thing

dis-o-blige v. act contrary to

dis-or-der n. breach of peace

dis-or-gan-ize v. destroy or break up unity

dis-own v. refuse to claim as one's own

dis-patch or **des-patch** v. to send on a particular destination dispatcher n.

dis-pense v. to give out

dis-perse v. to break up

dis-place v. to change the position of displacement n.

dis-play v. put in view

dis-please v. to cause disapproval or annoyance

dis-pute v. to debate or argue

dis-qual-i-fy v. to deprive of the required conditions

dis-qui-si-tion n. a type of formal inquiry

dis-re-gard v. to neglect

dis-re-pute n. the state of being held in low esteem

dis-re-spect n. lack of respect

dis-robe v. to undress

dis-rupt v. throw into disorder

dis-sat-is-fy v. fail to satisfy

dis-sect v. cut into pieces

dis-sen-sion n. difference of opinion -tious adj.

dis-sent v. to differ in opinion or thought

dis-serv-ice n. ill turn

dis-sim-i-lar adj. unlike

dis-solve v. to cause to fade away; to melt

dis-tance n. the separation in time or space

dis-tem-per n. contagious viral disease of dogs

dis-till v. to give off in drops by distillation

dis-til-late n. a condensed substance that is separated by distillation

dis-tinc-tive adj. serving to give style

dis-tin-guish v. to recognize as being different

dis-tort v. to twist or to bend out of shape distortion n.

dis-tract v. to divert one's attention distraction n.

dis-traught adj. agitated with anxiety; crazed

dis-tress v. cause suffering of mind or body

dis-trib-ute v. to give out

dis-trict n. section of a territory

dis-trust v. suspicion; doubt

dis-turb v. to bother

dis-u-ni-ty n. discord; unrest

dis-use n. state of not using

ditch n. trench in the earth

dith-er n. state of nervousness

dive v. plunge into water head-first

di-verge v. move in different directions divergence n.

di-verse adj. unlike in characteristics diversely adv.

di-ver-si-fy v. give variety to

di-ver-sion n. act of diverting from an activity; pastime

di-ver-si-ty n. variety

di-vide v. separate into parts

div-i-dend n. individual share distributed

di-vine adj. to be pertaining to

God **divinely** adv.

di-vorce n. the legal end to a marriage

div-ot n. a square of turf or sod

do v. to bring about

doc-ile adj. being easily managed; fame

dock n. landing pier for boats; deduct pay

dock-yard n. a shipyard

doc-tor n. the person who is trained in medicine

doc-tor-ate n. the degree or title of a doctor

doc-u-ment n. an official paper documentation n.

dodge v. to avoid by moving suddenly

doe n. mature female deer

does-n't contr. does not

dog n. the domesticated carnivorous mammal

dog-ged adj. being stubbornly determined

dog-ma n. rigidly held doctrine

dog-mat-ic adj. marked by authoritative assertion

dol-drums pl.,n. period of listlessness

dole n. distribution of money to the needy

dole-ful adj. filled with sadness

doll n. child's toy

dol-lar n. standard monetary unit of the U.S.

dol-ly n. low, flat frame on wheels

dol-men n. a type of prehistoric monument

do-lor-ous adj. marked by grief; mournful

dolt n. a stupid person

do-main n. territory of control

dome n. a round shaped roof

do-mes-tic adj. relating to the household domestically adv.

dom-i-nant adj. prevailing

dom-i-no n. mask; costume; block of wood with dots

done adj. completed

don-key n. domesticated mule

do-nor n. the one who gives or donates

don't contr. do not

doo-dle v. to aimlessly draw or scribble

doom n. one's destiny

door n. the means of entrance or exit

dope n. drug or narcotic

dor-mant adj. being asleep

dose n. quantity of medicine

dos-si-er n. the complete data about a person

dou-ble adj. twice as much

dou-ble joint-ed adj. having unusually flexible joints

dou-ble take n. delayed reaction to something unusual

dou-ble talk n. a meaningless speech despite intelligible words

doubt v. to be uncertain

dough n. mixture of flour and ingredients

dough-nut n. small cake made of dough

dove n. a small bird

down adv. moving from higher to lower

dowse v. to search for underground water

dozen n. twelve

drab adj. dull brown

draft n. current of air; a sketch

drag v. pull along by force

drag-on n. a mythical giant monster

drain v. to draw off liquid gradually

drake n. a male duck

dram n. small portion

dra-ma n. a play recounting a serious story

drape v. to cover something

dras-tic adj. extremely harsh

draw v. to cause to move toward position

draw-back n. a unwanted or undesirable feature

draw-bridge n. bridge that is raised or lowered

drawer n. a sliding box in furniture

draw-in n. picture; process of choosing lots

drawl v. to speak slowly using prolonged vowels

dray n. a low, heavy cart without sides, used for hauling things

dread v. to fear greatly; to anticipate with alarm, anxiety, or reluctance

dread-ful adj. to be inspiring dread; very distasteful

dreadfully adv., **-ness** n.

dream n. the series of images one has while sleeping

dreamlike adj., **-fulness** n.

drea·ry adj. gloomy and bleak **drearily** adv., **-iness** n.

dredge v. remove sand or mud from a river bottom

dregs n. the sediment of a liquid; least desirable part

drench v. wet thoroughly

dress n. the outer garment for women

drew v. the past tense of draw

drib·ble v. to drip; to slobber; to drool **dribbler** n.

drift v. to move about aimlessly

drill n. tool used in boring holes v. to train

drill-mas·ter n. a non-commissioned officer who instructs in military drill

drink v. to swallow liquid n. a beverage or liquid

drip v. to fall in drops

drip cof·fee n. coffee made by allowing boiling water to drip slowly through the ground coffee

drip--dry adj. made from fabric that dries without wrinkling

drive v. to operate a vehicle

drive-in n. place of business that serves customers in their vehicles

driv·el v. to slobber; to talk in a manner that is nonsensically

driz·zle n. the fine, gentle, and quiet rain

droll adj. whimsically comical

drom-e-dar·y n. one-humped camel which is mainly used in Africa and western Asia as a beast of burden

drone n. the male bee which has no sting and does not make honey

drool v. to let saliva dribble from the mouth

droop v. to hang downward **droopiness** n., **droopy** adj.

drop n. act of falling v. to deposit at a specified place

drop-sy n. disease where water collects in body tissues

dross n. an impurity which forms on the surface of molten metal

drought n. a prolonged period of dryness

drove n. herd being driven in a body; a crowd

drown v. to die by suffocating in a liquid

drowse v. to doze

drows-y adj. sleepy; tending to induce sleep

drub v. to hit with a stick

drudge n. the person who does menial tasks

drug n. substance used to treat a disease or illness

drum n. kind of musical percussion instrument

drum up v. to invent or devise; to go out and actively pursue new accounts or business

drunk adj. to be intoxicated with alcohol

drunk-ard adj. a person who is intoxicated

drupe n. a fruit, as a peach, usually having one large pit or seed

dry adj. being free from moisture or wetness

dry-ad n. a wood nymph

dry--clean v. to clean fabric with chemical solvents

dry goods pl., n. textile fabrics

du-al adj. made up of two parts **dualist**, **duality** n., **dualistic** adj.

du-al-ism n. the two opposing forces

dub v. to nickname; to give a new sound track to dubbing, dubbed v., **-er** n.

du-bi-ous adj. causing doubt **dubiousness** n., **-ly** adv.

du-cal adj. to be pertaining to a duke or his dukedom

du-cat n. coin of gold

duch-ess n. a wife or a widow of a duke

duch-y n. the area controlled by a duke

duck n. various swimming birds ducked adj.

duct n. tube or canal **-less** adj.

duc-tile adj. capable of being drawn and shaped into a fine strand

dud n. something which turns out to be a failure

dude n. a city person vacationing on a ranch

dudg-eon n. a displeased or indignant mood

due adj. being owed; payable

du-el n. the planned combat between two people -ist n.

du-et n. musical composition for two performers

duf-fel bag n. large cloth bag for carrying belongings

duff-er n. a dumb person

duke n. noble ranking below a prince dukedom n.

dul-cet adj. melodious; pleasing to the ear

dul-ci-mer n. musical stringed instrument played with two small picks

dull adj. to be stupid; no interest or curiosity

dullish adj., dullness n.

du-ly adv. a proper or due manner

dumb adj. unable to speak

dumbness n., dumbly adv.

dumb-bell n. the bar with two adjustable weights on either of its end

dumb-wait-er n. small hand elevator

dum-dum bullet n. a softnosed, small-arms bullet designed to expand on contact with something

dum-found v. to confound with amazement

dum-my n. one who is habitually silent; stupid

dump v. to discard

dump-ling n. a small mass of cooked dough

dun v. to press for payment

dunce n. a slow-witted person

dune n. a ridge or hill of sand

dung n. the excrement of animals; a manure

dun-ga-ree n. overalls; jeans

dun-geon n. a kind of underground chamber

dunk v. to dip food into liquid before eating

du-o n. an instrument duet

du-o-de-num n. first portion of the small intestine

dupe n. the person easily manipulated dupery n.

du-plex adj. double n. two family home

du-pli-cate n. an exact copy duplication, duplicator n.

du-ra-ble adj. continue for a prolonged time -bility n.

du-ra-tion n. period of time something lasts

du-ress n. forced restraint; constraint by fear or force

dur-ing prep. throughout the time of

dusk n. the earliest part of the evening, occurring just before dark

dust n. a fine, dry particles of matter

Dutch elm dis-ease n. a fungus which affects elm trees and eventually kills them

duty n., pl. -ties obligation; task

dwarf n. anything smaller than normal dwarfish adj.

dwell n. to live; brood; to focus one's attention dweller n.

dwell-ing n. a house or building in which one lives or is located in

dwin-dle v. waste away

dye v. to fix a color in dyeing, dyed v.

dye-stuff n. the materials used for dyeing something

dying adj. to be coming to the end of life

dy-nam-ic adj. marked by energy -cally adv., -cal adj.

dy-nam-ics n. the part of physics dealing with energy, force, etc.

dy-na-mite n. explosive which may be composed of nitroglycerin

dy-nas-ty n. the succession of rulers from the same family or group dynastic adj.

dys-en-ter-y n. the infection of the lower intestinal tract that produces pain, fever, and diarrhea

dys-lex-i-a n. impairment in one's ability to read

dys-pep-sia n. indigestion

dys-pep-tic adj. to suffer from dyspepsia

dys-pro-si-um n. a metallic element that is magnetic

dys-tro-phy n. various muscular disorders

E, e the fifth letter of the English alphabet

each adj everyone, separately considered

each oth-er pron. each in reciprocal action

ea-ger adj. being marked by enthusiasm; interested; yearing; earnest

eagerness n., **eagerly** adv.

ea-ger bea-ver n. an over zealous person

ea-gle n. the large, powerful bird of prey

ea-gle eye n. excellent vision; the ability to observe with keenness

ea-gle ray n. a large type of sting ray

ea-glet n. baby eagle

ear n., Anat. the hearing organ

ear-ache n. a pain in the ear

ear-drum n. the membrane that separates the external ear from the middle ear

eared adj. to have ears

eared seal n. type of seal having external ears

ear-ful n. a large amount of gossip or news

earl n. a British nobleman

ear-less seal n. the seal with no external ears, such as the hair seal

ear-ly adj. before the usual time **earliness** n.

ear-ly bird n. a person who arrives early

ear-mark n. on cattle, mark of ownership

ear-muff n. a cover to keep the ears warm

earn v. payment for work done; to get; to merit by service **earner** n.

ear-nest adj. serious intent; sincere **-ness** n., **-ly** adv.

earn-ings pl., n. something earned, such as a salary

ear-phone n. an instrument worn in the ear which transfers sound into the ear

ear-ring n. a decorative item worn in the ear

ear-shot n. the range of hearing something; the distance at which something can be heard

earth n. a globe, dirt or soil; the plant on which we live

earth-bound adj. firmly fixed to or in the earth; worldly

earth-en adj. to be made of dirt or of earth

earth-en ware n. dishes made of baked clay; crockery

earth-quake n. shaking or disturbance in the earth's crust

earth sci-ence n. the study of the earth

earth-ward adv. to move in the direction of the earth

earth-work n. building or structure made of earth

earth-worm n. segmented worms found in the ground; to be used as bait by a fisherman

earth-y adj. composed of soil or earth **earthiness** n.

ear-wax n. the yellowish wax-like substance that protects the ear from dirt

ease n. being comfortable; quiet; leisure; free from effort **easing, eased** v.

ea-sel n. the frame used by artists to paint or draw

ease-ment n. the right to cross or used another persons property

eas-i-ly adv. to be very easy in manner

east n. direction in which the sun rises **easterly** adv., **easternmost, eastern** adj.

East-er n. the Christian celebration that commemorates the resurrection of Jesus Christ

easy adj. little difficulty **easiness** n., **easier** adj.

eat v. chew and swallow food; to wear away **eatable** adj., **eater** n., **eatery** n.

eaves pl., n. the sloping edge of a roof that over hangs the wall of a structure

eaves-drop v. an act of listening to what is said in private **eavesdropper** n.

ebb v. to recede, as the tide; to flow back

eb-o-ny n. a dark, hard, colored wood; jet black

e-bul-lient adj. enthusiasm;

exuberant; overflowing

ec-cen-tric adj. strange eccentrically adv., -ity n.

ech-e-lon n. formation of military aircraft; level of command

e-chi-no-derm n. a starfish

ech-o n. repetition of a sound produced by sound waves echoer n., echoing adj.

e-clair n. long pastry filled with whipped cream and covered with chocolate

ec-lec-tic adj. to have components which are from a diverse source

e-clipse n. the partial blocking of one celestial body by another body

e-col-o-gy n. scientific study of the environment ecological, ecologic adj., ecologist n.

ec-o-nom-ic adj. relating to the necessities of life economical adj., -cally adv.

ec-o-nom-ics n. the science which treats the production of commodities

e-con-o-mize v. to manage thriftily economizer n.

e-con-o-my n. the management of money; controlled expenditures of money

ec-sta-sy n. an intense joy; abnormal emotion

ec-stat-ic adj. to be rapturous

ec-u-men-i-cal adj. world-wide ecumenicalism n., -cally adv.

ec-ze-ma n. skin condition that is characterized by itchiness

ed-dy n. the water current that is running against the main current; current of air

edge n. the thin cutting side of a blade

edg-y adj. to be nervous edginess n., edgily adv.

ed-i-ble adj. to be fit for consumption

e-dict n. public decree or law that is ordered by a king

ed-i-fy v. to instruct and improve edifying adj.

ed-it v. prepare for publication editor n.

e-di-tion n. form in which a book is published

ed-i-to-ri-al n. article in a newspaper editorially adv.

ed-u-cate v. supply with training or schooling educator, education n., educated adj.

e-duce v. to call or bring out; to develop -tion n., -ible adj.

eel n. a snake-like fish having an elongated body eely adj.

ee-rie adj. weird; scary; frightening eeriness n.

ef-face v. to remove or rub out effacer, effacement n.

ef-fect n. the power to produce a desired result

ef-fec-tive adj. producing an expected effect -ness n., effectively adv.

ef-fem-i-nate adj. woman-like quality; unmanly -ly adv.

ef-fer-ent adj. carrying away or outward

ef-fete adj. to be exhausted; being wornout

ef-fi-ca-cious adj. producing an intended effect

ef-fi-cient adj. being adequate in performance efficiency n.

ef-fi-gy n. the image or representation of a hated person

ef-flo-res-cence n. slow process of development

ef-flu-ence n. an act of flowing out

ef-fort n. earnest attempt or achievement; putting forth exertion of power or strength effortlessly adv.

ef-fron-ter-y n. a shameless; a boldness

ef-ful-gent adj. shining brilliantly effulgence n.

ef-fu-sion n. an unrestrained outpouring of feeling

egg n. the reproductive cell of female animals

egg-beat-er n. tool with rotating blades for mixing

egg-nog n. a drink of beaten eggs, sugar, and milk

egg-plant n. the plant with egg-shaped edible fruit

e-go n. thinking of oneself

e-go-ma-ni-a n. a self obsession

e-gre-gious adj. remarkably bad egregiously adv.

e-gress n. a means of departing something

eight n. cardinal number following seven

ei-ther *pron.* one or the other

e-jac-u-late *v.* eject abruptly **ejaculation** *n.*, **-tory** *adj.*

e-ject *v.* throw out or expel **-ment, -tion, -tor** *n.*

e-lab-o-rate *adj.* carried out with great detail **elaboration** *n.*, **-ly** *adv.*

e-lapse *v.* slip or glide away

e-las-tic *adj.* being capable of easy adjustment **elasticty** *n.*

e-late *v.* to make someone proud of **elated** *adj.*

el-bow *n.* outer joint of the arm between the upper arm and the forearm

eld-er *n.* a person who is older than the others **elderly** *adj.*, **eldership** *n.*

e-lect *v.* to choose or select by vote **election** *n.*

e-lec-tric *adj.* pertaining to electricity **electrically** *adv.*, **electrical** *adj.*

e-lec-tri-cian *n.* the person who maintains the electric equipment

e-lec-tric-i-ty *n.* attract or repel each other; form of energy

e-lec-tro-cute *v.* kill by electric current **electrocution** *n.*

e-lec-tron *n.* particle with a negative electric charge

e-lec-tro-type *n.* a plate used in printing

el-e-gance *n.* the refinement in appearance or manner

el-e-gy *n.* a poem expressing sorrow for one who is dead

el-e-ment *n.* the constituent part **elementally** *adv.*

el-e-men-ta-ry *adj.* fundamental essential

el-e-phant *n.* large mammal having a long trunk

e-le-vate *v.* lift up or raise

e-lev-en *n.* cardinal number equal to ten plus one

elf *n.* an imaginary being

e-lic-it *v.* to bring or draw out

e-lim-i-nate *v.* to get rid of or remove **elimination** *n.*

e-lite *n.* the most skilled members of a group

elk *n.* largest deer of Europe

e-lipse *n.* a closed curve

elm *n.* various valuable timber and shade trees

el-o-cu-tion *n.* art of effective public speaking

e-lope *v.* to run away to marry

el-o-quent *adj.* power to speak fluently **eloquently** *adv.*

else *adj.* different; other

else-where *adv.* in another place

e-lu-ci-date *v.* to make something clear **elucidation** *n.*

e-lude *v.* evade or avoid

em *n.* unit of measure for printed matter

e-ma-ci-ate *v.* to become extremely thin

em-a-nate *v.* to come forth

e-man-ci-pate *v.* to liberate someone **emancipator** *n.*

e-mas-cu-late *v.* to castrate

em-balm *v.* treat a corpse with preservatives to protect from decay

em-bar-go *n.* a restraint placed on trade

em-bark *v.* set out on a venture

em-bar-rass *v.* to feel self-conscious; to confuse

em-bas-sy *n.* the ambassador headquarters

em-bel-lish *v.* to adorn; to decorate **embellishment** *n.*

em-ber *n.* a piece of glowing, hot coal

em-bez-zle *v.* to take money fraudulently **-ment** *n.*

em-blem *n.* a symbol of something

em-bod-y *v.* to give something a bodily form

em-bold-en *v.* to encourage; to make bold

em-bo-lism *n.* a blockage of a blood vessel

em-boss *v.* to shape or decorate in relief

em-brace *v.* to hold or clasp in the arms

em-bro-cate *v.* rub with liquid medicine **embrocation** *n.*

em-broi-der *v.* to decorate with needlework **-dery** *n.*

em-broil *v.* to throw into a confusion **embroilment** *n.*

em-bry-o *n.* an organism in early development stage

em-cee *n.* the master of ceremonies

e-mend v. to correct or remove
faults emendation n.

em-er-ald n. type of bright-
green gemstone

e-merge v. come into existence

e-mer-gen-cy n. sudden and
unexpected situation

e-mer-i-tus adj. retired from
duty with honor

e-met-ic adj. medicine to in-
duce vomiting

em-i-grate v. move from one
country or region -tion n.

em-i-nent adj. being high in esteem

em-is-sar-y n. person who is on
a mission

e-mit v. to send forth

e-mol-lient n. substance used
for softening skin

e-mol-u-ment n. compen-
sation for something

e-mote v. to show emotion

e-mo-tion n. feelings of sorrow,
hate, and love

em-pa-thy n. understanding
feelings of another person

em-per-or n. the ruler of an
empire

em-pha-sis n. importance attached to anything

em-pire n. nations governed by
a single supreme authority

em-pir-i-cal adj. being gained
from experience -cally adv.

em-ploy v. engage the service of
employment n.

em-ploy-ee n. person who
works for another in return
for wages

em-pow-er v. to authorize

em-press n. emperor's wife

emp-ty adj. containing nothing;
vacant emptiness n.

em-u-late v. to imitate
-tion n., -tively adv.

e-mul-sion n. the light-sensitive
coating placed on photo-
graphic paper

en-a-ble v. supply power to
enabling adj., enabled v.

en-act v. to make into law

e-nam-el n. a glossy coating on
the teeth

en-camp v. to stay or to live in a
camp encampment n.

en-ceph-a-li-tis n. the inflammation of the brain

en-chant v. to put under a spell
enchantment n.

en-cir-cle v. to surround

en-close v. to form a circle
around something

en-co-mi-um n. high praise

en-com-pass v. to surround

en-core n. demand for repeat
performance

en-coun-ter n. an unexpected
meeting

en-cour-age v. inspire with
courage or hope -ment n.

en-croach v. to intrude upon
someone encroachment n.

en-cum-ber v. to hinder or to
burden someone

en-cy-clo-pe-di-a n. com-
prehensive work of
knowledge in a book

end n. terminal point where
something is concluded

en-dan-ger v. to expose to
danger endangerment n.

en-dear v. to make beloved

en-deav-or n. an attempt to at-
tain or do something

en-dem-ic adj. being peculiar to
a particular area

en-dog-e-nous adj. to be growing from within

en-dorse v. write one's signature on the back of a check

en-dow v. to bestow upon

en-dure v. to undergo; to
tolerate enduring adj.

en-e-ma n. injection of a liquid
into the rectum for the purpose of cleansing

en-e-my n. hostile force

en-er-gy n. vigor; strength

en-er-vate v. to deprive one of
strength

en-fee-ble v. to weaken

en-force v. to compel
obedience enforcement n.

en-fran-chise v. to give a fran-
chise to someone

en-gage v. to employ or hire

en-gen-der v. to exist

en-gine n. a type of mechanical
instrument

en-gorge v. to swallow greedily

en-grave v. etch into a surface

en-gross v. to occupy attention
engrosser, engrossment n.

en-gulf v. to enclose something
completely

en-hance v. to make greater

e-nig-ma n. anything puzzling; a riddle

en-join v. to prohibit

en-joy v. to feel pleasure

en-large v. make greater in size enlargement n.

en-light-en v. to give spiritual guidance to another

en-list v. to sign up for service with the armed forces

en-mesh v. to entangle

en-mi-ty n. a kind of deep hatred; hostility

en-no-ble v. to confer the rank of nobility ennoblement n.

e-nor-mity n. enormous; great wickedness

en-nui n. boredom

e-nor-mous adj. being very great in size

e-nough adj. adequate to satisfy demands

en-rage v. to put into a rage

en-rap-ture v. to delight

en-roll v. to place one's name in a register or roll

en-sconce v. to settle securely

en-sem-ble n. a group of complementary parts that are in harmony

en-shrine v. to hold sacred

en-sign n. an officer in the navy; a flag

en-slave v. to put in bondage

en-snare v. to catch or to trap something or one -ment n.

en-sue v. to follow

en-sure v. to make certain

en-tail v. have a necessary accompaniment or result

en-tan-gle v. to complicate something entanglement n.

en-ter v. go or come into

en-ter-prise n. a risky undertaking

en-ter-tain v. to amuse someone entertainment n.

en-thrall v. to fascinate

en-throne v. to place someone on a throne

en-thu-si-asm n. an intense feeling

en-thu-si-ast n. a person full of enthusiasm

en-thu-si-as-tic adj. being characterized by enthusiasm -tically adv.

en-tice v. arousing desire

en-tire adj. whole; complete entirely adv., entireness n.

en-ti-tle v. furnish with a right

en-ti-ty n. something that exists alone

en-tomb v. to place in a tomb

en-to-mol-o-gy n. study of insects entomologist n.

en-tou-rage n. the group of people that surround an important person

en-trails n. the internal parts of the body

en-trance n. the means or place of entry

en-trance v. fascinate

en-trap v. to catch in a trap

en-treat v. to make a request

en-trench v. fix or sit firmly on something entrenchment n.

en-trust v. transfer to another for care entrustment n.

en-try n. an opening used for entering

en-twine v. to twine together

e-nu-mer-ate v. to count off one by one enumerative adj.

e-nun-ci-ate v. to speak with clarity enunciation n.

en-ve-lope n. a paper case, especially for a letter

en-vi-a-ble adj. highly desirable enviableness n.

en-vi-ron-ment n. the physical surroundings -al adj.

en-vi-rons n. the surrounding neighborhood

en-vis-age v. to visualize

en-voy n. a type of diplomatic messenger

en-vy n. resentment for other's possessions

en-zyme n. proteins produced by living organisms that function in plants and animals

e-on n. an indefinite period of time

ep-au-let n. type of shoulder ornament, as one on a military uniform

e-phem-er-al adj. lasting a very short time ephemerally adv.

ep-ic n. a type of long narrative poem epical n.

ep-i-cen-ter n. the middle of an earthquake

ep-i-cure n. refined tastes

epicurism n., **-anism** adj.

ep-i-dem-ic adj. something widespread **-cally** adv.

ep-i-der-mis n. the outer layer of the skin **-ic** adj.

ep-i-gram n. brief pointed remark or observation

epigramatical, **-matic** adj.

ep-i-lep-sy n. type of nervous disorder

ep-i-lep-tic adj. state of having epilepsy

ep-i-logue n. short speech

ep-i-sode n. section of a movie, novel, etc.

-ically adv., **-ical**, **-ic** adj.

e-pis-tle n. a formal letter

ep-i-taph n. an inscription

epitaphist n., epithaphic adj.

ep-i-thet n. word used to characterize something

epithetical, epithetic adj.

e-pit-o-me n. concise summary of a book epitomize v.

ep-och n. a point in time

ep-ox-y n. a compound

equ-a-ble adj. being fair **-bility** n., **-ably** adv.

e-qual adj. of the same measurement **equalness**, **equalizer** n., **equally** adv.

e-qual-i-tar-i-an n. the ideas of all men are equal **-ism** n.

e-qual-i-ty n. being equal

e-qua-nim-i-ty n. one's composure

e-quate v. to consider or to make equal

e-qua-tion n. the process of things being equal

equationally adv., **-al** adj.

e-qua-tor n. great imaginary circle around the earth

e-qua-to-ri-al adj. to be referring to at or near the equator **equatorially** adv.

eq-uer-ry n. officer in charge of the horses of royalty

e-ques-tri-an n. one who rides horses

e-qui-lat-er-al adj. being equal sided

e-qui-li-brate v. balancing of something **-tor**, **-tion** n.

e-qui-lib-ri-um n. the state of balance

e-quine adj. pertaining to or like horse

e-qui-nox n. twice a year when days and nights are equal in time **-noctial** adj.

e-quip v. furnish with whatever is needed

equiper, **equipment** n.

eq-ui-ta-ble adj. impartial **-bly** adv., **-ness** n.

eq-ui-ty n. a fairness or an impartiality

e-quiv-a-lent adj. being equal **equivalence** n., **-ly** adv.

e-quiv-o-cal adj. questionable **equivocalness** n., **-cally** adv.

e-quiv-o-cate v. to use vague language **-tor**, **-tion** n.

e-ra n. period of time

e-rad-i-cate v. to remove **-tive**, **-tion**, **-tor** n.

e-rase v. to remove something written **-able** adj., **-bility** n.

e-rect adj. being of a vertical position **erection** n.

er-e-mite n. a hermit

er-go conj. & adj. consequently

er-mine n. weasel fur

e-rode v. to wear away gradually **erosion** n.

e-rog-e-nous adj. responsive to sexual stimulation

err v. make a mistake; to sin

er-rand n. a trip to take a message to someone

er-rant adj. search of adventure **errantly** adv.

er-rat-ic adj. to be irregular or different **erratically** adv.

er-ro-ne-ous adj. containing an error **-ness** n., **-ly** adv.

er-ror n. done incorrectly; wrongdoing **errorless** adj.

er-satz adj. artificial

er-u-dite adj. scholarly **eruditeness** n., **-ly** adv.

e-rupt v. burst forth violently with steam, lava, etc.

-tiveness, **-tion** n.,

-tive adj., **-tively** adv.

es-ca-la-tor n. type of moving stairway

es-cal-lop v. & n. a variation of scallop

es-ca-pade n. a kind of prankish trick

es-cape v. to break free from capture **escaper** n.

s-ca-role n. endive leaves, used in salads

s-carp-ment n. steep slope

s-chew v. to shun or avoid someone eschewer n.

s-cort n. one accompanying another person

s-crow n. written deed placed in the custody of a third party

soph-a-gus n. the tube leading to stomach

s-o-ter-ic adj. to be confidential esoterically adv.

s-pe-cial adj. having a special place

s-pi-o-nage n. act of spying to obtain secret information

s-pous-al n. adoption or support, as of a cause

s-pouse v. to give in marriage

s-prit n. mental liveliness

s-prit de corps n. a group's spirit

s-quire n. title of courtesy

s-say n. type of short composition essayer n.

s-sen-tial adj. to be necessary ly adv., -ness, -ity n.

s-tab-lish v. to make permanent establisher n.

s-tab-lish-ment n. place of residence or business

s-tate n. large piece of land containing a large home

s-teem v. to regard someone with respect

s-ti-ma-ble adj. worthy of respect -ly adv., -ness n.

s-ti-mate v. to give a approximate opinion on something estimation n.

s-trange v. to dissociate or to remove oneself -ment n.

s-tro-gen n. the female hormones

s-tu-ar-y n. wide mouth of a river

ch v. engrave by using acid -tcher, etching n.

-ter-nal adj. lasting indefinitely eternally adv.

-ter-ni-ty n. an existence without beginning or end

ther n., Chem. anesthetic the-re-al adj. delicate ness, -ity n., -ly adv.

h-ic n. moral values

eth-nic adj. being of a racial group ethnically adv.

e-ti-ol-o-gy n. study of causes or origins -ically adv., -ical adj., -ist n.

et-i-quette n. the prescribed rules for behavior

et-y-mol-o-gy n. the history of a word origin -ist n., -ical, -ic adj.

eu-ca-lyp-tus n. a large, native Australian tree with very aromatic leaves

eu-chre n. a card game for two to four players played with thirty two cards

eu-gen-ics n. the study of improving the physical qualities of something -ic adj., -cist n.

eu-lo-gize v. to write or to deliver an eulogy for someone in order to honor them eulogizer n.

eu-lo-gy n. the speech that honors a person

eu-nuch n. a castrated male

eu-phe-mism n. the substitution for a word -tic adj., -tically adv.

eu-pho-ny n. the agreeable sound of spoken words -ious adj., -iously adv.

eu-pho-ri-a n. the strong feeling of elation

eu-re-ka interj. an expression of triumph

eu-ro-pi-um n. a soft, silvery-white, rare-earth element used in nuclear research

eu-sta-chian tube n. the passage between the middle ear and the pharynx, equalizing the air pressure

eu-tha-na-sia n. the act of mercy killing

eu-then-ics n. the study of improving the physical and mental qualities of a person

e-vac-u-ate v. to leave a threatened area quickly evacuator, evacuation n.

e-vac-u-ee n. a person who is evacuated from a hazardous place or area

e-vade v. to baffle; to elude

e-val-u-ate v. to examine carefully; to appraise

evaluator, evaluation *n.*

ev-a-nesce *v.* to fade away; to disappear from somewhere

ev-a-nes-cent *adj.* vanishing or passing quickly; fleeting

ev-an-gel-ism *n.* preaching of the gospel -ically *adj.*

ev-an-gel-ist *n.* a zealous missionary evangelic *adj.*

e-vap-o-rate *v.* to remove the liquid from water, milk, etc. evaporator *n.*, -tive *adj.*

e-va-sive *adj.* being vague evasiveness, evasion *n.*

eve *n.* evening before a special day or holiday

e-ven *adj.* being level

eve-ning *n.* time between sunset and bedtime

e-vent *n.* something that takes place

e-ven-tu-al *adj.* happening in due time

e-ven-tu-al-i-ty *n.* a conceivable outcome

ev-er *adv.* at any time

ev-er-glade *n.* tract of low, swampy land

ev-er-green *adj.* a tree that has green foliage

ev-er-last-ing *adj.* to be lasting forever

ev-er-more *adv.* at all times to come

eve-ry *adj.* being without exceptions

eve-ry-body *pron.* every person

eve-ry-day *adj.* to be happening daily

eve-ry-one *pron.* every person

eve-ry-place *adv.* to be everywhere

eve-ry-thing *pron.* all things

eve-ry-where *adv.* at, to everyplace

e-vict *v.* to put out a tenant or a renter eviction *n.*

ev-i-dence *n.* the signs or facts on which a conclusion can be based

ev-i-dent *adj.* obvious

e-vil *adj.* morally bad or wrong

e-vince *v.* to indicate something clearly evincive *n.*

e-vis-cer-ate *v.* to remove the entrails of something

ev-i-ta-ble *adj.* avoidable

e-voke *v.* to call or summon

forth someone or thing

e-v-o-lu-tion *n.* gradua development evolutionist

e-volve *v.* to develop or to change gradually -ment *n.*

ewe *n.* a female sheep

ew-er *n.* large pitcher or jug

ex-act *adj.* being accurate every detail exactness *n.*

ex-act-ing *adj.* to be makin severe demands

ex-act-i-tude *n.* the act of bein exact

ex-ag-ger-ate *v.* to represe something as being greate than what it really is

ex-alt *v.* to increase the inter sity exaltation *n.*

ex-am-i-na-tion *n.* a test o one's knowledge

ex-am-ine *v.* to observe o inspect; look into

ex-am-ple *n.* a representative a sample

ex-as-per-ate *v.* to mak frustrated -ation *n.*

ex-ca-vate *v.* to dig a hole in the ground -vation *n.*

ex-ceed *v.* go beyond the limit

ex-cel *v.* to do better than others in something

ex-cel-lence *n.* the quality being superior

ex-cel-lent *adj.* having the be quality

ex-cel-si-or *n.* the wood shav ings of trees

ex-cept *prep.* aside from; ex clude exception *n.*

ex-cerpt *n.* a passage take from a book

ex-cess *n.* over indulgence

ex-ces-sive *adj.* extreme; mo than necessary

ex-change *v.* to trade

ex-cise *n.* tax on a sale of a commodity exciseable *adj*

ex-cise *v.* remove surgically.

ex-cite *v.* to stimulate the em tions excitement *n.*

ex-claim *v.* to utter somethin suddenly exclamation *n.*

ex-cla-ma-tion mark *n.* mar (!) to show strong feeling

ex-clude *v.* keep out

ex-clu-sive *adj.* being selectiv not shared

ex-co-ri-ate *v.* to censur

something harshly
x-cre-ment n. bodily waste
x-cre-ta pl., n. excretions from the body
x-cru-ci-at-ing adj. being painful; torturous
x-cul-pate v. free from wrong doing exculpation n.
x-cur-sion n. short trip
x-cuse v. to grant forgiveness
x-e-cra-ble adj. being extremely bad
x-e-crate v. to detest; to hate violently
x-e-cute v. put to death; perform execution n.
x-ec-u-tive n. administrator in an organization
x-em-plar n. an example
x-em-pla-ry adj. to be serving as a model
n-pli-fy v. to be made an example
x-empt v. free from obligation exemption n.
x-er-cise n. developing oneself; physical training
x-ert v. to use force -ion n.
x-hale v. to breathe out
x-haust v. extremely tired
x-hib-it v. to display
x-hi-bi-tion-ism n. calling attention to oneself
x-hil-a-rate v. to elate
x-hort v. to urge by earnest appeal exhortion n.
x-hume v. to remove a body from a grave
x-i-gen-cy n. necessity
x-ig-u-ous adj. being extremely small
x-ile n. separation from one's country or home
x-ist v. to live existence n.
x-is-ten-tial adj. based on experience
x-it n. a passageway out
x-o-dus n. the departure of a group of people
x-on-er-ate v. to free from blame
x-or-bi-tant adj. beyond usual and proper limits
x-or-cise v. to cast out an evil spirit
x-ot-ic adj. being strangely beautiful in character
x-pand v. to increase

ex-panse n. a wide, open stretch of land
ex-pa-tri-ate v. to banish
ex-pect v. to look forward to something; hope
ex-pec-tant adj. to be pregnant
ex-pec-to-rate v. to spit
ex-pe-di-ent adj. selfish interests expediency n.
ex-pe-dite v. to speed up progress of something
ex-pe-di-tious adj. being quick; being speedy
ex-pel v. to drive or force out
ex-pend v. to pay out or use up
ex-pend-a-ble adj. being available for spending
ex-pen-di-ture n. an amount that is spent
ex-pense n. the consumption of money
ex-pen-sive adj. high priced
ex-pe-ri-ence n. skill that is acquired from actual participation
ex-per-i-ment n. test to illustrate a truth
ex-pert n. person having great knowledge expertness n.
ex-pi-ate v. to atone
ex-pire v. to come to an end
ex-plain v. to make something understandable
ex-plic-it adj. plainly expressed
ex-plode v. to blow up violently explosion n.
ex-ploit n. a notable deed
ex-plore v. to travel unfamiliar territory exploration n.
ex-pose v. to reveal
ex-po-si-tion n. a public exhibition
ex-pos-tu-late v. to reason earnestly expostulation n.
ex-pound v. to give a detailed statement
ex-press v. to verbalize with another expressiveness n.
ex-press-way n. a type of multilane highway
ex-pro-pri-ate v. to deprive a person expropriation n.
ex-pul-sion n. an act of expelling someone
ex-pur-gate v. to remove obscene material from a book expurgator n.
ex-qui-site v. being highly

sensitive

ex-tant *adj.* still in existence

ex-tem-po-ra-ne-ous *adj.* having no advance preparation **-ly** *adv.*

ex-tem-po-rize *v.* to improvise, to meet circumstances

ex-tend *v.* to make longer or broader **extendible** *adj.*

ex-te-ri-or *adj.* external layer

ex-ter-mi-nate *v.* to destroy completely **-nation** *n.*

ex-ter-nal *adj.* being outside; exterior **externally** *adv.*

ex-tinct *adj.* no longer existing

ex-tin-guish *v.* put an end to

ex-tir-pate *v.* to destroy

ex-tol *v.* to praise highly

ex-tort *v.* to obtain money by threat **extortion** *n.*

ex-tra *adj.* over what is normal

ex-tract *v.* to pull out by force, such as a tooth

ex-tra-dite *v.* to surrender by extradition

ex-tra-mar-i-tal *adj.* being adulterous

ex-tra-ne-ous *adj.* to be coming from without **extraneously** *adv.*, **-ness** *n.*

ex-tra-or-di-nar-y *adj.* being beyond what is usual

ex-tra-sen-so-ry *adj.* to be beyond perception

ex-trav-a-gant *adj.* wasteful **-gance** *n.*, **-ly** *adv.*

ex-trav-a-gan-za *n.* a type of showy entertainment

ex-treme *adj.* going beyond the bounds of moderation **extremely** *adv.*, **-ness** *n.*

ex-trem-i-ty *n.* the utmost or the farthest point; the greatest degree of distress

ex-tri-cate *v.* to free from hindrance or difficulties

ex-trin-sic *adj.* from the outside **extrinsically** *adv.*

ex-tro-vert *n.* one who is an out going person

ex-trude *v.* to push or thrust out **-sion** *n.*, **-sive** *adj.*

ex-u-ber-ant *adj.* being full of high spirits **-ly** *adv.*

ex-ude *v.* to trickle forth sweat on the skin **exution** *n.*

ex-ult *v.* to be jubilant **-ly** *adv.*, **-tion** *n.*, **-ant** *adj.*

ex-ur-bi-a *n.* well-to-do residential area

eye *n.* an organ of vision o sight

eye-ball *n.* ball of the eye

eye-bank *n.* place where co neas removed from recent

eye-brow *n.* short hairs cove ing the bony ridge over th eye

eye-ful *n.* the total view o something

eye-glass *n.* corrective ler used to assist vision

eye-hole *n.* an opening to pass hook, pin, rope, etc.

eye-lash *n.* stiff, curved hai growing from the edge o the eyelids

eye-let *n.* perforation for hook or cord to fit throug in closing a fasten

eye-lid *n.* either of two folds o skin and muscle which wi open and close over an eye

eye-lin-er *n.* makeup used t highlight the outline of th eyes

eye--o-pen-er *n.* that whic opens the eyes **-ing** *adj.*

eye-piece *n.* combination lenses of an optical in strument

eye-shadow *n.* a cosmeti preparation applied to th eyelids for decoration

eye-sight *n.* the faculty o power of sight

eye-sore *n.* something ugly tha offends the sight

eye-stalk *n.* a movabl peduncles with an eye found in a decapod crus tacean

eye-strain *n.* discomfort of th eyes, due to excessiv misuse

eye-tooth *n.*, *pl.* teeth one of t canine teeth of the uppe jaw

eye-wash *n.* a lotion for clea ing the eye

eye-wit-ness *n.* the person wh has seen something and i able to testify to it firsthan as in a court of law

eyre *n.* English court o medieval times

F, f the sixth letter of the English alphabet

fa-ble n. a type of brief, fictitious story which conveys a moral at the end
fabled adj., **fablist** n.

fab-ric n. the cloth produced from fibers

fab-ri-cate v. to assemble; to manufacture a product
fabrication n., **-tive** adj.

fab-u-lous adj. wonderful; incredible; very pleasing
fabulously adv., **-ness** n.

fa-cade n., Arch. the face of a building or structure

face n. front surface of the head of someone or thing

face card in playing cards, a king, queen, or jack of a suit

face--lift-ing n. the plastic surgery to tighten facial tissues

face--off n. the action of facing off in hockey, starts games

face--saver n. something that preserves one's self-esteem or dignity

fac-et n. the polished surface of a gemstone **faceted** adj.

fa-ce-tious adj. humorous; being without serious intent
facetiousness n., **-ly** adv.

face val-ue n. the apparent value of something; the value printed on the face of a bill or bond

fa-cial adj. being near, of, or for the face, such as a cleanser **facially** adv.

fac-ile adj. to be requiring little effort for doing
facileness n., **facilely** adv.

fa-cil-i-tate v. to make easier
facilitation n., **-tive** adj.

fa-cil-i-ty n., pl. **-ies** doing something easily

fac-ing n. the lining or the covering sewn to a garment

fac-sim-i-le n. exact copy of a document or paper

fact n. something that actually occurred or exists

fact find-er n. the person who attempts to find the facts of a case

fac-tion n. self-seeking party within government **-ally** adv., **-alism** n., **-al** adj.

fac-tious adj. dissension; creating friction; relating to faction **factiousness** n.

fac-ti-tious adj. produced artificially; made by man
factitiousness n., **-ly** adv.

fac-tor n. the transacting business for commission

fac-tor-age n. a business of the factor

fac-to-ri-al adj. to be relating to a factor

fac-to-ize v. to factor

fac-to-ry n., pl. **-ies** place where goods are manufactured

fac-to-tum n. an all-around employee having diverse activities

fac-tu-al adj. consisting or containing facts
factually adv., **factualness** n.

fac-ul-ty n., pl. **-ies** one's natural ability; instructors

fad n. a temporary fashion, style, or interest
fadness n., **faddish** adj.

fade v. lose brightness, brilliance, or sound gradually

fade-a-way n. the act of something fading away

fade-less adj. able to resist fading **fadelessly** adv.

fag v. to exhaust by hard work or labor

fag end n. the frayed end of a rope or cloth

fag-ot or **fag-got** n. bundle of twigs for fuel

fag-ot-ing n. a method of ornamenting cloth by pulling out horizontal threads; style of embroidery

fa-ience n. earthenware that is decorated with a colorful opaque glaze

fail v. totally unsuccessful
failure n., **failingly** adv.

fail-ing n. a minor fault; a defect in something

faille n. a ribbed material of cotton, silk, or rayon

fail--safe adj. system to prevent equipment failure

fail-ure n. the fact or state of failing something

faint adj. little strength or vigor
faintness n., **faintly** adv.

faint-hearted adj. to be lacking

courage or conviction

faintheartedness n., **-ly** adv.

fair adj. light in coloring; not stormy **fairness** n.

fair ball n. a ball that remains in the area bounded by the foul lines

fair--haired adj. having blond or light colored hair

fair--mind-ed adj. just and impartial in character

fair-way n. the usual course through a channel

fair--weather adj. friendly only during good times

fair-y n., pl. **-ies** an imaginary being capable of working good or bad deeds

fair-y-land n. any delightful, enchanting place; the land of the fairies

fair-y tale n. story about fictitious creatures

fait ac-com-pli n. an accomplished fact or deed that is irreversible

faith n. belief and trust in God **faithful** adj., **faithfulness** n.

faith-less adj. not being true to one's obligations **faithlessly** adv., **-ness** n.

fake adj. to have false appearance **faker** n.

fal-con n. type of bird of prey

fall v. drop down; collapse

fal-la-cious adj. deceptive **fallaciousness** n., **-ly** adv.

fal-la-cy n., pl. **-ies** deception

fall-back n. a place or position to which one can retreat

fall guy n., Slang the person to blame

fal-li-ble adj. capable of making an error; liable to be deceived or to be misled **fallibility** n., **fallibly** adv.

fall-ing--out n. a disagreement, fight, or quarrel

fall-ing star n. a meteor, often visible as a result of being ignited by the atmospheric friction

fall--off n. a decrease in something

fal-lo-pi-an tube n. slender duct serving as a passage for the ovum from the ovary to the uterus

fall-out n. the decent of radioactive material

fal-low n. plowed ground; light brown in color

fal-low deer n. a European deer about three feet high at the shoulders

false adj. incorrect; untrue **falseness** n., **falsely** adv.

false face n. the type of mask worn at Halloween

false-hood n. act of lying; an intentional untruth

false ribs n. ribs that are not united directly with the sternum in one's body

fal-set-to n. high singing voice, usually male

fal-si-fy v. to misrepresent a fact **falsification** n.

fal-ter v. uncertain in action **falteringly** adv., **falterer** n.

fame n. the public esteem; a good reputation

fa-mil-iar adj. being well-acquainted with; having complete knowledge of something **familiarly** adv.

fa-mil-i-ar-i-ty n., pl. **-ties** knowledge of something; an established friendship

fa-mil-iar-ize v. to make oneself or someone familiar with something

fam-i-ly n. the group of people who are related by blood or marriage

fam-i-ly name n. a surname or last name of the family

fam-i-ly tree n. a genealogical drawing showing family decent

fam-ine n. a widespread scarcity of food

fam-ish v. to starve or cause one to starve **famished** adj.

fa-mous adj. being well-known or popular **famously** adv.

fan n. device for putting air into motion **fanlike** adj.

fa-nat-ic n. the one who is moved by enthusiasm **fanatically** adv., **fanatical** adj.

fan-ci-er n. a person having a special interest in something or someone

fan-cy n. a whimsical notion or idea **fancied** adj.,

fanciness n., **fancily** adv.

fan-cy–free adj. unattached; not in love; carefree

fan-cy-work n. decorative or ornamental needle work

fan-dan-go n. a Spanish dance in triple time

fan-fare n. a loud trumpet flourish

fang n. pointed tooth or tusk of an animal **fanged** adj.

fan-jet n. an aircraft with a turbojet engine

fan-ny n. the buttocks

fan mail n. mail receive by a public figure from the people who admire them

fan-tail n. any fan shaped tail or end; a variety of domestic pigeons having a fan like tail

fan-ta-sia n. composition according to composer's fancy

fan-ta-size v. to create mental pictures or images

fan-tas-tic adj. wildly fanciful

fan-ta-sy n. pl. **-ies** a creative imagination or thoughts

far adv. at a distance

far-a-way adj. very distant; remote; absentminded state of mind

farce n. theatre comedy

farcical adj., **farcically** adv.

fare n. the fee paid for transportation **farer** n.

fare–thee–well n. the most extreme degree; perfection

fare-well n. good-by

far–fetched adj. to be highly improbable

far–flung adj. being widely distributed over a great area or distance

fa-ri-na n. a fine meal obtained chiefly from nuts, cereals and used as a food

far-i-na-ceous adj. being composed of starch

farm n. land used for agriculture **farming** adj., **-er** n.

farm-house n. the house or homestead on a farm

farm-land n. land that is suitable for agricultural production of food

farm-stead n. a farm, including its land and all of the buildings on it

farm team n. a minor league baseball team

farm-yard n. the area surrounded by farm buildings and enclosed for confining the stock

far–off adj. distant; remote

far–out adj. to be very unconventional

far-ra-go n. confused mixture

far-row n. litter of pigs

far–sighted adj. see things at a distance clearly

far-sightedness n., **-ly** adv.

far-ther adv. at a more distant point **farthermost** adj.

far-thest adj. greatest distance

fas-ci-nate v. to captivate

fascination n., **-ingly** adv.

fas-cism n. one-party system of government

fascistic adj., **fascistically** adv.

fash-ion n. the mode or manner of dress

fashionable adj., **-ably** adv.

fast adj. being swift; being rapid **fastness** n.

fast-back n. car with a downward slope

fast-en v. to join something else fastening, **fastener** n.

fast–food adj. to be specializing in foods prepared and served quickly

fas-tid-i-ous adj. delicate; refined **fastidiousness** n.

fat adj. obese; plump **fatness** n., **fatly** adv.

fat-al adj. causing death **fatalist** n., **fatally** adv.

fa-tal-i-ty n. a death caused by a disaster or accident

fat cat n., Slang powerful and wealthy person

fate n. predetermined events **fated**, **fateful** adj.

fa-ther n. male parent Father a priest **-ly** adj., **-hood** n.

fath-om n. length equal to six feet **fathomless** adj.

fa-tigue n. extreme tiredness

fat-u-ous adj. silly and foolish **fatuousness** n., **fatuously** adv.

fau-cet n. the valve to draw liquids from a pipe

faugh interj. an exclamation of contempt

fault n. impairment or defect;

weakness -iness n., -ily adv.

faux pas n. a false step

fa-vor n. a helpful act

fa-vor-a-ble adj. advan-tageous favorableness n., -bly adv.

fa-vor-ite n. preferred above all others favoritism n.

fawn n. a young deer

faze v. to disconcert

fe-al-ty n. an allegiance owed to a feudal lord

fear n. anticipation of danger faerfully adv., -fulness n.

fear-less adj. brave fearlessness n., fearlessly adv.

fea-si-ble adj. to be able to be accomplished feasibility, feasibleness n., -bly adv.

feast n. meal; a banquet

feat n. a notable achievement

feath-er n. the protective covering of birds

feath-er-weight n. a light weight boxer

fea-ture n. appearance or shape of the face -less adj.

feb-ri-fuge n. medicine to reduce fever

feb-rile adj. being feverish

fe-ces pl. n. an excrement

feck-less adj. ineffective; weak

fe-cund adj. productive -ity n.

fed-er-al adj. agreement between states or groups federalism n., federally adv.

fed-er-ate v. unite in a union

fed-er-a-tion n. two or more states joining a confederacy

fe-do-ra n. soft felt hat

fed up adj. extremely annoyed

fee n. fixed charge

fee-ble adj. lacking strength; weak feebleness n., -bly adv.

fee-ble mind-ed adj. mentally deficient -ness n.

feed v. to supply one with food or nutrition feeder n.

feel v. perceive through touch feeling n., feelingly adv.

feet n. plural of foot

feign v. make a false show of -ed adj., -ingly adv., -er n.

feint n. deceptive movement

fe-lic-i-tate v. to wish happiness to someone felicitation n.

fe-line adj. relating to cats felinity n., felinely adv.

fell v. past tense of fall

fel-low n. boy or man

fel-low-ship n. the common interests of a group

fel-ly n. rim of a wooden wheel

fel-on n. person who committed a felony

fel-o-ny n. kind of serious crime felonious adj., feloniousness n., -iously adv.

felt n. a unwoven fabric

fe-male n. the sex that produces the eggs

fem-i-nine adj. to be pertaining to the female sex feminineness n., -ly adv.

fem-i-nism n. a movement granting equal rights to women feministic adj.

fen n. low, marshy land

fence n. boundary or barrier around something -er n.

fend v. to offer resistance

fen-nel n. an herb from the parsley family

fe-ral adj. not tame

fer-men-ta-tion n. decomposition of organic compounds

fe-ro-cious adj. extremely savage -ness n., -ly adv.

fer-ret n. a small, red-eyed polecat ferreter n.

fer-rous adj. containing iron

fer-rule n. cap at the end of a walking cane

fer-ry n. boat for transporting people, vehicles

fer-tile adj., Biol. ability to reproduce fertility n.

fer-til-ize v. to make something or one fertile

fer-vent adj. ardent; very hot fervency n., fervently adv.

fer-vid adj. being fervent to an extreme degree -ness n.

fer-vor n. a kind of great emotional warmth

fes-cue n. type of tough grass

fes-ter v. to generate pus

fes-ti-val n. type of celebration or party festivity n.

fes-toon n. garland of flowers

fet-a n. Greek cheese

fetch v. to go after and return with something fetcher n.

fetch-ing adj. very attractive

fete n. festival or feast

fet-id adj. having a foul odor fetidness n., fetidly adv.

et-ish *n.* object with magic powers -ism *n.*, -istic *adj.*

et-ter *n.* a chain used to prevent escape

e-tus *n.* unborn organism carried within the womb

eud *n.* quarrel between families feudal *adj.*

e-ver *n.* an abnormally high body temperature

feverish *adj.*, -ishly *adv.*

ew *adj.* small in number

ey *adj.* acting as if under a spell

ez *n.* red felt hat

i-as-co *n.* complete failure

i-at *n.* positive order or decree

ib *n.* trivial lie fibber *n.*

i-ber *n.* piece of synthetic material fibered *adj.*

i-ber-board *n.* a kind of pliable building material

i-ber-glass *n.* a flexible, non-flammable material

i-ber op-tics *pl., n.* the light transmitted through flexible glass rods

ck-le *adj.* changeable

ic-tion *n.* imaginary or created fictional *adj.*

ic-ti-tious *adj.* nonexistent; imaginary fictitiously *adv.*

id-dle *n.* violin fiddler *n.*

i-del-i-ty *n.* loyalty

dg-et *v.* move nervously fidgetiness *n.*, fidgety *adj.*

ef *n.* a feudal estate

eld *n.* piece of cultivated land

end *n.* evil spirit -ish *adj.*, ishness *n.*, -ishly *adv.*

erce *adj.* violent in nature fierceness *n.*, fiercely *adv.*

er-y *adj.* composed of fire fieriness *n.*, fierily *adv.*

-es-ta *n.* religious holiday

fe *n.* an instrument that is similar to a flute

if-teen *n.* cardinal number equal to 14 + 1

fth *n.* one of five equal parts

-ty *n.* cardinal number equal to 5 X 10

g *n.* tree bearing edible fruit

ght *v.* to argue or quarrel over something fighting *n.*

ght-er *n.* person who fights Milit. fast plane

g-ment *n.* an invention or fabrication

fig-u-ra-tive *adj.* containing a figure of speech figurativeness *n.*, -ly *adv.*

fig-ure *n.* the symbol which represents a number figurer *n.*, -ed, -ing *adj.*

fig-ure-head *n.* one with leadership but no power

fil-a-ment *n.* very finely spun fiber or thread -ous *adj.*

fil-bert *n.* edible nut of the hazel tree

filch *v.* to steal filcher *n.*

file *n.* a device for storing papers; grinding tool

fi-let mi-gnon *n.* a tender cut of beef and can be costly

fil-i-buster *n.* attempt to hinder legislative action

fil-i-gree *n.* ornamental wire of gold and silver

fill *v. & n.* supply fully; satisfy a need; put into

fil-lip *n.* snap of the finger

film *n.* photosensitive paper used in photography

film-strip *n.* strip of film for still projection on a screen

fil-ter *n.* device used to purify

fil-th *n.* dirty or foul filthy *adj.*, filthiness *n.*

fin *n.* extension of the body of a fish for swimming

fi-na-gle *v.*, *Slang* to trick or deceive another finagler *n.*

fi-nal *adj.* to be coming to the end or finish finalize *v.*

fi-na-le *n.* final scene in a play

fi-nal-ist *n.* the last person in a contest

fi-nance *n.* a science dealing with monetary affairs

fin-an-cier *n.* expert in large financial affairs

find *v.* to come upon unexpectedly finder *n.*

fine *adj.* superior in skill fineness *n.*, finely *adv.*

fin-er-y *n.* elaborate clothes

fi-nesse *n.* the tact in handling a situation

fin-ger *n.* one digit of the hand

fin-ger bowl *n.* bowl for cleansing the fingers

fin-ger-print *n.* a form of identification of someone

fin-ick-y *adj.* hard to please

fi-nis *n.* the end

fin-ish v. reach the end; conclude finishing n., -ed adj.

fi-nite adj. to be having limits or bounds finiteness n.

fir n. evergreen tree

fire n. chemical reaction of burning fireless adj.

fire-arm n. small weapon

fire-bug n. one who enjoys setting fires

fire drill n. a practice for escaping fires

fire es-cape n. structure for emergency exits

fire-fly n. winged insect that glows at night

fire-man n. person employed to extinguish fires

fire-plug n. hydrant for supplying water

fire tow-er n. forest fire lookout station

firm adj. solid; compact firmness n., firmly adv.

fir-ma-ment n. expanse of the heavens; the sky

first adj. ahead of all others

first aid n. the emergency medical care

first-rate adj. finest quality

fish n., pl. -es cold-blooded aquatic animal fisherman n.

fish-y adj. suspicious

fis-sion n. act of splitting into separate parts

fis-sure n. the narrow crack in a rock

fist n. tightly closed hand

fit v. proper size; good health; competent fitness n.

five n. cardinal number equal to 4 + 1

fix v. to mend; to repair fixer n., fixed adj.

fix-a-tion n. act of being fixed

fix-ture n. the part or appendage of a house

flab n. loose body tissue flabby adj., flabbiness n.

flab-ber-gast v. surprise

flac-cid adj. to be lacking in firmness flaccidness n.

flac-on n. type of small stoppered bottle

flag n. banner of a country

flag-el-lant n. whipping for sexual pleasure -lation n.

flag-rant adj. notorious; evil

flair n. dashing style

flak n. antiaircraft fire

flake n. piece peeled from the surface flaky adj., -ness n.

flam-boy-ant adj. ornate, showy -boyancy n., -ly adv.

flame n. burning vapor from a fire -ingly adv., -ing adj.

flame-out n. the combustion failure of a jet engine

fla-min-go n. pink, tropical wading bird

flank n. the fleshy part of the hip flanker n.

flan-nel n. woven wool fabric

flap-per n. woman of the 1920's

flare v. blaze with a bright light

flare-up n. sudden outburst

flash v. to burst into a bright fire flashiness n.

flash-back n. one's review of past events

flash-light n. small, battery powered lantern

flash-y adj. tastelessly showy flashiness n., flashily adv.

flask n. glass container

flat adj. no curvature; level

flatten v., flatness n.

flat-car n. railroad car

flat-ter v. praise favorably flattery n., flatteringly adv.

flat-u-lent adj. gas in the intestines flatulently adv.

flat-ware n. eating utensils

flaunt v. display showily flaunting n., flauntingly adv.

fla-vor n. distinctive taste flavoring n., flavorless adj.

flaw n. defect or blemish

flaw-less adj. without defects

flax n. plant yielding linseed o

flea n. bloodsucking insect

flea mar-ket n. place to sell used goods and antiques

fleck n. spot or streak

fledg-ling n. young bird

flee v. run away

fleece n. the wool covering sheep fleeced adj.

fleet n. number of warships

flesh n. tissue of the human body fleshiness n., -ly adv.

fleur-de-lis n., pl. fleurs-de-li heraldic emblem

flex v. contract a muscle

flex-i-ble adj. capable of bei flexed; pliable flexibly adv.

flick n. a quick sharp movement

flick-er v. to burn in an unsteady manner -ing n.

flight n. one's scheduled airline trip flightless adj.

flight-y adj. fickle -iness n., flightily adv.

flim-flam n. swindle; hoax

flim-sy adj. to be lacking in strength flimsiness n.

flinch v. to wince from pain inflicted flinchingly adv.

fling v. throw or toss

flip v. turn or throw suddenly

flip-pant adj. impudence flippancy n., flippantly adv.

flirt v. to make romantic overtures flirter n.

flit v. move abruptly flitter n.

float n. action of suspending on water floater n.

flock n. group of animals

floe n. large mass of floating ice

flog v. to beat hard with a whip flogger n.

flood n. the overflow of water or other liquid flooder n.

flood-light n. type of intense artificial light

floor n. the level base of a room

flop v. to fall down clumsily or sloppily flopper n.

flop-py disk n. flexible plastic disk to store computer data

flo-ra n. the plants in a specific region or area

flo-ral adj. to be pertaining to flowers

flor-id adj. to be covered with flowers floridity n.

flo-rist n. seller of flowers

floss n. thread to clean between teeth flossy adj.

flo-til-la n. fleet of vessels

flot-sam n. the debris from sunken ships

floun-der v. struggle clumsily

flour n. the ground meal of wheat floury adj.

flour-ish v. to thrive; to prosper flourishing adj.

flout v. show open contempt for someone flouter n.

flow v. move freely

flow-er n. a group or cluster of petals flowered adj.

fluc-tu-ate v. shift irregularly

flue n. pipe for escaping smoke

flu-ent adj. facile in speech fluently adv., fluency n.

flu-id n. flowing liquid fluidness n., fluidly adv.

fluke n. stroke of luck

flunk v., Slang fail a test

flu-o-res-cence n., Chem. an electromagnetic radiation

flu-o-rine n. gaseous element

flush v. flow out suddenly

flus-ter v. to become nervous or upset flustered adj.

flute n. woodwind instrument fluteist n., fluted adj.

flut-ter v. flap irregularly fluttery adj., flutteringly adv.

flux n. flowing

fly v. travel by air

fly-wheel n. rotating wheel to regulate speed

foal n. young horse

foam n. mass of bubbles foaminess n., foamy adj.

fo-cus n. point at which rays converge focuser n.

fod-der n. feed for livestock

foe n. the enemy

fog n. a mass of condensed water foginess n.

foil v. prevent from being successful; fencing sword

fold v. double or lay one part over another

fo-li-age n. leaves of plants

fo-li-o n. a folder for holding loose papers

folk n. ethnic group of people

folk lore n. the beliefs or customs of people

fol-li-cle n. a small cavity or hole follicular adj.

fol-low v. come after; pursue following adj., follower n.

fol-ly n. instance of foolishness

fo-ment v. to rouse; to incite someone fomentation n.

fond adj. to be cherished with affection fondly adv.

fon-dle v. to caress one affectionately fondler n.

font n. fountain for holy water

food n. substance used to sustain life and growth

fool n. a person who is lacking sense foolish adj.

foot n. the lower part of one's

leg; twelve inches

foot-bridge n. type of bridge used for pedestrians

foot-hill n. low hill at the base of a mountain

foot-ing n. stable position

foot-loose adj. having no ties

foot-note n. note of reference at bottom of page

foot-work n. use of the feet

for prep. on behalf of someone; in favor of

for-age n. the food used for cattle; seek food

for-bid v. prohibit by law forbidden adj., -ingly adv.

force n. energy; power; strength -ful adj.; -er n.

for-ceps n. forceps pl. tongs used in surgery

ford n. a shallow place in the water fordable adj.

fore adj. & adv. toward the front; golfer's warning

fore-bode v. warning in advance foreboding n.

fore-cast v. to predict something in advance -er n.

fore-close v. recall a mortgage in default foreclosure n.

fore-fa-ther n. ancestor

fore-go v. go before

fore-go-ing adj. previous

fore-gone adj. finished or gone

fore-ground n. part of picture nearest viewer

fore-hand n. stroke in tennis -forehanded adj., -edness n.

fore-head n. part of the face

for-eign adj. outside one's country foreigner n.

fore-man n. overseer

fore-most adj. & adv. first in rank or order

fore-noon n. time between sunrise and noon

fore-run-ner n. one sent to give notice of approach of others

fore-see v. to see something beforehand foreseer n.

fore-shad-ow v. warn beforehand foreshadower n.

fore-sight n. looking forward foresightedness n., -ed adj.

for-est n. land covered with trees forester n.

fore-stall v. to prevent by prior measures

for-est ran-ger n. officer protecting a public forest

fore-tell v. predict foreteller n.

for-ev-er adv. without end

fore-warn v. warn in advance

fore-word n. an introductory statement to something

for-feit n. something taken away

forge n. furnace to heat metals forgeable adj., forger n.

for-get v. lose the memory of forgetfully adv., forgetful adj.

for-give v. excuse; pardon forgiveable adj., -ness n.

for-go v. give up forgoer n.

fork n. utensil which is used for eating forked adj.

for-lorn adj. abandoned; hopeless forlornness n., -ly adv.

form n. shape; contour

for-mal adj. based on conventions formally adv., -ism n.

for-mat n. general layout of a publication

for-ma-tion n. a given arrangement

for-ma-tive adj. developed

for-mer adj. previous -ly adv.

for-mi-da-ble adj. extremely strong -bly adv., -ness n.

for-mu-la n. set of rules; infant's food

for-mu-late v. express in formula formulation n.

for-ni-ca-tion n. the sexual intercourse between unmarried people

for-sake v. abandon; give up forsaken adv., -en adj.

for-swear v. renounce -er n.

fort n. fortified structure

forte n. activity one excels in

forth adv. forward in order

forth-right adj. being direct being frank -ness n.

for-ti-fy v. to strengthen something fortifier n.

for-ti-tude n. strength of mind

fort-night n. every two weeks

for-tress n. fort

for-tu-i-tous adj. by chance -tuity n., fortuitously adv.

for-tu-nate adj. having good fortune fortunately adv.

for-tune n. a large amount of money or valuables

for-ty n., pl. -ies cardinal num

ber equal to four times ten

fo-rum n. judicial assembly

for-ward adj. toward a place

fos-sil n. remains of an animal

fos-ter v. give parental care to

foul adj. spoiled; offensive

found v. establish; set up

foun-da-tion n. base of building; make up base

found-ling n. abandoned infant

fount n. fountain

foun-tain n. a natural spring of water

four n. cardinal number that equals 3 + 1

four-score adj. being four times twenty

four-teen n. cardinal number that equals 13 + 1

fowl n. bird used as food or hunted as game

fox n. wild animal

fox-hole n. a shallow pit dug by a soldier as cover against enemy fire

fox-hound n. large hunting dog that is developed for hunting fox

fox terrier n. a small dog having a wiry coat

fox--trot n. ballroom dance

fox-y adj. being sly or crafty in one's character

foy-er n. lobby entrance

fra-cas n. noisy quarrel; a fight or dispute

frac-tion n. small part of; a quantity that is less than a whole number

frac-ture n. broken bone; the state of being broken

frag-ile adj. being easy to break or to damage; frail

frag-ment n. a detached part or section; part unfinished or incomplete

fra-grant adj. having a sweet odor or scent

frail adj. delicate; weak

frame v. to enclose with a border, such as picture

frame-up n. Slang make someone appear guilty

fran-chise n. license to market a company's goods

fran-gi-ble adj. breakable

frank adj. sincere and straightforward -ness n.

frank-furt-er n. smoked sausage; hot dog

frank-in-cense n. an aromatic gum resin

fran-tic adj. lose emotional control franticly adv.

fra-ter-nal adj. pertaining to brothers fraternity n.

frat-er-nize v. to associate with others in a friendly manner or way

frat-ri-cide n. the killing of one's brother or sister

fraud n. deception for unlawful gain fraudulently adv.

fraud-u-lent adj. marked by or practicing fraud

fraught adj. being full of or accompanied by something specified

fray n. brawl, or fight; a heated argument or dispute

fraz-zle v. to completely fatigue or tire

freak n. capricious event

freck-le n. dark, sun induced spots freckly adv.

free adj. under no obligation; without charge

free-dom n. the condition or the state of being free

free lance n. the services without commitments to any one employer

free-stand-ing adj. standing alone without any support

free trade n. the trade between nations which is unrestricted

free-way n. tollfree highway having more than two lanes

free will n. the ability to choose freely or do as one wishes

freeze v. to become solid ice

freeze-dry v. to preserve by drying in a frozen state and under a high vacuum

freez-er n. an insulated box for storing food

freight n. the manner or the way of shipping cargo

freight-er n. a cargo ship that carries goods to other places

French fries pl., n. strips of potatoes fried in deep fat

fren-zy n. a state of extreme excitement

fre·quent adj. to be happening often **frequently** adv.

fres·co n. art of painting on moist plaster

fresh adj. being newly made; not stale **freshness** n.

fresh·man n. a first year student of college or high school

fret v. anxious or irritated; worry **fretfully** adv.

fri·a·ble adj. easily crumbled

fric·as·see n. type of dish made of meat or poultry

fric·tion n. conflict or clash

friend n. a close companion

frig·ate n. type of square-rigged warship

fright n. feeling of alarm

fright·en v. scare; terrify

frig·id adj. very cold

frill n. decorative ruffle

fringe n. & v. ornate edging

frisk v. skip about; search for weapons

frit·ter v. squander or waste

friv·o·lous adj. being trivial or silly **frivolousness** n.

frock n. loose-fitting dress

frog n. aquatic, leaping amphibian

frol·ic n. playful, carefree jaunting **frolicing** v.

from prep. starting at a particular place

front n. the forward surface of an object or building

fron·tier n. unexplored area

frost n. the ice crystals on a cold surface

frost·bite n. the injury due to exposure to cold

frost·ing n. icing for a cake

froth n. mass of bubbles; foam

frown v. contract the eyebrow in displeasure

fro·zen adj. covered with or made into ice

fru·gal adj. being thrifty or economical **frugalness** n.

fruit n. edible berries

frump·y adj. dowdy; unfashionable **frumpiness** n.

frus·trate v. keep from attaining a goal; thwart **-tion** n.

fry v. cook in hot fat

fuch·sia n. tropical plant

fudge n. type of soft cooked chocolate candy

fuel n. combustible matter used to produce energy

fu·gi·tive adj. to be fleeing from arrest

ful·fill v. to carry out something or act; satisfy

full n. largest amount

fume n., often **fumes** irritating smoke or gas; show anger

fu·mi·gate v. to exterminate vermin or insects

func·tion n. occupation; duty

fund n. the source of money and supplies

fun·da·men·tal adj. basic or essential **fundamentaly** adv.

fu·ner·al n. the services for a dead person

fun·gus n., pl. **-gi** or **-guses** type of spore-bearing plants

fun·nel n. a hollow cone utensil for pouring liquid

fur·bish v. to make bright by rubbing; renovate

fu·ri·ous adj. angry; fit of rage

furl v. to roll up and secure something

fur·lough n. the permission to be absent from duty

fur·nace n. large device to produce intense heat

fur·nish v. equip or outfit

fur·ni·ture n. beds, lamps, sofas, chairs, etc.

fu·ror n. violent anger; rage.

fur·row n. long, narrow trench in the ground

fur·tive adj. obtained underhandedly; stolen

fu·ry n., pl. **-ies** uncontrolled anger; turbulence; an angry or spiteful person

fuse n. electrical safety device; device to detonate explosives

fu·sil·lage n. central section of an airplane that contains the wings and tail

fu·sil·lade n. a quick discharge of firearms

fus·tian n. a sturdy and stout cotton cloth

fu·tile adj. being of no avail; serving no purpose; ineffectual **futility** n.

fu·ture n. time yet to come

fuzz n. mass of loose fibers

G, g the seventh letter of the English alphabet

gab v., Slang talk or chat idly or in thoughtless manner

gab-ar-dine n. a type of cloth which is durable

gab-ber n. a person who talks too much

gab-ble v. to speak incoherently

gab-bro n. type of igneous rock composed of minerals

gab-by adj. too talkative

gab-er-dine n. a long smock

gad v. to wander about restlessly

gad-a-bout n., Slang person who seeks excitement

gad-fly n. type of fly which will bite livestock

gadg-et n., Slang small tool for various jobs

gad-o-lin-ite n. type of brown or black mineral

gad-wall n. a dabbling duck and is the size of a mallard

gaff n. sharp iron hook used for landing fish

gaf-fer n. an old man; lighting electrician on a television set

gag n. wadded cloth, forced into the mouth to prevent speech Slang practical joke

gage n. item deposited as a pledge of combat

gag-ger n. person that gags such as a joker

gag-gle n. flock of geese that is not in flight

gai-e-ty n., pl. -ies state of being happy; cheerfulness

gain v. to earn or acquire possession

gain-ful adj. producing profits

gain-say v. to deny; to contradict

gait n. manner of moving on foot

gai-ter n. covering of leather for the leg

ga-la n. festive celebration

gal-ax-y n., pl. -ies Astron. very large cluster of stars

gale n., Meteor. very powerful wind

gall n., Physiol. bitter fluid secreted by the liver; bile

gal-lant adj. polite and attentive to women

gal-lant-ry n. nobility and bravery

gall-blad-der or gall bladder n. small sac under the right liver that stores bile

gal-le-on n. large sailing ship

gal-ler-y n., pl. -ries group of spectators; building that displays works of art

gal-li-vant v. roam about in search of pleasure

gal-lon n. liquid measurement equal to four quarts

gal-lop n. horse's gait

gal-lows n. framework used for execution by hanging

gall-stone n., Pathol. small, stony mass that forms in the gall bladder

ga-lore adj. in great numbers overshoes

gal-va-nism n. electricity produced by chemical action

gal-va-nize v. to protect iron or steel with rust resistant zinc

gal-va-nom-e-ter n., Electr. apparatus that detects electric and its strength and direction

gam-bit n. an opening in chess where a piece is sacrificed

gam-ble v. to take a chance

gam-bol v. frolic, skip, or leap about in play

gam-ete n., Biol. mature reproductive cells

gam-in n. homeless child

gam-mer n. elderly woman

gam-ut n. whole range or extent of anything

gan-der n. male goose Slang quick glance

gang n. group of persons who work together or socialize regularly

gan-gling adj. tall and thin

gan-grene n., Pathol. the death and decay of tissue in the body

gap n. opening or wide crack

gape v. open the mouth wide

gar n. fish having a spearlike snout and elongated body

garb n. clothing

gar-bage n. food wastes; trash

gar·ble *v.* mix up or confuse

gar·den *n.* place for growing plants

gar·de·nia *n.* tropical shrub with fragrant white flowers

gar·gan·tu·an *adj.* of enormous size

gar·gle *v.* to cleanse or medicate the back of the mouth and throat

gar·ish *adj.* too showy and bright; gaudy

gar·land *n.* wreath of flowers or leaves

gar·lic *n.* plant having a strong odor, resembling an onion

gar·ment *n.* article of clothing

gar·ner *v.* gather and store

gar·net *n.* dark-red gemstone

gar·nish *v.* to add decoration

gar·ret *n.* room in an attic

gar·ri·son *n.* military post

gar·ter *n.* band worn to hold a stocking in place

gas *n., pl.* gases combustible mixture used as fuel; gasoline

gash *n.* long, deep cut

gas·ket *n., Mech.* seal to prevent the escape of fluid or gas

gas·o·hol *n.* fuel blended from unleaded gasoline and ethanol

gasp *v.* labored attempts to breathe

gas·tric *adj.* pertaining to the stomach

gas·tri·tis *n., Pathol.* inflammation of the stomach lining

gas·tron·o·my *n.* art of good eating

gate *n.* movable opening in a wall or fence

gath·er *v.* bring or come together into one place

gaud·y *adj.* too highly decorated for good taste

gauge *or* **gage** *n.* standard measurement

gaunt *adj.* thin in appearance

gaunt·let *or* **gant·let** *n.* challenge to fight

gav·el *n.* mallet used to call for order

ga·vi·al *n.* large crocodile

gawk *v.* to gape; to stare stupidly

gawk·y *adj.* clumsy or awkward

gay *adj.* merry; happy

gaze *v.* to look steadily at something to stare

ga·zette *n.* newspaper

gear *n., Mech.* toothed wheel

gee·zer *n., Slang* an old man

geld *v.* to castrate

gem·ol·o·gy *or* **gem·mol·o·gy** *n.* study of gems

gen·der *n.* quality of being either male or female

gene *n., Biol.* means by which hereditary characteristics are given

ge·ne·al·o·gy *n., pl.* -ies record or study of ones ancestory

gen·er·al *adj.* pertaining to the whole of something

gen·er·al·ize *v.* draw a general conclusion from facts or observations

gen·er·ate *v.* cause to be; to produce

gen·er·a·tion *n.* group of individuals born about the same time

ge·ner·ic *adj.* relating to an entire class or group; general

gen·er·ous *adj.* sharing freely; abundant

gen·e·sis *n., pl.* -ses act or state of originating

ge·net·ic *adj.* pertaining to the development of something

gen·ial *adj.* cheerful, pleasant and good-humored

gen·i·tals *pl.,n.* the external sexual organs

gen·i·tive *adj., Gram.* indicating origin, source, or possession

gen·ius *n., pl.* -ses exceptional intellectual ability a strong, natural talent

gen·o·cide *n.* systematic extermination of a race or cultural group

gen·teel *adj.* refined or well-bred

gen·tian *n.* annual or perennial plant

gen·tle *adj.* not harsh, mild in manner

gen·tle·man *n.* man of noble birth and social position

gen·try *n.* people of high social standing

gen-u-flect v. to bend down on one knee

gen-u-ine adj. real; not counterfeit

ge-o-cen-tric adj. relating to the earth's center

ge-og-ra-phy n., pl. -hies the scientific study of the earth's features and population

ge-om-e-try n., pl. ies mathematics dealing with lines, planes, and solids

ge-o-ther-mal adj. relating to the internal heat of the earth

ger-i-at-rics pl., n. medical study that deals with diseases and hygiene of old age

germ n. small cell from which a new organism may develop

ger-mane adj. relevant to what is being considered or discussed

germ cell n. egg or sperm cell

ger-mi-cide n. agent used to destroy or disease germs

ger-mi-nate v. to grow, develop, or sprout

gest n. notable deed or feat

ges-tic-u-late v. make expressive gestures

ges-ture n. bodily motion, especially with the hands in speaking

get v. to receive or come into the possession of

get-up n. an outfit; a costume

gey-ser n. natural spring that ejects hot water and steam

ghast-ly adj. horrible; terrifying

gher-kin n. very small pickle

ghet-to n. section of a city in which members of an ethnic group lives

gib-ber v. to talk or chatter incoherently or unintelligibly

gib-ber-ish n. meaningless speech

gib-bet n. a gallows v. To execute by hanging on a gibbet

gib-bon n. a slender, long-armed Asian ape

gibe v. to ridicule or make taunting remarks **-er** n.

gib-let n., or **giblets** the heart liver, and gizzard of a fowl

gid-dy adj. affected by a reeling or whirling sensation; dizzy **giddily** adv., **-giddiness** n.

gift n. something that is given from one person to another

gifted adj. having a special ability; talented

gi-gan-tic adj. of tremendous size; huge **gigamtically** adv.

gig-gle v. to laugh in high-pitched, repeated, short sounds **giggler** n., **-ly** adj.

gig-o-lo n., a man who is supported by a woman, who is not his wife

gild v. to coat with a thin layer of gold; to brighten or adorn **-ed** adj., **-ing**, **-er** n.

gill n., Zool. the organ, as of fishes and various other aquatic invertebrates, used for taking oxygen from water.

gilt adj. covered with, or of the color of gold

gim-crack n. a cheap and useless object of little or no value

gim-let n. a small, sharp tool with a bar handle and a pointed, spiral tip used for boring holes

gimp n., Slang a person who walks with a limp; a cripple

gin-ger n. a tropical Asian plant with a pungent aromatic root, used in medicine and cooking

gin-ger-ly adv. doing something very cautiously

ging-ham n. a cotton fabric woven in solid colors and checks

gin-gi-vi-tis n., Pathol. inflammation of the gums

gird v. to surround, encircle, or attach with or as if with a belt girded, **girding** v.

gird-er n. a strong, horizontal beam, as of steel or wood

gir-dle n. a cord or belt worn around the waist; supporting undergarment worn by women **girdle** v.

girl n. a female child or infant; a young, unmarried woman **girlish** adj.

girth n. the circumference or

distance around something

gis-mo n., Slang a part or device whose name is unknown or forgotten

gist n. the central or main substance

give v. to make a present of; to bestow; donate or contribute; to apply; to devote giving v.

giv-en adj. bestowed; presented

giz-zard n. the second stomach in birds

gla-brous adj., Biol. having no hair or projections -ness n.

glacial epoch Geol. a portion of geological time when ice sheets covered much of the earth's surface

glad adj. displaying, experiencing, or affording joy and pleasure; being happy

glad-den v. to make glad; to make happy

glade n. a clearing in a forest

glad-some adj. giving cheer

glam-or-ize or **glam-our-ize** v. to make glamorous

glam-our or **glam-or** n. alluring fascination or charm

glance v. to take a brief or quick look at something

gland n., Anat. any of various body organs which excrete or secrete substances

glare v. to stare fiercely or angrily

glau-co-ma n., Pathol. a disease of the eye

glau-cous adj. yellowish green

gleam n. a momentary ray or beam of light

glean v. to collect or gather facts by patient effort gleaner n., gleanings pl., n.

glee n. joy; merriment

glen n. a small, secluded valley

glib adj. spoken easily and fluently; superficial glibly adv., glibness n.

glide v. to pass or move smoothly with little or no effort glidingly adv.

glid-er n. one that glides; Aeron. an aircraft without an engine

glim-mer n. a faint suggestion; an indication; a dim unsteady light

glimpse n. a momentary look

glis-san-do n., pl. -di a rapid passing from one tone to another by a continuous change of pitch

glis-ten v. to shine softly as reflected by light

glitch n. a minor mishap or malfunction

glit-ter n. a brilliant sparkle

gloam-ing n. twilight

gloat v. to express, feel, or observe with great malicious pleasure or self-satisfaction gloater n.

glob n. a drop of something

glob-al adj. spherical; involving the whole world -ize v.

globe n. a spherical object; anything that is perfectly rounded

glob-u-lin n., Biochem. any of a class of simple proteins found widely in blood, milk, tissue, muscle and plant seeds

gloom n. partial or total darkness -ily adv., -iness n.

glop n., Slang a messy mixture of food; something that is considered worthless

glo-ri-fy v. to worship and give glory to glorification n.

glo-ri-ous adj. magnificent gloriously adv.

glory n., pl. -ies distinguished praise or honor

gloss n. the sheen or luster of a polished surface

glos-sa-ry n., pl. -ries a list of words and their meanings

glot-tis n., pl. -ises or -ides Anat. the opening or cleft between the vocal cords

glow v. to have a bright, warm, ruddy color

glow-er v. to look sullenly or angrily at; to glare

glox-in-i-a n. a tropical South American plant

glu-cose n., Chem. a substance less sweet than cane sugar, found as dextrose in plants and animals and obtained by hydrolysis

glut v. to feed or supply beyond

capacity n. an overabundance

glu·ten n. a mixture of plant proteins that is used as an adhesive **glutenous** adj.

glut·ton n. someone who eats immoderately

glyc·er·ol n., Chem. a sweet, oily, syrupy liquid derived from fats and oils

gly·co·side n., Chem. any of a group of carbohydrates which, when decomposed, produce glucose or other sugar

gnarl n. a hard, protruding knot on a tree **gnarled** adj.

gnash v. to grind or strike the teeth together

gnat n. a small, winged insect, specially one that bites or stings

gnaw v. to bite or eat away with persistence **gnawer** n.

gnome n. in folklore, a dwarf-like creature

go v. to proceed or pass along; to leave; pass, as of time n. an attempt; a try

goal n. a purpose

goat·ee n. a short, pointed beard on a man's chin

goat-skin n. the skin of a goat

gob n. a piece or lump of something

gob·ble v. to eat and swallow food greedily

gob·bler n. a male turkey

gob·let n. a drinking glass

gob·lin n. in folklore, an ugly, grotesque creature said to be mischievous and evil

god n. someone considered to be extremely important or valuable

God n. the Supreme Being

god·less adj. not recognizing a god **godlessness** n.

god·ly adj. filled with love for God

god·send n. something received unexpectedly that is needed or wanted

go·get·ter n. an enterprising, aggressive person

gog·gle n., pl. -gles spectacles or eyeglasses to protect the eyes

go·ing n. the act of moving, leaving, or departing

goi·ter n., Pathol. any abnormal enlargement of the thyroid gland **goitrous** adj.

gold n. a soft, yellow, metallic element that is highly ductile and resistant to oxidation

gold·en adj. made of or containing gold; bright yellow in color

gold·fish n. a reddish or brass-colored freshwater fish

Gol·go·tha n. the place near Jerusalem where Jesus was crucified; also known as Calvary

Go·li·ath n. in the Bible, a giant Philistine killed by David with a stone from a sling shot

gon·ad n., Anat. the male or female sex gland where the reproductive cells develop; an ovary or testis

gon·do·la n. a long, narrow, flat-bottomed boat

gong n. a heavy metal disk with a deep resonant tone

gon·o·coc·cus n., pl. -cocci the bacterium which causes gonorrhea **gonococcic** adj.

gon·or·rhe·a n., Pathol. a contagious venereal infection transmitted chiefly by sexual intercourse

goo n. any sticky substance

goo·ber n., Regional a peanut

good adj. having desirable or favorable qualities or characteristics; morally excellent

Good Book n. the Bible

good·by or **good-bye** interj. used to express farewell n. a farewell; a parting word

good-look·ing adj. handsome

good-na·tured adj. having an easygoing and pleasant disposition

good·ness n. the state or quality of being good

good·y n., pl. -ies something that is good to eat; a prissy person

goof n., Slang a mistake v. to blunder; to make a mistake

goof--off *n.* a person who shuns responsibility or work

goof-y *adj.* ridiculous; silly

gook *n., Slang* a slimy, sludgy, or dirty substance

goon *n., Slang* a thug or hoodlum hired to intimidate or injure someone

goose *n., pl.* **geese** a large water bird related to swans and ducks

go-pher *n.* a burrowing rodent with large cheek pouches

gore *v.* to stab or pierce *n.* blood that has been shed

gorge *n.* a deep, narrow ravine; deep or violent disgust **gorger** *n.*

gor-geous *adj.* beautiful; dazzling

go-ril-la *n.* a large African jungle ape

gorse *n.* a spiny plant bearing fragrant yellow flowers

go-ry *adj.* covered or stained with blood; resembling gore

gos-hawk *n.* a large, short-winged hawk formerly used in falconry

gos-ling *n.* a young goose

gos-pel *or* **Gos-pel** *n.* the teachings of Christ and the apostles

gos-sa-mer *n.* the fine film or strands of a spider's web floating in the air **gossamer** *adj.*

gos-sip *n.* idle, often malicious talk *v.* to spread or engage in gossip **gossiper** *n.*

got *v.* past tense of get

gour-mand *n.* a person who takes excessive pleasure in eating

gour-met *n.* someone who appreciates and understands fine food and drink

gout *n., Pathol.* a disease caused by a defect in metabolism and characterized by painful inflammation of the joints **gouty** *adj.*

gov-ern *v.* to guide, rule, or control by right or authority **governable** *adj.*

gov-ern-ment *n.* the authoritative administration of public policy and affairs of a nation, state or city **governmental** *adj.*

gov-er-nor *n.* one who governs, as the elected chief executive of any state in the United States **governorship** *n.*

grab *v.* to snatch or take suddenly **graber** *n.,* **grabby** *adj.*

gra-ben *n., Geol.* an elongated depression in the earth, caused by the downward faulting of a portion of the earth's crust

grace *n.* seemingly effortless beauty, ease, and charm of movement or form

gra-da-tion *n.* a gradual and orderly arrangement or progression according to quality, size, rank, or other value **gradational** *adj.*

grade *n.* a step or degree

gra-di-ent *n.* a slope or degree of inclination *Phys.* a rate of change in variable factors, as temperature or pressure

grad-u-al *adj.* moving or changing slowly by degrees **gradually** *adv.,* **-ness** *n.*

grad-u-ate *v.* to receive or be granted an academic diploma or degree upon completion of a course of study

grad-u-a-tion *n.* the state of graduating; a commencement ceremony

graf-fi-to *n., pl.* **graffiti** an inscription or drawing made on a public wall

gra-ham *n.* whole wheat flour

grail *n.* the legendary cup used by Christ at the Last Supper

grain *n.* a small, hard seed or kernel of cereal, wheat, or oats; the seeds or fruits of such plants as a group; texture; basic nature

grain alcohol *n.* ethanol

grain-y *adj.* having a granular texture **graininess** *n.*

gram *n.* a metric unit of mass and weight equal to 1/1000 kilogram and nearly equal to one cubic centimeter of water at its maximum density

gram-mar *n.* the study and description of the classes of words, their relations to each other, and their arrangement into sentences

gram molecule *n., Chem.* the quantity of a compound, expressed in grams, that is equal to the molecular weight of that compound

gran-a-ry *n., pl.* **ries** a building for storing threshed grain

grand *adj.* large in size, extent, or scope; magnificent

gran-deur *n.* the quality or condition of being grand

gran-dil-o-quent *adj.* speaking in or characterized by a pompous or bombastic style **grandiloquence** *n.*

gran-di-ose *adj.* impressive and grand; pretentiously pompous **grandiosely** *adv.*

grand mal *n., Pathol.* a form of epilepsy characterized by severe convulsions and loss of consciousness

gran-ite *n.* a hard, coarse-grained igneous rock composed chiefly of quartz, mica, and orthoclase

gran-ite-ware *n.* ironware utensils coated with hard enamel

gran-ny *or* **gran-nie** *n.* a grandmother; an old woman

gra-no-la *n.* rolled oats mixed with dried fruit and seeds

grant *v.* to allow; to consent to **granter, grantor** *n.*

gran-u-lar *adj.* composed or seeming to be composed of containing grains or granules **granularity** *n.*

gran-u-late *v.* to make or form into granules or crystals **granulation** *n.*

gran-ule *n.* a very small grain or particle

graph *n.* a diagram representing the relationship between sets of things

graph-ic *or* **graph-i-cal** *adj.* describing in full detail

graph-ite *n.* a soft black form of carbon having a metallic luster and slippery texture, used in lead pencils, lubricants, paints, and coatings **graphitic** *adj.*

graph-ol-o-gy *n.* the study of handwriting for the purpose of analyzing **graphologist** *n.*

grap-nel *n.* a small anchor with several flukes at the end

grap-ple *n.* an instrument with iron claws used to fasten an enemy ship along-side for boarding **grappler** *n.*

grasp *v.* to seize and grip firmly *n.* the power to seize and hold

grasp-ing *adj.* urgently desiring material possessions; greedy **-ly** *adv.,* **-ness** *n.*

grass *n.* any of numerous plants having narrow leaves and jointed stems *Slang* marijuana **grassy** *adj.*

grassiness *n.*

grate *v.* to reduce, shred or pulverize by rubbing against a rough or sharp surface *n.* a rasping noise **grater** *n.,* **grating** *adj.*

grate *n.* a framework or bars placed over a window or other opening

grate-ful *adj.* thankful or appreciative for benefits or kindnesses **gratefully** *adv.*

grat-i-fy *v.* to give pleasure or satisfaction to **-ication** *n.*

grat-ing *n.* a grate

grat-is *adv. & adj.* free

grat-i-tude *n.* the state of appreciation and gratefulness

gra-tu-i-tous *adj.* given or obtained without payment; unjustified **gratuitously** *adv.*

gra-tu-i-ty *n., pl.* **-ies** a gift given in return for a service rendered

gra-va-men *n., pl.* **-mens** *or* **-mina** in law, the part of an accusation or charge weighing most heavily against the accused

grave *n.* a burial place for a dead body *adj.* very serious or important in nature

grav-el *n.* loose rock fragments often with sand *Pathol.* the deposit of sand-like crystals that form in the kidneys

gra-vim-e-ter *n.* an implement for determining specific gravity **gravimetry** *n.*

grav-i-tate *v.* to be drawn as if by an irresistible force

grav-i-ta-tion *n., Physics* the force or attraction any two bodies exert towards each other **-ive** *adj.*, **-ally** *adv.*

grav-i-ty *n., pl.* **-ies** the gravitational force manifested by the tendency of material bodies to fall toward the center of the earth

gray-ling *n., pl.* **-ling** *or* **-lings** any of several freshwater food and game fish with a small mouth and a large dorsal fin

gray matter *n.* the grayish-brown nerve tissue of the spinal cord and brain

graze *v.* to feed upon growing grasses or herbage

grease *n.* melted or soft animal fat *v.* to lubricate or coat with grease

great *adj.* very large in size or volume; very good or firstrate **greatly** *adv.*

great-heart-ed *adj.* noble in spirit

greed *n.* selfish desire to acquire more than one needs or deserves

green-er-y *n., pl.* **-ies** green foliage or plants

green--eyed *adj.* jealous

green thumb *n.* a special skill for making plants thrive

greet *v.* to address someone in a friendly way; to welcome **greeter** *n.*

greet-ing *n.* a word of salutation

gre-gar-i-ous *adj.* habitually associating with others as in groups, flocks, or herds; sociable

grem-lin *n.* a mischievous elf

grew *v.* past tense of grow

grid *n.* an arrangement of regularly spaced bars

grid-dle *n.* a flat pan used for cooking

grid-i-ron *n.* a metal

framework used for broiling meat, fish, and other foods; a football field

grief *n.* deep sadness or mental distress caused by a loss

griev-ance *n.* a real or imagined wrong which is regarded as cause for complaint or resentment

grieve *v.* to cause, or feel sorrow **grievous** *adj.*

grille *or* **grill** *n.* a grating with open metalwork

grim *adj.* stern or forbidding in appearance or character; gloomy; dismal **grimly** *adv.*

grim-ace *n.* a facial expression of pain, disgust

grime *n.* dirt, especially soot clinging to or coating a surface **-iness** *n.,* **grimy** *adj.*

grin *v.* to smile broadly

grind *v.* to reduce to fine particles; to sharpen; *n.* a person who works hard

grip *n.* a firm hold; a grasp; the ability to seize or maintain a hold **gripper** *n.*

gripe *v.* to cause sharp pain or cramps in the bowels; to anger

grippe *n.* influenza **grippy** *adj.*

gris-ly *adj.* ghastly; gruesome

gris-tle *n.* cartilage of meat

grit *n.* small, rough granules; having great courage and fortitude **gritty** *adj.*

grits *pl., n.* coarsely ground hominy; coarse meal

griz-zle *v.* to become gray

grog-gy *adj.* dazed, weak, or not fully conscious, as from a blow **groggily** *adv.*

groom *n.* a male person hired to tend horses; a stableman; a bridegroom

gro-tesque *adj.* incongruous or ludicrous in appearance; bizarre; outlandish

grot-to *n., pl.* **-toes** *or* **-tos** a cave or cave-like structure

grouch *n.* an habitually irritable or complaining person **grouchily** *adv.*

ground *n.* the surface of the earth

ground *v.* past tense of grind

ground hog *n.* a woodchuck

group *n.* a collection or assemblage of people, or things

grov-el *v.* to lie or crawl face downward, as in fear; to act with abject humility

grow *v.* to increase in size, develop, and reach maturity; to expand; to increase **grower** *n.*

grub *v.* to dig up by the roots; to lead a dreary existence

grub-by *adj.* sloppy, unkempt

grudge *n.* a feeling of ill will, rancor, or deep resentment

gru-el *n.* a thin liquid made by boiling meal in water or milk

gru-el-ing *or* **gru-el-ling** *adj.* extremely tiring -ly *adv.*

grue-some *adj.* causing horror or fright **gruesomely** *adv.*

gruff *adj.* brusque and rough in manner; harsh in sound; hoarse -ly *adv.*, -ness *n.*

grum-ble *v.* to complain in low, throaty sounds; to growl **grumbler** *n.*

grump-y *adj.* irritable and moody; ill tempered

grun-gy *adj., Slang* dirty, run-down, or inferior in condition

grunt *n.* the deep, guttural sound of a hog

guar-an-tee *n.* the promise or assurance of the durability or quality of a product; something held or given as a pledge or security

guar-an-ty *n., pl.* -ies a pledge or promise to be responsible for the debt, duty, or contract of another person

guard *v.* to watch over or shield from danger or harm; to keep watch

guard-i-an *n.* one who is legally assigned responsibility for the care of a person unable to do so for himself **guardianship** *n.*

gub-ba *v., Slang* to playfully tickle the neck area of small children

guess *v.* to make a judgment or form an opinion on uncertain or incomplete knowledge

guest *n.* one who is the recipient of hospitality from another

guf-faw *n.* a loud burst of laughter **guffaw** *v.*

guid-ance *n.* the act, process, or result of guiding

guide *n.* one who leads or directs another **guider** *n.*

guilt *n.* the condition of having committed a crime

gul-let *n., Pathol.* the passage from the mouth to the stomach; esophagus; the throat

gul-li-ble *adj.* easily cheated

gul-ly *n., pl.* -ies a ditch cut in the earth by running water

gump-tion *n., Slang* boldness; initiative; enterprise

gust *n.* a sudden, violent rush of wind or air; a sudden outburst -ily *adv.*, -y *adj.*

gus-ta-to-ry *adj.* of or pertaining to the sense of taste

gus-to *n.* hearty enjoyment

guts-y *adj., Slang* courageous

guy *n., Slang* a man; a fellow

gym-na-si-um *n., pl.* -ums *or* -sia a building equipped for indoor sports

gy-ne-col-o-gy *n.* the branch of medicine dealing with the female reproductive organs **gynecological** *adj.*

gyp *v., Informal* to swindle, cheat *n.* a fraud **gypper** *n.*

gy-rate *v.* to rotate or revolve around a fixed point or axis *adj.* coiled or winding about **gyrator** *n.*, **gyratory** *adj.*

gy-ro-com-pass *n.* a compass that has a motor-driven gyroscope so mounted that its axis of rotation maintains a constant position with reference to the true or geographic north

gy-ro-scope *n.* a spinning wheel or disk whose spin axis maintains its angular orientation when not subjected to external torques

gy-ro-sta-bi-liz-er *n.* a gyroscopic instrument designed to reduce the rolling motion of ships

H, h the eighth letter of the English alphabet

ha-ba-ne-ra n. type of dance done in Cuba

ha-be-as cor-pus n. order to produce a prisoner in court

hab-er-dash-er n. the person dealing in mens clothing

hab-er-dash-er-y n. the goods sold by a haberdasher

hab-ile adj. being skillful or having an ability

ha-bil-i-ment n. characteristic clothing of rank or of an occassion

ha-bil-i-tate v. to make one capable **habilition** n.

hab-it n. the involuntary pattern of one's behavior

hab-it-a-ble adj. suitable for habitation or residing -ness n., -ably adv.

ha-bi-tant n. a settle being of French origin and of the farming class in Canada

hab-i-tat n. the region in which an animal or plant lives or grows; the place of residence of a person

hab-i-ta-tion n. the place of residence of someone or something

hab-it--form-ing adj. to be producing a kind of physiological addiction

ha-bit-u-al adj. acting according to habit **habitually** adv., **habitualness** n.

ha-bit-u-ate v. to familiarize oneself with something

ha-bit-u-a-tion n. the process of making something habitual

ha-cen-da-do n. one who owns a proprietor

ha-chure n. line used for the shading of surfaces on a relief map

ha-ci-en-da n. a large estate or ranch in Spanish-speaking countries or areas

hack v. to hit or strike with irregular blows; cough

hack-ber-ry n. a tree of the elm family having edible berries

hack-le n. the hair found on the back of a dog

hack-ney n. a horse of medium size for ordinary driving or for riding

hack-neyed adj. being trite; lacking freshness

hack-saw n. saw in a narrow frame for cutting metal

had v. past tense of have

had-dock n. food fish that is smaller than the related cod found in the Atlantic Ocean

had-n't cont. had not

haft n. handle of a weapon v. set in with a haft

hag n. a malicious, ugly, old woman; a witch

hag-gard adj. having a gaunt, worn-out, exhausted look **haggardness** n., **-ly** adv.

hag-gle v. to bargain on a price with another **haggler** n.

hag-i-og-ra-phy n. a biography of saints

hai-ku n. an unrhymed Japanese verse form with three short lines

hail n. the precipitation of small ice **hailer** n.

hail-stone n. a hard pellet of frozen snow and ice

hair n. the pigmented filaments that grow from the skin of most mammals **hairy** adj., **hairiness** n.

hair-breadth adj. being extremely close or narrow

hair-brush n. a brush used of grooming the hair

hair-cloth n. the wiry, stiff fabric of horsehair

hair-dress-er n. one who works on hair

hair--raising adj. to be causing fear or horror

hair-split-ting n. the process of making petty distinctions

hair-spring n. a kind of fine, coiled spring

hair trig-ger n. a gun trigger set to react to the slightest pressure

hake n. a marine fish which is related to the cod

hal-berd n. medieval weapon having an ax-like blade and a steel spike on the end of a long pole

hal-cy-on adj. to be calm and

tranquil in manner

hale *adj.* healthy

half *n.* two equal parts

half-back *n.* postion played in the game of football

half heart-ed *adj.* being discouraged; disinterested **half heartedness** *n.*, **-tly** *adv.*

half step *n.* in music, a semitone

half--track *n.* a vehicle propelled by continuous rear treads and front wheels

half--wit *n.* a mentally disturbed person **-ed** *adj.*

hal-i-but *n.* any of the edible flat fishes of the North Atlantic or Pacific waters

hal-ite *n.* a large crystal or masses of salt

hal-i-to-sis *n.* a condition of having bad breath

hall *n.* large room for the holding of meetings

hal-le-lu-jah *interj.* a word used to express one's joy

hall-mark *n.* an official mark on something genuine

hal-low *v.* to sanctify; to make holy **hallowed** *adj.*

hal-lu-ci-na-tion *n.* an illusion of something **-tory** *adj.*

hal-lu-ci-no-gen *n.* type of drug that causes or produces hallucinations

ha-lo *n.* the aura of glory

hal-o-gen *n.* a nonmetallic element including chlorine, bromine, iodine, and also flourine **halogenous** *adj.*

halt *v.* to stop doing something **halting** *adj.*

hal-ter *n.* the strap used for leading an animal

halve *v.* to divide into two equal parts

hal-yard *n.* the rope that is used to lift sails

ham *n.* the meat of a hog's thigh **hammy** *adj.*

ham-burg-er *n.* ground beef

ham-let *n.* a little town or group of houses

ham-mer *n.* the tool used to strike forcefully

ham-mer-head *n.* a large shark of warm water

ham-mer-toe *n.* a toe that is

bent downward and malformed

ham-mock *n.* a hanging bed

ham-per *v.* to interfere with

ham-ster *n.* a rodent with large cheek pouches

ham-string *n.* the two tendons which are located at the back of the human knee

hand *n.* the lower part of the arm; for grasping items

handful *n.*, **handed** *adj.*

hand-bag *n.* a woman's purse

hand-ball *n.* court game

hand-bill *n.* a hand-distributed advertisement

hand-book *n.* type of small reference book

hand-cuff *v.* to put on handcuffs on someone

hand-ful *adj.* the most a hand will hold or contain

hand-gun *n.* a gun that can be held and fired in one hand

hand-i-cap *n.* a physical disability **-ped** *v.*, **-per** *n.*

hand-i-craft *n.* skill done with the hands

hand-ker-chief *n.* a cloth used for wiping the nose

han-dle *v.* touch, pick up, or hold **handler** *n.*, **-ing** *v.*

han-dle-bar *n.* the curved bar of a bicycle that is used to guide it

hand-made *adj.* made by the hands or a hand process

hand-maid-en *n.* a girl who is a servent to someone

hand--me--down *n.* a used article that is passed from one person to another

hand-out *n.* the food or other items which are given freely to other people

hand--pick *v.* to select for a purpose **hand-picked** *adj.*

hand-rail *n.* a rail that is used as support

hand-shake *n.* the grasping of hands between two people

hand-some *adj.* very goodlooking **-ness** *n.*, **-ly** *adv.*

hand-spring *n.* acrobatic feat

hand--to--hand *adj.* in close touch or at close range

hand-stand *n.* standing on the hands with feet in the air

hand-work n. the work which is done by the hands

hand-writ-ing n. cursive style of writing

hand-y adj. helpful or useful

hang v. suspended -**able** adj.

hang-ar n. an aircraft building

han-ger n. a device from which something may be hung

hang-nail n. the loose skin from the root of a fingernail

hand-up n. emotional problem

hank n. a piece of hair, thread or yarn

han-ker v. craving something **hankering, hankerer** n.

han-som n. a two-wheeled vehicle pulled by a horse

Ha-nuk-kah n. the eight-day Jewish holiday

hap-haz-ard adj. occurring by accident -**ly** adv., -**ness** n.

hap-less adj. unfortunate; un-lucky **haplessly** adv.

hap-pen v. discover by chance

hap-pen-ing n. a spontaneous performance

hap-pen-stance n. something that occures by chance

hap-pi-ness n. the quality of being content

hap-py adj. contentment **happier** adj., **happiness** n.

hap-py--go--luck-y adj. being not worried about what may happen

ha-ra-ki-ri n. a Japanese sui-cide ritual

ha-rangue n. a lecture **haranguement** n., -**ed** v.

ha-rass v. to disturb or annoy **harassment, harasser** n.

har-bin-ger n. the sign of com-ing events

har-bor n. the anchorage used for ships **harborer** n.

hard adj. being difficult; solid texture **hardness** n.

hard-back n. type of book bound with a firm back

hard--bit-ten adj. tough by hard experiences

hard--boiled adj. to be cooked in a shell to a hard state

hard--core adj. very tough in nature; unyielding

hard copy n. the printed data from a computer

hard-en v. to become physi-cally or mentally tough

hard-head-ed adj. being a stubborn character

hard-heart-ed adj. unfeeling

har-di-hood n. daring

hard-ly adj. very little

hard-nosed adj. being stubborn

hard palate n. the bony palate of the mouth roof

hard-pan n. the hard and clay-like subsoil

hard-ship n. difficult condition

hard-ware n. the metal household utensils

har-dy adj. being bold and robust **hardily** adv.

hare n. the mammal which is related to rabbits

hare-brained adj. being foolish or silly

har-em n. the residence of the sultan's wives

hark v. to listen closely

har-le-quin n. a pantomime comic character

har-lot n. a prostitute -**ry** n.

harm n. physical damage or in-jury **harmful** adj., -**ness** n.

harm-less adj. without harm **harmlessly** adv., -**ness** n.

har-mon-ic adj. concordant

har-mon-i-ca n. small rectan-gular musical instrument

har-mo-ni-ous adj. being pleas-ing to the ear -**ly** adv.

har-mo-ny n. in tune **harmonize** v., -**ious** adj.

har-ness n. the gear that is used to guide a horse

harp n. string instrument **harpist** n., **harper** n.

har-poon n. a large spear which is used to kill large whales and animals

har-py n. a greedy person

har-ri-dan n. a vicious woman

har-row n. kind of tool for breaking up soil

har-row-ing adj. to cause emo-tional or mental distress to someone

har-ry v. to harass

harsh adj. disagreeable **harshness** n., **harshly** adv.

hart n. fully grown male deer

har-um--scar-um adj. reckless

har-vest n. the gathering of

crops, such as corn

has-been n. a person who has passed the time of greatest achievement

hash n. a meat that has been cooked with vegetables

hasp n. a hinged fastener

has-sle n. quarrel or argument

has-sock n. type of cushioned footstool

haste n. speed; quickness

has-ten v. to move with speed

hast-y adj. swift; rapid **hastily** adv., **hastiness** n.

hat n. covering for the head

hatch v. bring forth, as an egg

hatch-er-y n. the place or building for hatching eggs

hatch-et n. a small ax

hatch-way n. the opening in a ship's deck

hate v. dislike intensely **hateful** adj., **hater** n.

haugh-ty adj. arrogantly proud **haughtily** adv., **-tiness** n.

haul v. pull or draw with force

haul-age n. the process or act of hauling items

haunch n. the hip

haunt v. to visit or see frequently **haunted** adj.

haunt-ing adj. hard to forget

have v. to hold or own

ha-ven n. a safe secure place

hav-er-sack n. a bag used for carrying supplies

hav-oc n. mass confusion

hawk n. predatory birds **hawkish** adj., **hawkness** n.

hawk n. a large bird of prey

haw-ser n. a heavy cable used for towing

hay n. an alfalfa

hay fever n. an acute allergy

hay-fork n. hand tool used to move hay

hay-loft n. upper loft in a barn

hay-mow n. large mound of stored hay

hay-stack n. the hay which is stored outdoors

hay-wire n. being emotionally out of control

haz-ard n. a risk **-ous** adj., **-ously** adv., **-ousness** n.

haze n. a fine mist

ha-zel n. tree with edible nuts; a reddish-brown color

haz-y adj. lacking clarity; vague

H-bomb n. the hydrogen bomb

head n. the upper part of the one's body **heading** n.

head-ache n. a pain which is located in the head

head-band n. the cloth worn around the head

head-board n. a frame standing at the head of a bed

head-dress n. ornamental head covering usually worn during special ceremonies

head-first adv. having the head in a forward position

head-gear n. the covering used for the head as protection

head-ing n. the title that acts as a beginning of a story

head-land n. cliff projecting into the water

head-less adj. having no head

head-line n. a caption or a summarizing words

head-most adj. being foremost

head-long adv. headfirst

head-mas-ter n. the school principal or leader

head-piece n. a covering for the head usually for the purpose of decoration

head-quar-ters pl., n. the center of operations

head-set n. pair of headphones

head-stall n. the part of a bridle that goes over a horse's head

head start n. an advance start

head-stone n. marker at the head of a grave

head-strong adj. obstinate

head-waiter n. person who supervises a restraunt

head-wat-ers n. the source or beginning of a river

head-way n. move forward

head-y adj. to be headstrong **headiness** n.

heal v. restore to good health **healer** n., **healable** adj.

health n. the physical well-being of a person **-ful** adj.

health-y adj. being in a state of good health **healthily** adv.

heap n. a large quantity

hear v. to perceive a sound by the ear **hearer** n.

hear-ing n. the range by which

sound can be heard

hear-ing aid *n.* device used to amplify sound

heark-en *v.* to listen carefully

hear-say *n.* a rumor

hearse *n.* the vehicle for transporting the dead

heart *n.* the blood pumping body organ

heart-ache *n.* emotional grief

heart attack *n.* acute malfunction of the heart

heart-beat *n.* the pulsation of the heart

heart-break *n.* a great sorrow; a deep grief -ing *adv.*

heart-brok-en *adj.* to be grieved deeply

heart-burn *n.* burning sensation in the esophagus and stomach

heart-felt *adj.* deeply felt

hearth *n.* floor of a fireplace

heart-land *n.* an important central region

heart-less *adj.* no sympathy **heartlessness** *n.,* -ly *adv.*

heart-rend-ing *adj.* to be causing great distress

heart-sick *adj.* being profoundly dejected

heart-throb *n.* tender emotion

heart--to--heart *adj.* sincere

heart--warm-ing *adj.* having a feeling of warm sympathy

heart-wood *n.* the no longer active center part of a tree

heart-y *adj.* nourishing

heat *n.* the degree of warmth of something **heated** *adj.*

hea-then *n.* the one who is without a religion

heat light-ning *n.* the electric flashes from the sky occurring without thunder

heat stroke *n.* collapse of a person caused by heat

heave *v.* to lift forcibly

heaves *n.* the lung disease of horses

heav-en *n.* the paradise located above earth **heavenly** *adj.*

heavy *adj.* great weight

heavy--du-ty *adj.* to be designed for hard use

heavy--heart-ed *adj.* being sad; being depressed

heavy--set *adj.* having a stocky build or body

He-brew *n.* a language of Israel

heck-le *v.* to badger or annoy someone **heckler** *n.*

hec-tic *adj.* intensely rushed

he'd *conj.* he had; he would

hedge *n.* boundry of shrubs

hedge-row *n.* the dense row of bushes

he-don-ism *n.* an entire devotion to pleasure

heed *v.* to pay attention

heel *n.* the back section of the human foot

heft-y *adj.* being bulky

he-gem-o-ny *n.* the leadership or dominance

he-gi-ra *n.* journey to flee an undesirable situation

heif-er *n.* a young cow

height *n.* degree of tallness

height-en *v.* increase height

hei-nous *adj.* being extremely wicked **heinousness** *n.*

heir *n.* the inheritance of something, such as money

heir-ess *n.* the female heir

heir-loom *n.* a family possession which is handed down to each generation

heist *v.* to steal; to take from

hel-i-cop-ter *n.* aircraft propelled by rotors

hel-i-port *n.* area for helicopters to land and take off

he-li-um *n.* the light nonflammable gas

hell *n.* the abode of damned souls **hellish** *adj.*

he'll *contr.* he will

helm *n.* the steering wheel for a ship **helmsman** *n.*

hel-met *n.* the protective covering for the head

helms-man *n.* the one who guides a ship

help *v.* assist or aid -ful *adj.*

help-ing *n.* a serving of food

help-less *adj.* lacking strength

help-mate *n.* a partner

hel-ter--skel-ter *adv.* to be done in a confused manner

helve *n.* handle of an axe

hem *n.* the finished edge of the fabric **hemming** *v.*

he--man *n.* the man who is marked by strength

he-ma-tol-o-gy *n.* the science

dealing with blood

hem-i-sphere n. half of earth

hem-lock n. evergreen tree

he-mo-phil-i-a n. the inherited blood disease of spontaneous bleeding

hem-or-rhage n. an excessive bleeding

hem-or-rhoid n. the swollen anal tissue and veins

he-mo-stat n. the agent that stops bleeding

hemp n. Asian herb **-en** adj.

hem-stitch n. an ornamental sewing stitch

hen n. mature female bird

hence-forth adv. being from this time on

hench-man n. a loyal and faithful follower

hen-peck v. persistent nagging

hep-a-rin n. substance found in liver tissue prolonging the clotting of blood

he-pat-ic adj. of or like the liver

hep-a-ti-tis n. the inflammation of the liver

her-ald n. news announcer

her-ald-ry n. the art of tracing genealogies

herb n. kind of plant used for seasoning foods

her-ba-ceous adj. with herbs

herb-age n. a grass used especially for grazing

her-bi-cide n. the agent used to kill weeds

her-biv-o-rous adj. feeding on plant life

her-cu-le-an adj. unusual size

herd n. number of cattle kept together **-er** n., **-sman** n.

here adv. at the particular place or point

here-af-ter adv. from now on

he-red-i-tar-y adj. passing from an ancestor to a legal heir **-ily** adv., **-iness** n.

here-in adv. in or into this place

here-of n. belief that conflicts with orthodox religious beliefs

her-e-sy n. an opinion contrary to orthodox opinion

her-i-tage n. the property that is inherited

her-maph-ro-dite n. person

having both male and female reproductive organs

her-met-ic adj. tightly sealed

her-mit n. one who lives in complete seclusion

he-ro n. one with exceptional courage **heroism** n.

her-o-in n. addictive narcotic

her-o-ism n. heroic behavior

her-on n. bird with a long slender bill, legs and neck

her-pe-tol-o-gy n. scientific study of reptiles

her-ring n. valuable food fish

her-ring-bone n. a pattern of slanting parallel lines

hes-i-tant adj. lacking certainty

hes-i-tate v. to pause

hew v. to make or shape with

hex n. the one who is held to bring bad luck

hex-a-gon n. shape having six sides and six angles

hi-a-tus n. lapse in time

hi-ba-chi n. a portable grill used for cooking

hi-ber-nate v. to sleep during the winter **hibernation** n.

hi-bis-cus n. kind of plant with large flowers

hic-cup n. spasm in the throat

hick-o-ry n. kind of North American tree

hi-dal-go n. Spanish nobleman

hid-den adj. to be concealed

hide v. keep out of sight **-er** n.

hi-er-o-glyph-ic n. the pictorial symbol representing words

high adj. extending upward

high-ball n. an alcoholic drink

high-bred adj. to be from superior breeding

high-brow n. one claiming to have superior knowledge

high-er--up n. the person with more authority

high-fa-lu-tin adj. being extravagant in manner

high fi-del-i-ty n. the reproduction of sound

high fre-quen-cy n. band from three to thirty megacycles

high--hand-ed adj. to be overbearing **-ness** n.

high jump n. a jump in height in athletics

high-light v. to give emphasis

to something

high-ness n. state of being high

high--pres-sure adj. using persuasive methods

high rise n. an extremely tall building or structure

high-road n. the main road

high--spir-it-ed adj. energetic **high-spiritedly** adv., **-ness** n.

high--strung adj. very excitable

high--test adj. relating to gas with a high octane number

high-way n. the main and wide road or street

hi-jack v., Slang to seize while in transit **hijacker** n.

hike v. to take a lengthy walk through the woods

hi-lar-i-ous adj. being cheerful; to be very funny **hilariously** adv., **-ness** n.

hill n. an elevation of land

hill-bil-ly n. a country person usually from the back country

hill-ock n. a small mound

hill-side n. the side or the slope of a hill

hill-top n. the highest point or top of a hill

hilt n. handle of a sword

him pron. objective case of the pronoun he

hind n. the female deer after the third year

hin-der v. to interfere; to obstruct something

hin-drance n. act of state of being hindered

hind-most adj. to be farthest in back or behind

hind-sight n. the comprehension of something after it has happened

hinge n. a device which allows a door to open

hint n. an indication or a suggestion **hinter** n.

hip n. projecting thigh part

hip-bone adj. referring to the bone which forms a lateral half of the pelvis

hip joint n. joint between the hipbone and thighbone

hip-po-pot-a-mus n. kind of large, aquatic mammal

hire v. to service another for payment **hirer** n.

his adj. pronoun of he

His-pan-ic adj. to be relating to the cultures of Spain

hir-sute adj. covered with hair

hiss n. the sound of the letter s made by forcing air pass the upper teeth

his-ta-mine n. the substance in plant tissue

his-tol-o-gy n. study of tissues

his-tor-i-cal adj. of the past

his-to-ry n. the past events

his-tri-on-ics n. theatrical arts

hit v. to strike with a force

hitch v. to fasten **hitcher** n.

hitch-hike v. to travel by obtaining rides from passing drivers **hitchhiker** n.

hith-er adv. to this place

hive n. the habitation for the honeybees

hives pl., n. the itchy welts on the body

hoar adj. having gray hair

hoard n. something which is stored for future use **-er** n.

hoarse adj. gruff, voice **hoarseness** n., **hoarsely** adv.

hoar-y adj. being ancient

hoax n. a trick **hoaxer** n.

hob-ble v. to walk with a limp

hob-by n. activity for pleasure

hob-by-horse n. a child's rocking horse

ho-bo n. a tramp; a vagrant

hock n. leg joint of an animal

hock-ey n. game played on ice

hoe n. the tool for weeding

hog n. a large pig

hog-gish adj. selfish **hoggishness** n., **-ly** adv.

hogs-head n. large barrel

hog-wash n. any nonsense

hoist v. to haul or raise something up **hoister** n.

hold v. to grasp

hold-ing n. personal property

hold-up n. robbery at gun point

hole n. opening in a solid mass

hol-i-day n. day of celebration

ho-li-ness n. state of being holy

hol-ler v. to shout loudly

hol-low adj. having space within **hollowness** n.

hol-o-caust n. total destruction

hol-o-graph n. a type of handwritten document

hol-ster n. case designed to

hold a pistol or gun

ho-ly *adj.* being characterized by power **holily** *adv.*

hom-age *n.* the great respect or honor one has

home *n.* one's residence

home-bod-y *n.* one who prefers to stay at home

home-com-ing *n.* to return to one's home

home e-co-nom-ics *n.* principles of home management

home-ly *adj.* having plain features **homeliness** *n.*

home-made *adj.* made at home and not purchased

home plate *n.* the area where a batter stands

home-sick *adj.* to be yearning for home **homesickness** *n.*

home-word *n.* work assigned by a teacher that is to be completed at home

hom-i-cide *n.* a person killed by another **homicidal** *adj.*

hom-i-ly *n.* a sermon

hom-i-ny *n.* kernels of hulled and dried corn

ho-mo-ge-ne-ous *adj.* of the same nature **-ly** *adv.*

ho-mog-e-nize *v.* process milk

ho-mol-o-gous *adj.* related in structure or origin

hom-o-nym *n.* word that has the same sound as another but a different meaning

hon-cho *n.* the main person in charge of others

hon-est *adj.* not lying, or cheating **honestly** *adv.*

hon-ey *n.* a sweet, sticky substance made by bees

honey-bee *n.* type of bee living in colonies and producing honey

honey-comb *n.* a structure made by bees to store honey

honey-moon *n.* trip taken by newly married couple **-er** *n.*

honey-suck-le *n.* vine with highly fragrant flowers

honk *n.* the harsh sound made by a goose

hon-or *n.* a high regard or respect of someone

honor-able *adj.* being worthy of honor **honorably** *adv.*

hon-or-if-ic *adj.* to be convey-

ing honor

hood *n.* covering for the head

-hood *suff.* quality or state of

hood-lum *n.* a young, destructive kid

hoo-doo *n.* a jinx

hood-wink *v.* deceive **-er** *n.*

hoof *n.* covering of a mammals foot **hoofed** *adj.*, **hoofer** *n.*

hook *n.* to catch

hook-er *n.* a prostitute

hook-worm *n.* a parasitic intestinal worm

hoop *n.* a circular band

hoop-la *n.* the noise and excitement

hoot *n.* insignificant amount

hooter *n.*, **hootingly** *adv.*

hop *v.* to take short leaps on one foot

hope *v.* wish for something

hope-ful *adj.* full of hope

hopefully *adv.*, **hopelessness** *n.*

horde *n.* a large crowd

ho-ri-zon *n.* line which the earth and sky meet

hor-i-zon-tal *adj.* parallel to the horizon **horizontally** *adv.*

hor-mone *n.* internal secretion

horn *n.* musical instrument

hor-net *n.* various wasps that inflict a sever sting

hor-o-scope *n.* the zodiac signs

hor-rid *adj.* being horrible

hor-ror *n.* an extreme fear

hors d'oeu-vre *n.* appetizer served before dinner

horse *n.* large hoofed mammal

horse chest-nut *n.* trees with chestnut-like fruit

horse-fly *n.* kind of large fly that annoys horses and other animals

horse-hide *n.* leather made from a horse's hide

horse-man *n.* the person who rides horseback

horse sense *n.* common sense

horse-shoe *n.* metal plate that is attached to the hoof of a horse to give protection

horse-shoe crab *n.* marine arthropod having a rounded body and stiff pointed tail

hor-ti-cul-ture *n.* act of tending to a garden

hose *n.* tube for carrying fluids

ho-sier-y *n.* a stocking; socks

hos-pice *n.* the lodging used by travelers

hos-pi-ta-ble *adj.* treating guests with generosity

hos-pi-tal *n.* the place for medical care

hos-pi-tal-i-ty *n.* a hospitable treatment

host *n.* the one who entertains guests at a party

hos-tage *n.* person held as security kidnapping

host-ess *n.* woman who greets

hos-tile *adj.* being antagonistic

hos-til-i-ty *n.* a very deep-seated hatred

hot *adj.* excessive heat

hot-el *n.* place for lodging

hot-house *n.* a heated greenhouse for plants

hot line *n.* direct telephone line

hot plate *n.* portable electric plate for cooking

hound *n.* longeared dogs

hour *n.* sixty minutes

hour-ly *adj.* every hour

house *n.* the living quarters for families

house-boat *n.* a boat containing comforts of home

house-bro-ken *n.* animals that have been trained to excrete in a proper place

house-hold *n.* family members

house-holder *n.* the owner of a house

house-keeper *n.* a person paid to clean and care for another's home **-keeping** *n.*

house-work *n.* the household duties or tasks

hous-ing *n.* a shelter or lodging provided for people

how *adv.* in what manner or way

how-dy *interj.* a greeting

how-ev-er *adv.* in whatever manner

how-it-zer *n.* a short cannon

howl *v.* to utter a loud sound

howl-er *n.* one that howls

hua-ra-che *n.* a sandal

hub *n.* the center of a wheel

hub-bub *n.* an uproar

hub-cap *n.* a removable covering for a wheel and axle

hud-dle *n.* a crowd together

hue *n.* a color; a shade

huff *v.* to breathe heavily

hug *v.* to embrace **hugger** *n.*

huge *adj.* great size, or extent **hugely** *adv.*, **hugeness** *n.*

hu-la *n.* the dance of Hawaii

hulk *n.* a heavy, bulky object

bulk-ing *adj.* being awkward

hull *n.* outer cover of fruit

hul-la-ba-loo *n.* great uproar

hum *v.* sing with the lips closed

hu-man *adj.* being relating to mankind

hu-mane *adj.* being marked by compassion for others

hu-man-i-tar-i-an *n.* the person who is concerned for human welfare **-ism** *n.*

hu-man-i-ty *n.* the quality of being human

hum-ble *adj.* unpretentious; not being assertive

hum-bug *n.* a fraud

hu-mid *adj.* being characterized by moisture

hu-mil-i-ate *v.* to reduce one's dignity or one's pride

hum-mock *n.* a rounded hill of snow or dirt

hu-mor *n.* something amusing

hump *n.* rounded lump

hunch *n.* one's strong intuitive feeling

hun-dred *n.* cardinal number equal to ten times ten

hun-ger *n.* the strong need for food or fluids

hunk *n.* large portion or piece of something

hunk-y--do-ry *adj.*, *Slang* very satisfactory; all right

hunt *v.* to chase, to search or to hunt for food **hunter** *n.*

hunts-man *n.* a person who hunts things

hur-dle *n.* barrier used to jump over in a race **hurdler** *n.*

hurl *v.* throw with great force

hur-rah *interj.* to express approval

hur-ri-cane *n.* type of tropical storm with high winds

hur-ri-cane lamp *n.* lamp having a protective glass chimney that shields the fire from wind

hur-ry *v.* move with haste; to proceed or act in a hastily or quick manner **hurrier** *n.*

hurt n. a physical or an emotional pain **hurter** n.

hur-tle v. to rush; to move rapidly

hus-band n. a married man

hush v. to make quiet; to silence; to still

hush--hush adj. very confidential; secret

hush-pup-py n. cornmeal and onion mixture formed into a ball a deep fried

husk n. the dry outer cover of certain vegetables, fruits, and seeds **husker** n.

husk-y adj. burly or robust

hus-sy n. a brazen woman; mischievous girl

hus-tle v. to move hurriedly along; Slang to obtain or to sell by questionable means or tactics

hut n. a shack; dwelling; cabin; or temporary housing

hutch n. the compartment used for storage

hy-a-cinth n. bulbous plant that has a cluster of colored and fragrant flowers

hy-brid n. two animals of different species

hy-drant n. valve from which water is drawn

hy-drate n. a chemical compound formed by the union of water and another substance **hydration** n.

hy-drau-lic adj. operated, by means of water **-cal** adj.

hy-drau-lics n. the scientific study that deal with practical applications of liquids in motion

hy-dro-gen n. a highly flammable gas

hy-dro-gen bomb n. a bomb that is extremely destructive

hy-dro-gen peroxide n. a colorless, unstable liquid used as an antiseptic solution and as a bleach

hy-dro-pho-bi-a n. the fear of water **hydrophobic** n.

hy-dro-plane v. to skim over the top of water

hy-dro-ponics n., pl. method of growing plant rooted in chemical solutions instead

of soil **hydroponic** adj.

hy-dro-scope n. optical instrument that enables an observer to see object under the surface of water

hy-dro-stat n. an electrical device that detects the presence of water

hy-e-na n. kind of carnivorous mammal of Africa and Asia

hy-giene n. good health **hygienic** adj., **-ically** adv.

hy-grom-e-ter n. instrument that measures the degree of moisture in the atmosphere

hy-la n. type of tree frog

hy-men n. the membrane almost closing the internal vaginal orifice

hymn n. a song giving praise to God **hymnal** n.

hype v. to stimulate

hyper pref. excessive action

hy-per-ac-tive adj. being abnormally active

hy-per-ten-sion n. an abnormally high blood pressure

hy-phen n. the mark, (-), to show connection between two words

hy-phen-ate v. to join by a hyphen **hyphenation** n.

hyp-no-sis n. a state that resembles sleep but it is induced by another

hyp-no-ther-a-py n. treatment of disease with hypnotism

hyp-no-tism n. the act of inducing hypnosis

hyp-no-tize v. to be dazzled; put into a hypnotic state

hy-po-chon-dri-a n. type of mental depression

hys-ter-ec-to-my n. a type of female surgery dealing with the uterus

hys-ter-ia n. uncontrolled emotional outburst

hys-ter-ic n. the person suffering from hysteria

hys-ter-i-cal adj. being emotionally out of control

hys-ter-o-gen-ic v. to produce hysteria in someone

hys-ter-oid adj. resembling hysteria

hys-ter-ot-o-my n. surgery that involves opening the uterus

I, i the ninth letter of the English alphabet

I *pron.* person speaking or writing; n. the self

i-amb *or* **i-am-bus** *n.* a metrical foot consisting of a short or unstressed syllable followed by an accented syllable

i-at-ro-gen-ic *adj.* induced inadvertently by a physician

i-bex *n.* a wild goat living in high mountain areas

i-bis *n.* a long-billed wading bird related to the heron

ice *n.* solidly frozen water **iceiness** *n.*, **iceily** *adv.*

ice age *n.* a period in time of widespread glaciation

ice bag *n.* a waterproof bag used to hold and apply coldness to the body

ice-berg *n.* thick mass of floating ice separated from a glacier

ice-boat *n.* vehicle with runners and usually a sail

ice-bound *adj.* obstructed or covered by ice

ice-box *n.* structure made to hold ice and keep food cold

ice-break-er *n.* a ship used to clear ice from channels

ice cap *n.* the covering of ice and snow on land

ice cold *adj.* very cold

ice cream *n.* frozen desert made from cream, sugar and eggs

ice-fall *n.* a waterfall which has frozen

ice fog *n.* fog containing particles of ice

ice hoc-key *n.* hockey that is played on ice

ice-house *n.* place where ice is stored for use

ice milk *n.* food like ice cream, made with skim milk

ice pack *n.* mass of floating, compacted ice

ice pick *n.* pointed tool used for breaking ice

ice skate *n.* shoe having a runner on the bottom for gliding on ice

ich-thy-ol-o-gy *n.* zoological study of fishes

i-ci-cle *n.* hanging spike of ice

ic-ing *n.* frosting on cakes

icky *adj.* distasteful; offensive to the senses

i-con *n.* an idol

i-con-o-clast *n.* one who opposes use of sacred images

i-cy *adj.* relating to cold

id *n.* unconscious part of the psyche

I'd *contr.* I had; I should; I would

i-de-a *n.* a thought; a design; a plan of action

i-de-al *n.* a concept; standard of beauty or perfection **idealness** *n.*, **idealess** *adj.*

i-de-al-ism *n.* tendency to view things in an ideal form and not for what they really are

i-de-al-ize *v.* to give an ideal value to **-ization** *n.*

ide-ate *v.* to form an idea of

i-dem *adj.* the same

i-den-ti-cal *adj.* being the same; having the same origin or cause **identically** *adv.*, **identicalness** *n.*

i-den-ti-fi-ca-tion *n.* the act of identifying

i-den-ti-fy *v.* to recognize one's identity **identifyable** *adj.*

i-den-ti-ty *n.* the state of recognizing

id-e-o-gram *n.* pictorial symbol used in writing to represent an idea

i-de-ol-o-gy *n.* body of ideas that influences a culture

id-i-o-cy *n.* mental deficiency

id-i-om *n.* a form of expression

id-i-om-at-ic *adj.* peculiar to a certain style

id-i-o-syn-cra-sy *n.* a peculiarity **-cratic** *adj.*

id-i-ot *n.* mental deficiency; ignorant person **-cally** *adv.*

i-dle *adj.* inactive **-ness** *n.*

i-dol *n.* a symbol

i-dol-a-try *n.* worship of idols

idol-ize *v.* to admire someone to an excess **idolization** *n.*

i-dyll *n.* poem about a country life

if *conj.* in case or condition that something happens

if-fy *adj.* being uncertain

ig-loo *n.* Eskimo dwelling

ig-ne-ous adj. relating to fire

ig-nite v. start a fire

ig-ni-tion n. the act of igniting

ig-no-ble adj. dishonorable ignobleness n., ignobly adv.

ig-no-min-i-ous adj. being characterized by shame ignominiously adv., -ness n.

ig-no-mi-ny n. a disgraceful, personal humiliation

ig-no-ra-mus n. a person who acts ignorantly to others

ig-no-rant adj. to be lacking education -ly adv., -ness n.

ig-nore v. to not pay attention; refuse to notice

i-gua-na n. an American lizard

il-e-i-tis n. inflammation of the ileum

ilk n. kind or sort

ill adj. not healthy; sick

I'll contr. I will

ill--ad-vised adj. lack of sufficient counseling

ill--bred adj. ill-mannered; raised incorrectly

il-le-gal adj. contrary to law; unlawful -ly adv., -ity n.

il-leg-i-ble adj. being un-readable; not legible -bly adv., -ness, -ity n.

il-le-git-i-mate adj. born out of wedlock -ly adv., -cy n.

ill--fat-ed adj. being unlucky; being unfortunate

ill--fa-vored adj. unattractive; offensive; unpleasant

ill--got-ten adj. obtained in an illegal of dishonest way

ill--hu-mored adj. irritable or cross in mood

il-lic-it adj. not permitted by law illicitly adv.

il-lit-er-ate adj. being un-educated illiteracy n.

ill-man-nered adj. lacking or showing lack of good manners; being rude

ill--na-tured adj. unpleasant disposition

ill-ness n. sickness

il-log-i-cal adj. not having much sense or logic -ic n.

ill tem-per adj. to be moody -edly adv., -edness n., -ed adj.

il-lu-mi-nate v. to give light; to make something clear -ing adj., illuminator n.

ill--use v. to treat someone cruelly or unjustly

il-lu-sion n. false reality; overly optimistic idea or belief -sive, -sory adj.

il-lus-trate v. to explain something

il-lus-tra-tion n. the act of illustrating something

il-lus-tra-tive adj. serving to illustrate something

il-lus-tri-ous adj. celebrated illustriousness n., -ly adv.

ill will n. hostile feelings

I'm contr. I am

im-age n. representation of something

im-age-ry n. mental pictures

im-ag-in-a-ble adj. capable of being imagined

im-ag-i-nar-y adj. existing only in the imagination

im-ag-i-na-tion n. power of forming mental images

im-ag-ine v. to form or create a mental picture

i-ma-go n. insect in its sexually mature adult stage

im-bal-ance n. lack of functional balance

im-be-cile n. mental de-ficiency -ity n., -ly adv.

im-bibe v. to drink or to take something in imbiber n.

im-bri-cate adj. with edges that overlap one another

im-bro-glio n. complicated situation or disagreement

im-bue v. to saturate, as with a dye or stain

im-i-ta-ble adj. capable or worthy of imitation

im-i-tate v. to copy the actions of another imitator n.

im-i-ta-tion n. a copy; counterfeit; not the real thing

im-mac-u-late adj. impeccably clean; no blemish, error or flaw -ly adv., -ness n.

im-ma-nent adj. existing within; restricted to the mind; subjective

im-ma-te-ri-al adj. lacking material body or form

im-ma-ture adj. bring not fully grown -ness n., -ly adv.

im-mea-sur-able adj. unable to

measure -ly adv., -ness n.

im-me-di-a-cy n. quality of being immediate; directness

im-me-di-ate adj. acting at once -ness n., -ly adv.

im-me-mo-ri-al adj. beyond the limits of memory

im-mense adj. exceptionally large -ness n., -ly adv.

im-merse v. to put completely into a liquid immersion n.

im-mi-grant n. one who leaves his country to settle in another country

im-mi-grate v. leave one country and settle in another immigrator n.

im-mi-nent adj. about to happen imminence n.

im-mo-bile adj. not moving -lize v., -lity n.

im-mo-bi-lize v. to render something motionless

im-mod-er-ate adj. exceeding normal bounds

im-mod-est adj. lacking modesty -ty n., -ly adv.

im-mo-late v. to kill, as a sacrifice; destroy

im-mor-al adj. being sinful

im-mor-al-i-ty n. one's lack of morality

im-mor-tal adj. being exempt from death

im-mov-a-ble adj. not capable of being moved immovably adv., -bility n.

im-mune adj. not affected

im-mu-nize v. to make someone immune

im-mu-nol-o-gy n. study of immunity to diseases

im-mure v. to confine by or as if by walls

im-mu-ta-ble adj. unchanging

imp n. mischievous child

im-pact n. a sudden force experienced by something

im-pac-ted adj. wedged together, such as a tooth

im-pac-tion n. something wedged in a part of a body

im-pair v. diminish in quality impairment, impairer n.

im-pa-la n. kind of large African antelope

im-pale v. to pierce one with a sharp point impaler n.

im-pal-pa-ble adj. not perceptible to touch

impalpably adv., -bility n.

im-part v. to make known; to communicate

im-par-tial adj. being unbiased -ly adv., impartiality n.

im-pass-a-ble adj. impossible to travel over or across

im-passe n. a road with no exit; a difficult situation

im-pas-sioned adj. being filled with passion

im-pas-sive adj. unemotional -ness n., impassively adv.

im-pa-tient adj. unwilling to wait; to be restlessly eager -ly adv., impatience n.

im-peach v. to charge someone with misconduct in a public office impeachment n.

im-pec-ca-ble adj. having no flaws; being not capable of sin -ly adv., -bility n.

im-pe-cu-ni-ous adj. having no money; broke

im-pede v. to slow down the progress of something

im-ped-i-ment n. one that stands in the way

im-ped-i-men-ta n. things that impede or encumber

im-pel v. to drive forward; to spur into action

im-pend v. to hover threateningly

im-pen-e-tra-ble adj. not capable of being penetrated

im-per-fect adj. not perfect -ness n., imperfectly adv.

im-pe-ri-al n. the empire of emperor imperially adv.

im-per-il v. to endanger someone imperilment n.

im-per-ish-able adj. not subject to decay; lasting permanently imperishability n.

im-per-ma-nent adj. being temporary -ly adv.

im-per-son-al adj. no personal reference impersonally adv.

im-per-son-ate v. to imitate -tor, impersonation n.

im-per-ti-nent adj. being overly bold impertinently adv.

im-per-turb-a-ble adj. being

calm in manner -ly adv.
im-per-vi-ous adj. being incapable of being affected -ness n., -ly adv.
im-pe-ti-go n. a kind of contagious skin disease
im-pet-u-ous adj. impulsive -ness n., -ly adv.
im-pe-tus n. driving force
im-pinge v. strike or collide impinger, impingement n.
im-pish adj. mischievous
im-plac-a-ble adj. not capable of being appeased -ly adv., impacableness n.
im-plant v. to set something in firmly implanter n.
im-plau-si-ble adj. unlikely -bility n., -ly adv.
im-ple-ment n. utensil or tool -ation n., -tal adj.
im-pli-cate v. to involve
im-plic-it adj. without doubt -ness n., -ly adv.
im-plore v. to plead urgently for something -ation n.
im-ply v. express indirectly
im-po-lite adj. being rude -ness n., impolitely adv.
im-port v. to bring in goods from another country importer n., importable adj.
im-por-tance n. significance
im-por-tant adj. having value
im-por-tune v. repeated requests importuner n.
im-pose v. to burden another
im-pos-ing adj. being awesome in manner and style
im-pos-si-ble adj. not capable of happening or occurring -ly adv., impossibility n.
im-post n. a tax or duty
im-pos-tor n. false identity
im-po-tent adj. having no power impotently adv.
im-pound v. to seize and to keep someone or thing
im-pov-er-ish v. to make poor; impoverishment n.
im-prac-ti-cal adj. unwise to put into effect -able adj.
im-preg-nate v. to make one pregnant impregnator n.
im-press v. to apply with pressure -ible adj., -er n.
im-pres-sion n. a feeling retained in the mind -ist n.

im-pres-sion-a-ble adj. easily influenced -bly adv.
im-pris-on v. to put someone in prison imprisonment n.
im-promp-tu adj. planning or preparation
im-prop-er adj. unsuitable -ness n., improperly adv.
im-prove v. to make or become better improveable adj., improvement n.
im-pro-vise v. to make something up improviser n.
im-pru-dent adj. being unwise in character -ly adv.
im-pu-dent adj. being disrespectful to others -ly adv.
im-pugn v. to cast doubt on
im-pulse n. a spontaneous urge impulsion n.
im-pul-sive adj. uncalculated
im-pure adj. not pure; unclean impureness n., impurely adv.
in-ac-tive adj. out of current use -ity n., inactively adv.
in-ad-e-quate adj. not adequate
in-ad-ver-tent adj. being unintentional -ly adv.
in-ane adj. without sense inaneness n., inanely adv.
in-an-i-mate adj. not having life
in-ar-tic-u-late adj. unable to speak -ness n., -ly adv.
in-au-gu-rate v. put into office
in-be-tween adj. intermediate
in-cal-cu-la-ble adj. to be indeterminate -bly adv.
in-can-des-cent adj. giving off light when heated incandescently adv., -cence n.
in-can-ta-tion n. recitation of magic or spells
in-ca-pac-i-tate v. to disable
in-car-cer-ate v. to place someone in a jail -tion n.
in-cen-di-ary adj. causing fires
in-cense v. make angry
in-cep-tion n. beginning
in-ces-sant adj. to be continuous in character -ly adv.
in-cest n. intercourse between related people -uous adj., -uousness n., -uously adv.
inch n. unit of measurement
in-ci-dent n. an event
in-ci-den-tal adj. occurring as a result incidentally adv.
in-cin-er-ate v. to burn up with

fire incinerator *n.*

in-cip-i-ent *adj.* to be just beginning **incipiently** *adv.*

in-ci-sion *n.* surgical cut

in-cite *v.* provoke to action **inciter, incitement** *n.*

in-clem-ent *adj.* stormy or rainy **-ly** *adv.*, **-ency** *n.*

in-cli-na-tion *n.* an attitude

in-cline *v.* to slant **incliner** *n.*

in-clude *v.* to contain **-sion** *n.*, **includable** *adj.*

in-cog-ni-to *adv.* & *adj.* one's identity hidden

in-co-her-ent *adj.* lacking order **-ly** *adv.*, **-ence** *n.*

in-come *n.* the money received for work

in-com-ing *adj.* coming in

in-com-mu-ni-ca-do *adv.* & *adj.* not able to communicate with others

in-com-pat-i-ble *adj.* being not suitable **-bly** *adv.*, **-bility** *n.*

in-com-pe-tent *adj.* not able

in-com-plete *adj.* not finished **-tion, -ness** *n.*, **-ly** *adv.*

in-con-gru-ous *adj.* disagreeing **-ness** *n.*, **incongruously** *adv.*

in-con-sid-er-ate *adj.* thoughtless **-ness** *n.*, **-ly** *adv.*

in-con-spic-u-ous *adj.* not readily seen or noticed **-ness** *n.*, **inconspicuously** *adv.*

in-con-ti-nent *adj.* being uncontrolled **-ly** *adv.*

in-con-ven-ience *v.* to bother

in-cor-po-rate *v.* to form a legal corporation **-tor, incorporation** *n.*

in-cor-ri-gi-ble *adj.* incapable of being corrected **-bly** *adv.*

in-crease *v.* to make or become larger **-ingly** *adv.*, **increasable** *adj.*

in-cred-i-ble *adj.* unbelievable **-bly** *adv.*, **-ness** *n.*

in-cred-u-lous *adj.* disbelieving **-ly** *adv.*, **-ness** *n.*

in-cre-ment *n.* an increase in something **incremental** *adj.*

in-crim-i-nate *v.* involve in a crime **-tor, -tion** *n.*, **incriminatory** *adj.*

in-cu-bate *v.* to warm and hatch eggs **incubation** *n.*

in-cul-pate *v.* to incriminate someone **inculpation** *n.*

in-cum-bent *adj.* resting on something else **-ly** *adv.*, **incumbency** *n.*

in-cur *v.* become liable

in-cu-ri-ous *adj.* to be lacking in interest

in-debt-ed *adj.* obligated to another **indebtedness** *n.*

in-de-cent *adj.* morally offensive to good taste **-ly** *adv.*, **indecency** *n.*

in-de-ci-sion *n.* inability to make up one's mind

in-dec-o-rous *adj.* to be lacking in good taste

in-deed *adv.* most certainly

in-def-i-nite *adj.* unclear **-ness** *n.*, **indefinitely** *adv.*

in-del-i-ble *adj.* not able to be erased **-bly** *adv.*, **-ness** *n.*

in-del-i-cate *adj.* tactless **-ly** *adv.*, **indelicateness** *n.*

in-dem-ni-ty *n.* security against hurt, or loss

in-dent *v.* to set in from the margin

in-de-pend-ence *n.* being independent **independency** *n.*

in--depth *adj.* detailed

in-de-scrib-a-ble *adj.* surpassing description **-ness, -bility** *n.*, **-bly** *adv.*

in-dex *n.* list for aiding reference **indexer** *n.*

in-di-cate *v.* to point something out **indication** *n.*

in-dict *v.* accuse of an offense **-tor, -ter** *n.*, **-able** *adj.*

in-dif-fer-ent *adj.* impartial **-ly** *adv.*, **-ist** *n.*

in-dig-e-nous *adj.* living naturally in an area **-ness** *n.*, **indigenously** *adv.*

in-di-gent *adj.* being impoverished **indigently** *adv.*

in-di-ges-tion *n.* discomfort in digesting food **-tive** *adj.*

in-dig-nant *adj.* filled with indignation **indignantly** *adv.*

in-dig-ni-ty *n.* something that offends one's pride

in-di-go *n.* blue dye obtained

in-di-rect *adj.* not taking a direct course **-ness** *n.*, **indirectly** *adv.*

in-dis-creet *adj.* lacking discretion **indiscreetly** *adv.*

in-dis-pen-sa-ble *adj.* necessary

in-dis-posed *adj.* mildly ill

in-di-vid-u-al *adj.* a single human being -ly *adv.*

in-di-vis-i-ble *adj.* not able to be divided

in-doc-tri-nate *v.* instruct in a doctrine -tor *n.*

in-do-lent *adj.* lazy

in-duce *v.* cause to occur

in-duct *v.* to admit as a new member of a club

in-dulge *v.* give into the desires

in-dus-tri-ous *adj.* working steadily and hard

in-dus-try *n.* a branch of manufacturing

in-e-bri-ate *v.* to intoxicate

in-ef-fi-cient *adj.* being wasteful of time

in-ept *adj.* not suitable

in-eq-ui-ty *n.* unfairness

in-ert *adj.* not able to move

in-ev-i-ta-ble *adj.* not able to be avoided

in-ex-pe-ri-ence *n.* the lack of experience

in-ex-pli-ca-ble *adj.* not capable of being explained

in-ex-tre-mis *adv.* at the point of death

in-ex-tri-ca-ble *adj.* too complex to resolve

in-fal-li-ble *adj.* not capable of making mistakes

in-fa-my *n.* evil notoriety

in-fan-cy *n.* the time of being an infant

in-fant *n.* a baby

in-fan-ti-cide *n.* act of killing an infant

in-fan-try *n.* foot soldiers

in-fat-u-ate *v.* to foolishly love

in-fect *v.* to contaminate

in-fer *v.* conclude by reasoning

in-fer-ence *n.* the conclusion based on facts

in-fe-ri-or *adj.* to be located under or below

in-fer-nal *adj.* to be like, or relating to hell

in-fer-no *n.* the place suggestive of hell

in-fil-trate *v.* to pass through something gradually

in-fi-nite *adj.* being immeasurably large

in-fin-i-tes-i-mal *adj.* being immeasurably small

in-firm *adj.* physically weak

in-flame *v.* to set on fire

in-flam-ma-tion *n.* localized redness in which is a response to an injury

in-flate *v.* to fill with gas or air

in-fla-tion *n.* increase in the monetary supply

in-flect *v.* to vary the tone of the voice

in-flex-i-ble *adj.* not subject to change

in-flict *v.* cause to be suffered

in-flu-ence *n.* power to produce effects

in-flu-en-za *n.* acute, infectious viral disease

in-flux *n.* things coming in

in-for-ma-tive *adj.* to be providing information

in-frac-tion *n.* the violation of a rule

in-fringe *v.* to encroach

in-fu-ri-ate *v.* make very angry

in-gen-ious *adj.* to be showing great ability

in-gen-u-ous *adj.* being frank and straightforward

in-gest *v.* take or put food into the body

in-got *n.* mass of cast metal shaped in a bar

in-grained *adj.* deep-seated

in-grate *n.* one who is ungrateful

in-grat-i-tude *n.* the lack of gratitude

in-gre-di-ent *n.* a part of anything

in-grown *adj.* to be growing into the flesh

in-hab-it *v.* to reside in

in-hale *v.* to breathe into the lungs

in-her-ent *adj.* forming an essential element

in-her-it *v.* receive something by a will

in-hib-it *v.* hold back

in-hu-mane *adj.* lacking compassion or pity

in-im-i-cal *adj.* to be harmful opposition

in-im-i-ta-ble *adj.* incapable of being matched

in-iq-ui-ty *n.* the grievous violation of justice

in·i·tial *n.* first letter of a name or word

in·i·ti·ate *v.* begin or start

in·i·ti·a·tive *n.* action of taking the first step

in·ject *v.* force a drug into the body through a blood vessel with a hypodermic syringe

in·junc·tion *n.* authoritative command or order

in·jure *v.* cause physical harm

in·ju·ri·ous *adj.* causing injury, damage or hurt

in·ju·ry *n.* damage or harm inflicted

in·jus·tice *n.* violation of another person's rights

ink *n.* any of variously colored liquids or paste

ink·ling *n.* a slight suggestion or hint

ink·y *adj.* resembling ink in color; dark; black

in·land *adj.* located in the interior of a country

in·law *n.* relative by marriage

in·let *n.* bay or stream that leads into land

in·mate *n.* person who is confined in a prison

inn *n.* place of lodging

in·nate *adj.* being inborn and not acquired

in·ner *adj.* situated or occurring inside

in·ner·most *adj.* most intimate

in·ning *n.* one of nine divisions of a regulation baseball game

in·no·cent *adj.* free from sin, or moral wrong

in·noc·u·ous *adj.* having no harmful qualities

in·no·vate *v.* to begin something new

in·nu·en·do *n.* indirect or oblique comment

in·nu·mer·a·ble *adj.* too much to be counted

in·oc·u·late *v.* protect against disease by vaccination

in·op·er·a·ble *adj.* incapable of being treated

in·or·di·nate *adj.* exceeding proper or normal limits

in·or·gan·ic *adj.* not having living organisms

in·put *n.* the data which is put in a computer

in·quest *n.* legal investigation into the cause of death

in·quire *v.* to ask a question

in·quir·y *n.* request or question for information

in·qui·si·tion *n.* an investigation

in·quis·i·tive *adj.* to be curious; probing

in·sane *adj.* having a serious mental disorder

in·san·i·tar·y *adj.* not hygienic or clean and dangerous to one's health

in·scribe *v.* to engrave something on a surface

in·scru·ta·ble *adj.* difficult understand

in·sect *n.* tiny animal such as ant, flea, etc.

in·sec·ti·cide *n.* substance for killing insects

in·se·cure *adj.* feeling of being unsafe

in·sem·i·nate *v.* to make one pregnant

in·sen·si·ble *adj.* being incapable of feeling

in·sep·a·ra·ble *adj.* incapable of being separated

in·sert *v.* to put in place

in·shore *adj.* near the shore

in·side *n.* space that lies within

in·sid·i·ous *adj.* deceitful

in·sight *n.* the hidden nature of things

in·sig·ni·a *n.* a badge or emblem

in·sin·cere *adj.* hypocritical

in·sin·u·ate *v.* to suggest something by giving a hint

in·sip·id *adj.* lacking flavor

in·sist *v.* demand or assert

in·so·far *adv.* to such an extent

in·sol·u·ble *adj.* incapable of being dissolved

in·sol·vent *n.* to be unable to meet debts

in·som·ni·a *n.* chronic inability to sleep

in·spect *v.* examine very carefully for flaws

in·spire *v.* to guide by a divine influence

in·sta·bil·i·ty *n.* lacking stability

in·stall *v.* put in position for

service

in-stall-ment *n.* payments due at specified intervals

in-stance *n.* illustrative example

in-stant *n.* very short time

in-stan-ta-ne-ous *adj.* instantly

in-stead *adv.* lieu of that just mentioned

in-sti-gate *v.* to provoke

in-still *v.* to introduce by gradual instruction

in-stinct *n.* unlearned action

in-sti-tute *v.* to establish

in-sti-tu-tion *n.* organization which performs a particular job

in-struct *v.* impart knowledge

in-struc-tor *n.* one who instructs or teaches

in-stru-ment *n.* a device used to produce music

in-stru-men-tal-ist *n.* person who plays music

in-sub-or-di-nate *adj.* not obedient

in-suf-fi-cient *adj.* inadequate

in-su-late *v.* prevent loss of heat or sound

in-su-lin *n.* hormone released by the pancreas

in-sult *v.* abuse verbally

in-su-per-a-ble *adj.* not able to be overcome

in-sur-ance *n.* protection against loss, or ruin

in-sur-mount-a-ble *adj.* to be incapable of being overcome

in-sur-rec-tion *n.* open revolt

in-sus-cep-ti-ble *adj.* immune

in-tact *adj.* remaining whole

in-take *n.* act of absorbing

in-tan-gi-ble *adj.* indefinite to the mind

in-te-gral *adj.* being essential and part of a whole

in-te-grate *v.* open to people of all races

in-teg-ri-ty *n.* honesty

in-tel-lect *n.* power to understand

in-tel-li-gence *n.* capacity to comprehend meaning

in-tend *v.* have a plan in mind

in-tense *adj.* profound

in-ten-si-fy *v.* to make something more intense

in-ten-si-ty *n.* being intense

in-ten-sive care *n.* hospital care for a gravely ill patient

in-tent *n.* purpose of goal

in-ten-tion *n.* plan of action

in-ten-tion-al *adj.* deliberately

in-ter *v.* place in a grave

in-ter-act *v.* act on each other or with each other

in-ter-cede *v.* argue or plead on another's behalf

in-ter-cept *v.* interrupt the path or course

in-ter-ces-sion *n.* entreaty or prayer on behalf of others

in-ter-com *n.* two-way communication system

in-ter-com-mu-ni-cate *v.* to communicate with each other

in-ter-course *n.* mutual exchange between persons

in-ter-dict *v.* to forbid by official decree

in-ter-est *n.* curiosity about something

in-ter-face *n.* common boundary between adjacent areas

in-ter-fere *v.* to get in the way

in-ter-ga-lac-tic *adj.* between galaxies

in-ter-im *n.* time between events

in-te-ri-or *adj.* away from the coast or border

in-ter-ject *v.* go between other parts or elements

in-ter-jec-tion *n.* exclamation to express emotion

in-ter-lace *v.* to intertwine

in-ter-lock *v.* join closely

in-ter-lope *v.* intrude the rights of others

in-ter-lude *n.* period of time that occurs in and divides some longer process

in-ter-me-di-ar-y *n.* a mediator

in-ter-me-di-ate *adj.* situated in the middle

in-ter-min-gle *v.* to become mixed together

in-ter-mis-sion *n.* temporary break between events

in-ter-mit-tent *adj.* coming at intervals

in-tern *n.* medical school graduate

in-ter-nal *adj.* to be pertaining to others

in-ter-na-tion-al *adj.* involving two or more nations

in-ter-nist *n.* specialist in internal medicine

in-ter-pose *v.* to place or put between parts

in-ter-pret *v.* to convey the meaning of something

in-ter-ra-cial *adj.* affecting different races

in-ter-re-late *v.* to have a mutual relationship

in-ter-ro-gate *v.* to question one formally

in-ter-rupt *v.* break in on conversation

in-ter-sect *v.* divide

in-ter-sec-tion *n.* the place of crossing

in-ter-sperse *v.* to scatter

in-ter-twine *v.* to unite by twisting together

in-ter-ur-ban *adj.* among connecting urban areas

in-ter-val *n.* time between two points or object

in-ter-vene *v.* to come between something

in-ter-view *n.* meeting arranged for one person to question another

in-ter-weave *v.* weave together

in-tes-tate *adj.* having made no valid will

in-tes-tine *n.* the section of the stomach

in-ti-mate *adj.* close friendship

in-tim-i-date *v.* to frighten

in-to *prep.* the inside

in-tol-er-ant *adj.* to be not able to endure

in-tone *v.* to chant

in-tox-i-cate *v.* make drunk

in-tra-cel-lu-lar *adj.* being within a cell

in-tra-cra-ni-al *adj.* being within the skull

in-tra-mu-ral *adj.* taking place within a school

in-tra-mus-cu-lar *adj.* being within a muscle

in-tra-state *adj.* within a state

in-tra-ve-nous *adj.* being within a vein

in-trep-id *adj.* courageous

in-tri-cate *adj.* complex

in-trigue *v.* arouse interest

in-trin-sic *adj.* inherent

in-tro-duce *v.* to make acquainted with

in-tro-vert *n.* very shy person

in-trude *v.* to come in without being asked

in-tu-i-tion *n.* having insight

in-un-date *v.* overwhelm

in-ure *v.* to accept something undesirable

in-vade *v.* enter by force

in-va-lid *n.* disabled person

in-val-i-date *v.* to nullify

in-val-u-able *adj.* priceless

in-var-i-able *adj.* constant

in-vei-gle *v.* win over by flattery

in-vent *v.* to create by original effort

in-ven-tion *n.* the process of inventing

in-ven-to-ry *n.* list of items

in-verse *adj.* reversed in order

in-vert *v.* turn upside down

in-ver-te-brate *adj.* to be lacking a backbone

in-vest *v.* purchase of stocks to obtain profit

in-ves-ti-gate *v.* to examine carefully

in-vig-o-rate *v.* give strength

in-vin-ci-ble *adj.* being incapable of being defeated

in-vi-o-la-ble *adj.* being safe from assault

in-vi-o-late *adj.* not harmed

in-vis-i-ble *adj.* being not open to view

in-vite *v.* request the presence

in-vit-ing *adj.* tempting

in-voice *n.* the itemized list of merchandise

in-voke *v.* call upon for aid

in-vol-un-tar-y *adj.* not done by choice

in-volve *v.* include as a part

in-vul-ner-a-ble *adj.* to be immune to attack

in-ward *adj.* being toward the inside, center

i-o-dine *n.* a grayish-black, corrosive, poisonous element

i-on *n.* an electrically charged atom

i-on-ize *v.* to convert completely into ions

i-ras-ci-ble *adj.* being easily provoked to anger

i-rate *adj.* raging angry

ir-i-des-cent *adj.* shifting hues of color

i-ris *n.* the pigmented part of the eye

irk *v.* to annoy

i-ron-bound *adj.* being bound with iron

i-ron-clad *adj.* covered with protective iron plates

i-ron-stone *n.* heavy, white, glazed pottery

ir-ra-di-ate *v.* subject to ultraviolet light

ir-ra-tion-al *adj.* being unable to reason

ir-rec-on-cil-a-ble *adj.* not able or willing to be reconciled

ir-re-deem-a-ble *adj.* not capable of being recovered

ir-re-duc-i-ble *adj.* not having the capabilities of reduction

ir-ref-ra-ga-ble *adj.* cannot be refuted

ir-re-fut-able *adj.* cannot be disproved

ir-reg-u-lar *adj.* not according to the general rule

ir-rel-e-vant *adj.* not related to the subject matter

ir-re-lig-ious *adj.* to be lacking in religion

ir-re-mov-a-ble *adj.* being not removable

ir-rep-a-ra-ble *adj.* unable to be repaired

ir-re-place-a-ble *adj.* unable to be replaced

ir-re-press-i-ble *adj.* being impossible to hold back

ir-re-proach-a-ble *adj.* being blameless

ir-re-sist-i-ble *adj.* completely fascinating

ir-res-o-lute *adj.* to be lacking firmness

ir-re-spec-tive *adj.* regardless

ir-re-spon-si-ble *adj.* lacking in responsibility

ir-re-triev-a-ble *adj.* unable to be recovered

ir-rev-er-ence *n.* the lack of reverence

ir-rev-o-ca-ble *adj.* unable of being turned in the other direction

ir-ri-gate *v.* water the land or crops artificially

ir-ri-ta-ble *adj.* easily annoyed

ir-ri-tate *v.* annoy or bother

ir-ri-ta-tion *n.* the act of irritating; a condition of roughness, inflammation, or soreness of a bodily part

ir-ri-ta-tive *n.* produced by or accompanied with irritation

ir-rupt *v.* burst or rush in

is *v.* third person, singular, present tense of the verb to be

is-land *n.* the piece of land which is completely surrounded by water

isle *n.* small island

is-n't *contr.* is not

i-so-late *v.* to set apart one from the others

i-so-la-tion-ism *n.* national policy of avoiding political economic alliances

i-so-therm *n.* line on a map linking points that have the same temperature

i-so-tope *n.* element form

i-so-trop-ic *adj.* same value in all directions

is-sue *n.* act of giving out

isth-mus *n.* land which connects two larger pieces of land

it *pron.* used as a substitute for a specific noun

i-tal-ic *adj.* style of printing type in which the letters slant

i-tal-i-cize *v.* print in italics

itch *n.* skin irritation which causes a desire to scratch

-ite *suffix* native or inhabitant

i-tem *n.* separately-noted unit included in a category

item-iza-tion *n.* the act of itemizing something

i-tem-ize *v.* specify by item

i-tin-er-ant *adj.* traveling from place to place; marked by recurrence or repetition

i-tin-er-ar-y *n.* scheduled route of a trip

it'll *contr.* it will

its *adj.* possessive case of the pronoun it

i-vo-ry *n.* the white tusks on an elephant and walrus

i-vy *n.* climbing plant having glossy evergreen leaves

J, j the tenth letter of the English alphabet

jab v. to poke or thrust sharply with short blows; a rapid punch jabbingly adv.

jab-ber v. to speak quickly or without making sense; one who jabs

jab-i-ru n. a large white bird resembling the stork

jab-o-ran-di n. leaves of the shrubs of the rue family that are a source of pilocarpine

jab-ot n. ruffle or decoration on the front of a blouse, dress, or shirt

ja-bot-i-ca-ba n. a shrubby tree of the tropics

ja-cal n. a small hut made of clay and poles

jac-a-mar n. an insectivorous bird usually iridescent green in color

jacks n. game played with a set of six-pronged metal pieces and a small ball

jack-al n. an African or an Asian dog-like, carnivorous mammal

jack-a-napes n. an impudent person

jack-ass n. a male donkey or ass; a stupid person or one who acts in a stupid fashion

jack-boot n. a heavy military boot which reaches above the knee

jack-daw n. a glossy, black, crow-like bird

jack-et n. a short coat worn by men and women; an outer protective cover for a book; the skin of a cooked potato jacketed adj. jacketless adj.

Jack Frost n. a name given to frost or winter weather

jack-hammer n. a tool operated by air pressure, used to break pavement and to drill rock

jack-in-the-box n. a toy consisting of a small box from which a puppet springs up when the lid is unfastened

jack-in-the-pul-pit n. a common herb which grows from a turnip-shaped bulb

jack-knife n. a large pock-etknife

jack-leg adj. deficient in skill; an amateur

jack-of-all-trades n. a person who is able to do many types of work

jack-o--lan-tern n. a lantern made from a hollowed out pumpkin which has been carved to resemble a face

jack pine n. large pine tree

jack-pot n. any post, prize, or pool in which the amount won is cumulative

jack rabbit n. a large American hare with long back legs and long ears

jade n. hard, translucent, green gemstone **jade** v.

jad-ed adj. fatigued; dulled; worn-out

jag n. a very sharp projection or point Slang a binge or spree

jag-ged adj. having jags or sharp notches; serrated

jaggedly adv., jaggedness n.

jag-uar n. large, spotted, feline mammal of tropical America with a tawny coat and black spots

jai alai n. game similar to handball in which players catch and throw a ball with long, curved, wicker baskets strapped to their arms

jail n. a place of confinement for incarceration

jail-bird n., Slang a prisoner or exprisoner

jail-break n. prison escape using force

jail-er n. the officer in charge of a jail and its prisoners

ja-lop-y n., pl. -ies Slang an old, rundown automobile

ja-lou-sie n. a window, blind, or door having adjustable horizontal slats

jam v. to force or wedge into a tight position Mus. to be a participant in a jazz session Slang to be in a **jam** n. a preserve of whole fruit boiled with sugar

jamb n. the vertical sidepiece of a door

jam-ba-lay-a n. a food dish

made of rice, vegetables and various kinds of meats

jam-bo-ree *n.* a large, festive gathering

jam session *n.* an informal gathering of a group of jazz musicians

jan-gle *v.* to make a harsh unmusical sound *n.* a discordant sound

jan-i-tor *n.* person who cleans and cares for a building **janitorial** *adj.*

ja-pan *n.* black varnish used for coating objects

jape *v.* to joke; to make fun of or mock by words or actions **japer, japery** *n.*

jar *n.* deep, cylindrical vessel with a wide mouth; a harsh sound *v.* to strike against or bump into; to affect one's feelings unpleasantly

jar-di-niere *n.* decorative pot or stand for flowers or plants

jar-gon *n.* technical or specialized vocabulary used among members of a particular profession **jargonistic** *adj.*

jas-mine or **jes-sa-mine** *n.* a shrub with fragrant yellow or white flowers

jas-per *n.* an opaque red, brown, or yellow variety of quartz

ja-to *n.* takeoff of an airplane which is assisted by an auxiliary rocket engine

jaun-dice *n., Pathol.* a diseased condition of the liver due to the presence of bile pigments in the blood

jaunt *n.* short journey for pleasure **jaunt** *v.*

jaun-ty *adj.* having a buoyantly carefree and self-confident air or matter about oneself **-ily** *adv.* **-iness** *n.*

Ja-va *n., Slang* coffee

jave-lin *n.* a light spear thrown as a weapon

jaw *n., Anat.* either of the two bony structures forming the framework of the mouth and holding the teeth

jaw-bone *n.* one of the bones of the jaw, especially the lower jaw

jaw-break-er *n.* very hard piece of candy. *Slang* A word which is hard to pronounce

jay *n.* any of various corvine birds of brilliant coloring

jay-walk *v., Slang* to cross a street carelessly, violating traffic regulations and or signals **jaywalker** *n.*

jazz *n.* kind of music which has a strong rhythmic structure with frequent syncopation and often involving ensemble and solo improvisation **jazzer** *n.*, **jazzy** *adj.*

jeal-ous *adj.* suspicious or fearful of being replaced by a rival; resentful or bitter **jealously** *adv.*, **jealousness,** *n.*

jean *n.* strong, twilled cotton cloth **jeans** pants made of denim

jeep *n.* small, military, and civilian vehicle with four-wheel drive

jeer *v.* speak or shout derisively **jeerer** *n.*, **jerringly** *adv.*

Je-ho-vah *n.* God, in the Christian translations of the Old Testament

je-june *adj.* lacking in substance or nourishment; immature

je-ju-num *n., pl.* **-na** *Anat.* part of the small intestine which extends from the duodenum to the ileum

jel-ly *n. pl.* **-ies** food preparation made with pectin or gelatin and having a somewhat elastic consistency

jel-ly bean *n.* small candy having a hard, colored coating over a gelatinous center

jel-ly-fish *n., pl.* fishes any of a number of free-swimming marine animals of jelly-like substance

jeop-ard-ize *v.* to put in jeopardy; to expose to loss or danger

jeop-ar-dy *n.* exposure to loss or danger

jer-bo-a *n.* any of a type of small, nocturnal rodent of Asia and Africa with long hind legs

jer-e-mi-ad *n.* lament or prolonged complaint

Jer-emi-ah *n.* Hebrew prophet of the seventh century B.C.

jerk *v.* give a sharp twist or pull to *n.* sudden movement, as a tug or twist *Physiol.* involuntary contraction of a muscle resulting from a reflex action **jerky, jerkily** *adv.* **jerkiness** *n.*

jer-kin *n.* close-fitting jacket, usually sleeveless

jerk-wa-ter *adj.* of little importance

jer-ry--build *v.* build flimsily and cheaply **jerry-builder** *n.*

jer-sey *n., pl.* **-seys** a soft ribbed fabric of wool, cotton, or other material; a knitted sweater, jacket, or shirt; fawn-colored, small dairy cattle which yield milk rich in butter fat

jest *n.* action or remark intended to provoke laughter; a joke; a playful mood **jester** *n.*

Jes-u-it *n.* member of the Society of Jesus, a religious order founded in 1534

Jesus *n.* founder of Christianity, son of Mary and regarded in the Christian faith as Christ the son of God, the Messiah; also referred to as Jesus Christ or Jesus of Nazareth

jet *n.* sudden spurt or gush of liquid or gas emitted through a narrow opening; a jet airplane **jet** *adj.*

jet lag *n.* mental and physical fatigue resulting from rapid travel through several time zones

jet set *n.* international social group of wealthy individuals who travel from one fashionable place to another for pleasure **jet setter** *n.*

jet stream *n.* high-velocity wind near the troposphere, generally moving from west to east often at speeds exceeding 250 mph.; a high-

speed stream of gas or other fluid expelled from a jet engine or rocket

jet-ti-son *v.* throw cargo overboard; to discard a useless or hampering item

jet-ty *n., pl.* **-ies** wall made of piling rocks, or other material which extends into a body of water to protect a harbor or influence the current; a pier

Jew *n.* descendant of the ancient Hebrew people; a person believing in Judaism

jew-el *n.* precious stone used for personal adornment; a person or thing of very rare excellence or value *v.* furnish with jewels **jewelry** *n.*

jew-eler *or* **jew-el-ler** *n.* person who makes or deals in jewelry

Jew's harp *n.* small musical instrument held between the teeth when played, consisting of a U-shaped frame with a flexible metal piece attached which is plucked with the finger to produce twanging sounds

jib *n., Naut.* triangular sail set on a stay extending from the head of the foremast to the bowsprit

jif-fy *or* **jiff** *n.* short time

jig *n.* any of a variety of fast, lively dances; the music for such a dance *Mech.* device used to hold and guide a tool **jig** *v.*

jig-ger *n.* small measure holding 1 1/2 oz. used for measuring liquor *Naut.* small sail in the stern of a sailing craft

jig-gle *v.* move or jerk lightly up and down *n.* jerky, unsteady movement

jig-saw *n.* saw having a slim blade set vertically, used for cutting curved or irregular lines

jigsaw puzzle *n.* puzzle consisting of many irregularly shaped pieces which fit together and form a picture

jilt *v.* discard a lover *n.* woman

or girl who discards a lover

jim-my *n., pl.* **-ies** short crowbar, often used by a burglar *v.* to force open or break into with a jimmy

jim-son-weed *n.* tall, coarse, foul-smelling, poisonous annual weed with large, trumpet-shaped purplish or white flowers

jin-gle *v.* make a light clinking or ringing sound *n.* short, catchy song or poem, as one used for advertising

jin-go-ism *n.* extreme nationalism which is marked by a belligerent foreign policy **jingoist** *n.*, **jingoistic** *adj.*

jinn *n., pl.* **jin-ni** in the Moslem legend, a spirit with supernatural powers

jinx *n., Slang* person or thing thought to bring bad luck

jit-ney *n.* vehicle carrying passengers for a small fee

jit-ter *v., Slang* to be intensely nervous **jittery** *adj.*

jit-ter-bug *n., Slang* lively dance or one who performs this dance **jitterbug** *v.*

jit-ters *n.* nervousness

jive *n., Slang* jazz or swing music and musicians

job *n.* anything that is done; work that is done for a set fee; the project worked on; a position of employment **jobless** *adj.*, **joblessness** *n.*

job-ber *n.* one who buys goods in bulk from the manufacturer and sells them to retailers; a person who works by the job; a pieceworker

job-name *n. Computer Science.* code that is assigned to a specific job instruction in a computer program, for the operator's use

jock *n., Slang* male athlete in college; a person who participates in athletics

jock-ey *n.* person who rides a horse as a professional in a race

joc-u-lar *adj.* marked by joking; playful **jocularity** *n.*,

jocularly *adv.*

joc-und *adj.* cheerful; merry; suggestive of high spirits and lively mirthfulness **jocundity** *n.*, **jocundly** *adv.*

jog *n.* slight movement or a slight shake; the slow steady trot of a horse; to exercise by running at a slow but steady pace **jogger** *n.*

jog-gle *v.* move or shake slightly **joggle** *n.*

john *n., Slang* toilet; a prostitute's client

John *n.* one of the twelve Apostles

John Doe *n., Law* person in a legal proceeding whose true name is unknown

john-ny-cake *n.* thin bread made with cornmeal

John the Baptist *n.* baptizer of Jesus Christ

join *v.* bring or put together so as to form a unit

join-er *n.* person whose occupation is to build articles by joining pieces of wood

joint *n.* place where two or more things or parts are joined; a point where bones are connected *adj.* marked by cooperation, as a joint effort

join-ture *n., Law* settlement of property arranged by a husband which is to be used for the support of his wife after his death

joist *n.* any of a number of small parallel beams set from wall to wall to support a floor

joke *n.* something said or done to cause laughter, such as a brief story with a punch line; something not taken seriously *v.* to tell or play jokes **jokingly** *adv.*

jok-er *n.* person who jokes; a playing card

jol-li-fi-ca-tion *n.* merrymaking.

jol-ly *adj.* full of good humor; merry **jollity** *n.*, **jolly** *v.*

jolt *v.* knock or shake about *n.* sudden bump or jar, as from a blow **jolty** *adj.*

jon-quil *n.* widely grown species of narcissus related to the daffodil

josh *v., Slang* make good-humored fun of someone

joss *n.* Chinese idol or image

jos-tle *v.* make one's way through a crowd by pushing, elbowing, or shoving

jot *v.* make a brief note of something *n.* tiny bit

jounce *v.* bounce; to bump; to shake **jouncy** *adj.*

jour-nal *n.* diary or personal daily record of observations and experiences; in book-keeping, a book in which daily financial transactions are recorded

jour-nal-ese *n.* vocabulary and style of writing supposedly characteristic of most newspapers

jour-nal-ism *n.* occupation, collection, writing, editing, and publishing of newspapers and other periodicals **-ist** *n.*, **-istic** *adj.*, **journalistically** *adv.*

jour-ney *n.* trip from one place to another over a long distance

jour-ney-man *n., pl.* **-men** worker who has served an apprenticeship in a skilled trade

joust *n.* formal combat between two knights on horseback as a part of a medieval tournament

Jove *Interj.* mild expression of surprise or emphasis

jo-vi-al *adj.* good-natured; good-humored; jolly **joviality** *n.*

jowl *n.* fleshy part of the lower jaw; the cheek **jowly** *adj.*

joy *n.* strong feeling of great happiness; delight **-fully** *adv.*, **-fulness** *n.*, **-less** *adj.*, **-lessly** *adv.*,

joy-ous *adj.* joyful; causing or feeling joy **joyously** *adv.*

joy ride *Slang* ride taken for pleasure only

joy stick *Slang* control stick of an airplane or video game

ju-bi-lant *adj.* exultantly joyful or triumphant; expressing joy **jubilance** *n.*, **jubilantly** *adv.*

ju-bi-la-tion *n.* rejoicing; exultation

ju-bi-lee *n.* special anniversary of an event; any time of rejoicing

Ju-da-ism *n.* religious practices or beliefs of the Jews; a religion based on the belief in one God

judge *v., Law* public officer who passes judgment in a court *v.* decide authoritatively after deliberation

judg-ment or **judge-ment** *n.* ability to make a wise decision or to form an opinion; the act of judging *Law* sentence or determination of a court **judgmental** *adj.*

ju-di-ca-ture *n.* function or action of administration of justice; law, courts, or judges as a whole

ju-di-cial *adj.* pertaining to the administering of justice, to courts of law, or to judges **judicially** *adv.*

ju-di-ci-ar-y *adj.* of or pertaining to judges, courts, or judgments *n.* department of the government which administers the law

ju-di-cious *adj.* having, showing, or exercising good sound judgement **judiciously** *adv.*, **-ness** *n.*

ju-do *n.* system or form of self-defense, developed from jujitsu in Japan

jug *n.* small pitcher or similar vessel for holding liquids

jug-ger-naut *n.* destructive force or object

jug-gle *v.* keep several objects continuously moving from the hand into the air; to practice fraud or deception **juggler** *n.*

jug-u-lar *adj., Anat.* of or pertaining to the region of the throat or the jugular vein

jugular vein *n., Anat.* one of the large veins on either side of the neck

juice *n.* liquid part of a

vegetable, fruit, or animal *Slang* electric current

juic-er *n.* device for extracting juice from fruit

juic-y *adj.* full of; abounding with juice; full of interest; richly rewarding, especially financially **juiciness** *n.*

ju-jit-su *or* **ju-jut-su** *n.* Japanese system of using holds, throws, and stunning blows to subdue an opponent

juke box *n.* large, automatic, coin-operated record player equipped with push buttons for the selection of records

ju-lep *n.* mint julep

ju-li-enne *adj.* cut into thin strips *n.* clear meat soup containing vegetables chopped or cut into thin strips

jum-ble *v.* to mix in a confused mass; to throw together without order

jum-bo *n.* very large person, animal, or thing *adj.* extremely large

jump *v.* spring from the ground, floor, or other surface into the air by using a muscular effort of the legs and feet; to move in astonishment

jump-er *n.* one who or that which jumps; a sleeveless dress, usually worn over a blouse

jump-y *adj.* nervous; jittery **jumpiness** *n.*

jump suit *n.* one piece clothing worn by parachutes

jun-co *n.* any of various small birds of North America

junc-tion *n.* place where lines or routes meet, as roads or railways; the process of joining or the act of joining

junc-ture *n.* point where two things join; a crisis; an emergency; a point in time

June beetle *or* **June bug** *n.* large, brightly colored beetle which flies in June and has larvae that live in the soil and often destroy crops

jun-gle *n.* densely covered land

with tropical vegetation, usually inhabited by wild animals

jun-gle fe-ver *n.* disease of tropical regions where fever accompanies sickness

jun-gle-gym *n.* a structure with bars upon which children can climb

jun-gle rot *n.* skin disease, such as a fungus

jun-ior *adj.* younger in years or rank, used to distinguish the son from the father of the same first name; the younger of two *n.* third year of high school or college

junior college *n.* college offering a two year course which is equivalent to the first two years of a four year college

junior high school *n.* school which includes the 7th, 8th, and 9th grades

ju-ni-per *n.* evergreen shrub or tree of Europe and America with dark blue berries, prickly foliage, and fragrant wood

jun-ket *n.* party, banquet, or trip **junketeer** *n.*

junk-ie *or* **junk-y** *n., Slang* drug addict that uses heroin

ju-ry *n., pl.* **-ies** group of legally qualified persons summoned to serve on a judicial tribunal

just *adj.* fair and impartial in acting or judging; morally right **justly** *adv.*, **-ness** *n.*

jus-tice *n.* principle of moral or ideal rightness; conformity to the law

jus-ti-fy *v.* to be just, right, or valid; to declare guiltless; to adjust or space lines to the proper length

jut *v.* extend beyond the main portion; to project

ju-ve-nile *adj.* young; youthful; not yet an adult *n.* a young person; an actor who plays youthful roles

jux-ta-pose *v.* put side by side; to place together

jux-ta-po-si-tion *n.* the instance or act of placing two or more objects side by side

K, k the eleventh letter of the English alphabet

ka-bob *n.* small cubes of meat cooked with vegetables

ka-bu-ki *n.* traditional Japanese drama in which dances and songs are performed in a stylized fashion

kaf-fee-klatsch *n.* informal conversation or gathering over coffee

kai-nite *n.* a natural occurring salt used as a fertilizer

ka-ka *n.* a parrot that is olive brown in color and can be found in New Zealand

ka-ka-po *n.* New Zealand parrot which is nocturnal

kame *n.* short ridge of gravel and sand that remains after glacial ice melts

kan-ga-roo *n.*, *pl.* **-roo** various herbivorous marsupials, of Australia, with short forelegs, large hind limbs, capable of jumping, and a large tail

kangaroo court *n.* self-appointed, illegal court, usually marked by incompetence or dishonesty

ka-o-lin *or* **ka-o-line** *n.* fine clay used in ceramics

ka-pok *n.* silky fiber manufactured from the fruit of the silk-cotton tree and used for stuffing cushions and life preservers

ka-put *adj.*, *Slang* destroyed or out of order

kar-a-kul *n.* any of a breed of fat-tailed sheep of central Asia having a narrow body and coarse wiry, brown fur

kar-at *n.* unit of measure for the fineness of gold

ka-ra-te *n.* Japanese art of self-defense

kar-ma *n.* over-all effect of one's behavior, held in Hinduism and Buddhism to determine one's destiny in a future existence **kar-mic** *adj.*

ka-ty-did *n.* various green insects related to grasshoppers and crickets, having specialized organs on the wings of the male that make a shrill sound when rubbed together

kay-ak *n.* watertight Eskimo boat with a light frame and covered with sealskin **kayaker** *n.*

ka-zoo *n.* toy musical instrument with a paper membrane which vibrates symathelically when a player hums into the tube

kedge *n.* small anchor *v.* pull a ship by the rope of an anchor

keel *n.* central main stem on a ship or aircraft which runs lengthwise along the center line from bow to stern, to which a frame is built upwards *v.* to capsize *keel over* fall over suddenly; turn upside down **keeled** *adj.*

keelless *adj.*

keel-haul *v.* drag a person under the keel of a ship as a form of punishment

keel-son *n.*, *Naut.* structural member fastened above and parallel to the keel to give additional strength

keen *adj.* having a sharp edge or point; acutely painful or harsh; intellectually acute; strong; intense *Slang* great *n.* wailing lament especially for the dead **keenly** *adv.*, **keenness** *n.*

keep *v.* to have and hold; to not let go; to maintain, as business records; to know a secret and not divulge it; to protect and defend

keep-sake *n.* memento or souvenir

keg *n.* small barrel

keg-ler *n.* bowler

kelp *n.* any of a large brown seaweeds

kel-pie *n.* sheep dog originally bred in Australia

Kel-vin *adj.* designating or relating to the temperature scale having a zero point of approximately -273 15 degree C

ken-nel *n.* shelter for or a place where dogs or cats are bred, boarded, or trained

kennel v.

ke-no n. game of chance resembling bingo; a lottery game

kep-i n. French military cap having a flat, round top and a visor

ker-a-tin n. fibrous protein which forms the basic substance of nails, hair, horns, and hoofs **keratinous** adj.

ker-a-ti-tis n. inflammation of the cornea

ker-chief n. piece of cloth usually worn around the neck or on the head; scarf; a handkerchief **kerchiefed** adj.

ker-nel n. grain or seed, as of corn, enclosed in a hard husk; the inner substance of a nut; the central, most important part

ker-o-sene or **ker-o-sine** n. oil distilled from petroleum or coal and used for illumination

kes-trel n. small falcon, with gray and brown plumage

ketch n. small sailing vessel with two masts

ketch-up n. thick, smooth sauce made from tomatoes

ket-tle n. pot used for cooking

ket-tle-drum n. musical instrument with a parchment head which can be tuned by adjusting the tension

key n. an instrument by which the bolt of a lock is turned adj. of general importance

key-board n. bank of keys, as on a piano, typewriter, or computer terminal v. to set by means of a keyed typesetting machine; to generate letters by means of a word processor **keyboarder** n.

key club n. private club that offers entertainment amd serves liquor

key-note n., Mus. first and harmonically fundamental tone of a scale; main principle or theme

keynote address n. opening speech that outlines issues for discussion

key-punch n. machine operated from a keyboard that uses punched holes in tapes or cards for data processing systems

keypunch n., **keypuncher** v.

key-stone n. wedge-shaped stone at the center of an arch that locks its parts together; an essential part

key-stroke n. stroke of a key, as of a typewriter

key-way n. groove for a key

kg abbr. kilogram

khak-i n. yellowish brown or olive-drab color; a sturdy cloth being khaki in color **khakis** uniform of khaki cloth **khaki** adj.

khan n. Asiatic title of respect; a medieval Turkish, Mongolian or Tartar ruler **khanate** n.

khe-dive n. ruler of Egypt from 1867 to 1914 governing as a viceroy of the sultan of Turkey

kibble n. coarsely ground grain

kib-itz v. Slang look on and offer meddlesome advice to others **kibitzer** n.

kick n. sudden forceful thrust with the foot

kick-stand n. metal rod for holding up a two-wheeled bike

kick up n. provoke; to stir up

kid n. young goat; leather made from the skin of a young goat Slang child; youngster v. mock or tease playfully to deceive for fun; to fool **kidder** n.

kid leather n. soft pliable leather made from goatskin or lambskin

kid-nap v. seize and hold a person; unlawfully, often for ransom **kidnapper** n.

kid-ney n., pl. **neys** either of two organs situated in the abdominal cavity of vertebrates whose function is to keep proper water balance in the body and to excrete wastes in the form of urine

kidney bean n. bean grown for its edible seeds

kidvid n., Slang television programming for children

kiel·ba·sa n. smoked Polish sausage

kill n. put to death; nullify; cancel; to slaughter for food

kill·deer n., pl. -deer, -deers bird characterized by a plaintive, penetrating cry

killer whale n. black and white carnivorous whale, found in the colder waters of the seas

kil·lick n. small anchor usually made from a stone

kill·joy n. one who spoils the enjoyment of others

kiln n. oven or furnace for hardening or drying a substance, especially one for firing ceramics, pottery, etc.

ki·lo n. kilogram

kil·o·bit n. in computer science, one thousand binary digits

ki·lo·cy·cle n. unit equal to one thousand cycles, one thousand cycles per second

kil·o·gram n. measurement of weight in the metric system equal to slightly more than one third of a pound

kil·o·ton n. one thousand tons; an explosive power equal to that of one thousand tons of TNT

kil·o·watt n. unit of power equal to one thousand watts

kil·o·watt-hour n. unit of electric power consumption of one thousand watts throughout one hour

kilt n. knee-length wool skirt with deep pleats, usually of tartan, worn especially by men in the Scottish Highlands

kil·ter n. good condition; proper or working order

ki·mo·no n. loose, Japanese robe with a wide sash; a loose robe worn chiefly by women

kin n. one's relatives by blood

kin·der·gar·ten n. school or class for young children

from the ages of four to six

kin·der·gart·ner n. child who attends kindergarten

kind·heart·ed adj. a sympathetic nature -ly adv.

kindheartedness n.

kin·dle v. ignite; to catch fire; to stir up; to arouse; to excite, as the feelings

kindler n.

kin·dling n. easily ignited material such as, sticks, wood chips, etc. used to start a fire

kin·dred n. a person's relatives by blood adj. having a like nature; similar

kindredness n.

kin·e·mat·ics n. the branch of dynamics that deals with motion considered apart from force and mass -al adj., -ally adv.

kin·e·scope n. cathode-ray tube in a television set which translates received electrical into a visable picture on a screen; a film of a television on broadcast

ki·net·ic adj. of, or pertaining to, or produced by motion

king-bolt n. verticle central vehicle to the front axle

king crab n. large crablike crustacean common in the coastal waters of Japan, Alaska, and Siberia

king·pin n. foremost pin of a set arranged in order for playing bowling or tenpins; the most important or essential person

kink n. tight twist or knotlike curl; a sharp painful muscle cramp; a mental quirk v. to form or cause to form a kink

kink·a·jou n. tropical American mammal having large eyes, brown fur and a long prehensile tail

kink·y adj. tightly curled; sexually uninhibited

kinkily adv., **kinkiness** n.

ki·osk n. small building used as a refreshment booth or newsstand

kip n. untanned skin of a calf, a lamb and or an adult of any small breed

kip-per n. salted and smoked herring or salmon v. to cure by salting, smoking, or drying

kir-tle n. woman's long skirt

kis-met n. fate; appointed lot

kitch-en n. room in a house or building used to prepare and cook food

kite n. light-weight framework of wood and paper designed to fly in a gentle breeze at the end of a string; any of various predatory birds of the hawk family having a long, usually forked tail

kith or **kin** n. acquaintances or family

kitsch n. anything that is pretentious and in poor taste

kit-ten n. young cat

kit-ty-cor-nered adj. diagonally; cater-cornered

ki-wi n. flightless bird, of New Zealand having vestigil wings and a long, slender bill; a vine, native to Asia, which yields a fuzzy-skinned, edible fruit; the fruit of this vine

ki abbr. kiloliter

klep-to-ma-ni-a n. obsessive desire to steal or impulse to steal, especially without economic motive

klutz n., Slang stupid or clumsy person **klutziness** n., **klutzy** adj.

km abbr. kilometer

knack n. natural talent; aptitude

knack-wurst or **knock-wurst** n. thick or short, heavily seasoned sausage

knap-sack n. supply or equipment bag, as of canvas or nylon, worn strapped across the shoulders

knave n. tricky; or dishonest person **knavish** adj., **-ishly** adv., **-ishness** n.

knead v. work dough into a uniform mass; to shape by or as if by kneading

knee n. joint in the human body which connects the

calf with the thigh

knell v. sound a bell, especially when rung for a funeral; to toll n. act or instance of knelling; a signal of disaster

knick-ers pl. n. short loose-fitting pants gathered at the knee

knick-knack n. trinket; trifling article

knight n. medieval soldier serving a monarch; a chess piece bearing the shape of a horse's head **knighthood** n., knightly adj.

knish n. baked or fried dough stuffed with meat, cheese, or potatoes

knit v. to form by intertwining thread or yarn, by interlocking loops of a single yarn by means of needles; to fasten securely; to draw together **knit** n.

knitting needle n. long, slender, pointed rod for knitting

knob n. rounded protuberance; a lump; a rounded mountain; a rounded handle **knobbed** adj.

knock v. hit or strike with a hard blow; to criticize; to collide; to make a noise, as that of a defective engine Slang **knock out** to render unconscious **knock** n.

knock-down adj. designed to be easily assembled for storage or shipment

knockdown-drag-out adj. extremely violent or bitter

knock-er n. one who or that which knocks; as a metal ring for knocking on a door

knock-knee n. condition in which one or both knees turn inward and knock or rub together while walking **knock-kneed** adj.

knoll n. small round hill; a mound

knot n. interwinding as of string or rope; a fastening made by tying together lengths of material as string; a unifying bond, especially of marriage; a hard node on a tree from which a branch grows *Naut.* unit of speed, also called a nautical mile which equals approximately 1.15 statute miles per hour **-ness** *n.*, **knotty** *adj.*

knot-hole *n.* hole in lumber left by the falling out of a knot

knout *n.* whip or scourge for flogging criminals **knout** *v.*

know *v.* perceive directly as fact or truth; to believe to be true; to be certain of **knowable** *adj.*, **knowledge** *n.*

ko-a-la *n.* Australian marsupial which has large hairy ears, gray fur, and feeds on eucalyptus leaves

kohl-ra-bi *n.*, *pl.* **-ies** variety of cabbage having a thick stem and eaten as a vegetable

kook *n.*, *Slang* crazy or eccentric person **kookiness** *n.*

Ko-ran *n.* sacred book of Islam, accepted as containing the revelations made to Mohammed by Allah through the angel Gabriel

ko-sher *adj.* conformant to eat according to Jewish dietary laws *Slang* appropriate; proper

kow-tow *v.* show servile deference

kryp-ton *n.* white, inert gaseous chemical used mainly in fluorescent lamps; symbolized by Kr

ku-dos *n.* acclaim or prestige resulting from notable achievement or high position

kum-quat *n.* small, round orange fruit having a sour pulp and edible rind

kwash-i-or-kor *n.* severe malnutrition, especially in children, caused by protein deficiency

ky-ack *n.* a packsack for either side of a packsaddle

ky-pho-sis *n.* the abnormal backward curve of the spine

ky-rie *n.* a short prayer that consists of the words "Lord, have mercy"

L, l the twelfth letter of the English alphabet; the Roman numeral for fifty

lab *n.* laboratory

lab-da-num *n.* fragrant bitter oleoresin used in making perfumes

la-bel *n.* something that identifies or describes **label** *v.*

la-bel-lum *n.* terminal section of the labrun of some insects

la-bi-al *adj.* pertaining to or of the labia or lips

la-bia ma-jo-ra *n.* outer fold of the vulva

la-bia mi-no-ra *n.* inner fold of the vulva

la-bi-ate *n.* the plant in the mint family

la-bi-um *n.*, *pl.* **labia** any of the four folds of the vulva

la-bor *n.* physical or manual work done for hire

lab-o-ra-to-ry *n.*, *pl.* **-ies** a place equipped for conducting scientific experiments, research, or testing

lab-y-rinth *n.* a system of winding, intricate passages; a maze **labyrinthine** *adj.*

lac-er-ate *v.* to open with a jagged tear **laceration** *n.*

lach-ry-mal or **lac-ri-mal** *adj.* relating to or producing tears

lack *n.* the deficiency or complete absence of something

lack-a-dai-si-cal *adj.* lacking life, interest, or spirit; melancholy **-ly** *adv.*

lack-ey *n.* a male servant of very low status

lack-lus-ter *adj.* lacking sheen

lac-tate *v.* to secrete or to milk **lactation** *n.*

lac-te-al *adj.* of, resembling, or like milk

lac-tic acid *n.* a limpid, syrupy acid that is present in sour milk, molasses, some fruits, and wines

lac-tose *n.*, *Biochem.* a white, odorless, crystalline sugar

la-cu-na *n.*, *pl.* **-nas**, **-nae** a space from which something is missing

lad *n.* a boy or young man

lad-der n. an implement used for climbing up or down

lad-en adj. heavily burdened; oppressed; loaded **laden** v.

lad-ing n. cargo; freight

la-dle n. a cup-shaped vessel with a deep bowl and a long handle **ladle** v.

la-dy n., pl. **ladies** a woman showing refinement, cultivation, and often high social position

lag v. to stray or fall behind; to move slowly

la-gniappe n. a small gift which is given to a purchaser by a storekeeper

la-goon n. a body of shallow water separated from the ocean by a coral reef or sandbars **lagoonal** adj.

laid v. past tense of lay

lain v. past tense of lie

lais-sez--faire n. a policy stating that a government should exercise very little control in trade and industrial affairs

la-i-ty n. laymen, as distinguished from clergy

lake n. a large inland body of either salt or fresh water

La-maze method n. a method of childbirth in which the mother is prepared psychologically and physically to give birth

lamb n. a young sheep; the meat of a lamb used as food

lam-baste or **lambast** v., Slang to thrash or beat

lam-bent adj. lightly and playfully brilliant **lambency** n.

lame adj. disabled or crippled **lamely** adv., **lameness** n.

la-me n. a brocaded fabric woven with gold or silver thread

la-ment v. to express sorrow

lam-i-na n., pl. **-nae**, **-nas** a thin scale or layer Bot. the blade or flat part of a leaf

lam-i-nate v. to form or press into thin sheets **-ed** adj.

lamp n. a device for generating heat or light

lam-poon n. a satirical, but often humorous, attack in verse or prose

lam-prey n. ,pl. **preys** an eel-like fish

land n. the solid, exposed surface of the earth as distinguished from the waters

lan-dau n. a four-wheeled vehicle with a closed carriage and a back seat with a collapsible top

land-er n. a space vehicle for landing on a celestial body

land-scape n. a view or vista of natural scenery as seen from a single point

lane n. a small or narrow path between walls, fences, or hedges

lan-guage n. the words, sounds, pronunciation and method of combining words

lan-guid adj. lacking in energy **-ly** adv., **-ness** n.

lan-guish v. to become weak

lank adj. slender; lean

lan-o-lin n. wool grease obtained from sheep's wool and refined for use in ointments and cosmetics

lan-yard n. a piece of rope or line used to secure objects on ships

lap-in n. rabbit fur that is sheared and dyed

lap-is laz-u-li n. a semiprecious stone that is azure blue in color

lap-pet n. a flap or fold on a headdress or on a garment

lapse n. a temporary deviation or fall to a less desirable state **lapse** v.

lar-ce-ny n., pl. **-ies** the unlawful taking of another person's property

lar-der n. a place, such as a pantry or room, where food is stored

large adj. greater than usual or average in amount or size

lar-gess or **lar-gesse** n. liberal or excessive giving to an inferior; generosity

lar-go adv., Mus. in a very slow, broad, and solemn manner **largo** adj. & n.

lar-i-at n. a long, light rope

with a running noose at one end to catch livestock

lark n. a bird having a melodious ability to sing

lar-va n., pl. **larvae** the immature, wingless, often wormlike form of a newly hatched insect

lar-yn-gi-tis n. inflammation of the larynx

lar-ynx n., pl. **larynges** or **larynxes** the upper portion of the trachea which contains the vocal cords

lash v. to strike or move violently or suddenly

lass n. a young girl or woman

las-si-tude n. a condition of weariness; fatigue

last adj. following all the rest; of or relating to the final death

• **Last Supper** n. the last meal eaten by Jesus Christ and his disciples, before his crucifixion

latch n. a device used to secure a gate or door, consisting of a bar that usually fits into a notch **latch onto** to grab onto

latch-et n. a narrow leather strap or thong used to fasten a shoe

latch-key n. a key for opening an outside door

late adj. coming, staying, happening after the proper or usual time; having recently died **-ness** n., **-ly** adv.

lat-er-al adj. relating to or of the side **laterally** adv.

la-tex n. the milky, white fluid that is produced by certain plants, such as the rubber tree

lath n. a thin, narrow strip of wood nailed to joists, rafters, or studding

lathe n. a machine for holding material while it is spun and shaped by a tool

lat-i-tude n. the angular distance of the earth's surface north or south of the equator

la-trine n. a public toilet

lat-ter adj. being the second of two persons or two things

laud v. to praise; to extol **-able** adj., **-ably** adv.

laugh v. to express amusement, satisfaction **laughable** adj.

laun-dry n., pl. **-ies** an establishment where laundering is done professionally

lau-re-ate n. a person honored for his accomplishment

la-va n. molten rock which erupts or flows from an active volcano

lav-a-to-ry n., pl. **-ies** a room with permanently installed washing and toilet facilities

lav-en-der n. an aromatic plant having spikes of pale violet flowers **lavender** adj.

lav-ish adj. generous and extravagant in giving or spending **lavisher** n., **-ly** adv.

law n. a rule of conduct or action, recognized by custom or decreed by formal enactment, considered binding on the members of a nation, community, or group

law-ren-ci-um n. a short-lived radioactive element

law-suit n. a case or proceeding brought before a court of law for settlement

law-yer n. a person trained in the legal profession who acts for and advises clients or pleads in court

lax adj. lacking disciplinary control **laxity**, **laxness** n.

lax-a-tive n. a medicine taken to stimulate evacuation of the bowels **laxative** adj.

lay v. to cause to lie; to place on a surface; past tense of lie

lay-er n. a single thickness, coating, or covering that lies over or under another **layered** adj., **layer** v.

lay-ette n. the clothing, bedding, and equipment for a newborn child

lay-off n. a temporary dismissal of employees

la-zy adj. unwilling to work; sluggish **-ily** adv., **-iness** n.

la-zy-bones n. Slang a lazy person

L--do·pa n. a drug used in treating Parkinson's disease

lea n., *Poetic.* a grassy field or meadow

leach v. to cause a liquid to pass through a filter

lead v. to go ahead so as to show the way; to control the affairs or action of

lead poisoning n. poisoning of a person's system by the absorption of lead or any of its salts

leaf n., pl. **leaves** a flat outgrowth from a plant structure or tree

leaf·let n. a part or a segment of a compound leaf; a small printed handbill or circular

league n. an association of persons, organizations, or states for common action or interest

leak n. an opening, as a flaw or small crack, permitting an escape or entrance of light or fluid

leakage, leakiness n.

lean v. to rest or incline the weight of the body for support -ly adj., -ness n.

lean·ing n. an inclination

learn n. the process of acquiring knowledge **learner** n.

lease n. a contract for the temporary use or occupation of property or premises in exchange for payment of rent

leash n. a strong cord or rope for restraining a dog or other animal **leash** v.

least-wise adv., *Slang* last way

leath·er n. an animal skin or hide with the hair removed

leave v. to go or depart from

leav·en n. an agent of fermentation, as yeast, used to cause batters and doughs to rise **leaven** v.

lech·er·y n. unrestrained indulgence in sexual activity -er n., -ous adj., -ously adv.

lec·i·thin n. any of a group of phosphorus containing compounds found in plant and animal tissues

lec·tern n. a stand or tall desk, usually with a slanted top

lec·ture n. a speech on a specific subject

led v., p.t. & p.p. past tense of lead

ledg·er n. a book in which sums of money received and paid out are recorded

lee n. the side of a ship sheltered from the wind

leech n. any of various carnivorous or bloodsucking worms

leek n. a culinary herb of the lily family, related to the onion

leer n. a sly look or sideways glance expressing desire

lee·way n., *Naut.* the lateral drift of a plane or ship away from the correct course

left adj. pertaining to or being on the side of the body that faces north when the subject is facing east

leg·a·cy n., pl. -ies personal property, money, and other valuables that are bequeathed by will

le·gal adj. of, pertaining to, or concerned with the law or lawyers -ity, -ization n., legalize v., legally adv.

le·gal·ism n. a strict conformity to the law, especially when stressing the letter and forms of the law rather than the spirit of justice

le·ga·tion n. the official diplomatic mission in a foreign country, headed by a minister

le·ga·to adv., *Music* smooth and flowing with successive notes connected

legato adj. & n.

leg·end n. an unverifiable story handed down from the past **legendary** adj.

leg·horn n. a hat made from finely plaited wheat straw

leg·i·ble adj. capable of being read -ility n., -ly adv.

le·gion n. any various honorary or military organizations

leg·is·late v. to pass or make laws

leg·is·la·tion n. the act or procedures of passing laws

leg-is-la-ture n. a body of persons officially constituted and empowered to make and change laws

leg-ume n. a plant of the pea or bean family

lei n., pl. **leis** a wreath of flowers worn around the neck; the customary greeting of welcome in the state of Hawaii

lei-sure n. the time of freedom from work or duty **leisurely** adj. & adv.

lem-on n. an oval citrus fruit grown on a tree

lem-on-ade n. a drink made from water, lemon juice, and sugar

lend v. to allow the temporary use or possession of something **lender** n.

length n. the linear extent of something from end to end

length-wise adv. & adj. of or in the direction or dimension of length

le-ni-ent adj. gentle, forgiving, and mild **leniently** adv.

len-i-tive adj. having the ability to ease pain

lent v. past tense of lend

len-til n. a leguminous plant, having broad pods and containing edible seeds

leop-ard n. a large member of the cat family of Africa and Asia

le-o-tard n. a close-fitting garment worn by dancers and acrobats

lep-er n. one who suffers from leprosy

lep-re-chaun n. a mischief-making elf of Irish folklore

lep-ro-sy n., Pathol. a chronic communicable disease characterized by nodular skin lesions and the progressive destruction of tissue **leprotic** adj.

les-bi-an n. a homosexual woman **lesbian** adj.

lese maj-es-ty or n. an offense against a ruler or supreme power of state

le-sion n., Pathol. an injury; a wound

less adj. smaller; of smaller or lower importance or degree **-less** suffix. without; lacking

les-see n. one who leases a property

les-son n. an instance from which something is to be or has been learned

let v. to give permission; to allow

le-thal adj. pertaining to or being able to cause death

leth-ar-gy n., Pathol. a state of excessive drowsiness or abnormally deep sleep; laziness **lethargic** adj.

let's contr. let us

let-ter n. a standard character or sign used in writing or printing to represent an alphabetical unit or speech

leu-ke-mi-a n., Pathol. a generally fatal disease of the blood **leukemic** adj.

le-vee n. an embankment along the shore of a body of water, built to prevent overflowing

lev-el n. a relative position, rank, or height on a scale v. to make or become flat or level **leveler**, **levelness** n.

lever n. a handle that projects and is used to operate or adjust a mechanism

lev-i-tate v. to rise and float in the air in apparent defiance of gravity **levitation** n.

Le-vit-i-cus n. the third book of the Old Testament

lev-i-ty n., pl. **-ies** lack of seriousness; frivolity; lightness

lev-y v. to impose and collect by authority or force, as a fine or tax **levy** n.

lewd adj. preoccupied with sex; lustful **lewdness** n.

lex-i-cog-ra-phy n. the practice or profession of compiling dictionaries

lex-i-con n. a dictionary; a vocabulary or list of words that relate to a certain subject, occupation, or activity

li-a-bil-i-ty n., pl. **-ies** the condition or state of being liable

li-a-ble adj. legally or rightly

responsible

li-ai-son *n.* a communication, as between different parts of an armed force or departments of a government

li-ar *n.* a person who tells falsehoods

li-bel *n., Law* a written statement in published form that damages a person's character or reputation

lib-er-al *adj.* characterized by generosity or lavishness in giving; abundant; ample; inclining toward opinions or policies that favor progress or reform, such as religion or politics

liberal arts *pl. n.* academic courses that include literature, philosophy, history, languages, etc

lib-er-ate *v.* to set free, as from bondage, oppression

lib-er-ty *n., pl.* -ies the state of being free from oppression

li-bi-do *n.* one's sexual desire or impulse; the psychic energy drive that is behind all human activities

li-brar-i-an *n.* a person in charge of a library

li-brar-y *n., pl.* -ies a collection of books, pamphlets, magazines, and reference books kept for reading, reference, or borrowing

lice *n.* plural of louse

li-cense *n.* an official document that gives permission to engage in a specified activity or to perform a specified act

li-cen-ti-ate *n.* a person licensed to practice a specified profession

li-cen-tious *adj.* lacking in moral restraint; immoral

li-chen *n.* any of various flowerless plants consisting of fungi, commonly growing in flat patches on trees and rocks lichened, -ous *adj.*

lic-it *adj.* lawful licitly *adv.*

lick *v.* to pass the tongue over or along the surface of something

lick-e-ty--split *adv.* full speed

lic-o-rice *n.* a perennial herb of

Europe, the dried root of which is used to flavor medicines and candy

lid *n.* a hinged or removable cover for a container; an eyelid lidded, lidless *adj.*

lie *v.* to be in or take a horizontal recumbent position; to recline *n.* a false or untrue statement

liege *n.* a feudal lord or sovereign

lien *n.* the legal right to claim, hold, or sell the property of another to satisfy a debt or obligation

lieu *n.* place; stead. **in lieu of** in place of

lieu-ten-ant *n.* a commissioned officer

life *n., pl.* **lives** the form of existence that distinguishes living organisms from dead organisms or inanimate matter in the ability to carry on metabolism, respond to stimuli, reproduce, and grow

lifer *n.* Slang a person sentenced to life in prison

life-time *n.* the period between one's birth and death

life zone *n.* a biogeographic zone

lift *v.* to raise from a lower to a higher position; to elevate; to take from; to steal

liftoff *n.* the vertical takeoff or the instant of takeoff of an aircraft or spacecraft

lig-a-ment *n.* a tough band of tissue joining bones or holding a body organ in place ligamentous *adj.*

li-gate *v.* to tie with a ligature

lig-a-ture *n.* something, as a cord, that is used to bind

light *n.* electromagnetic radiation that can be seen by the naked eye; a source of fire, such as a match lightness *n.*

light-ning *n.* the flash of light produced by a high-tension natural electric discharge into the atmosphere

lig-ne-ous *adj.* of or resembling wood; woody

lig-nite *n.* a brownish-black

soft coal

lig-ro-in *n.* a volatile, flammable fraction of petroleum used as a solvent

lik-en *v.* to describe as being like; to compare

like-ness *n.* resemblance; a copy

like-wise *adv.* in a similar way

lilt *n.* a light song; a rhythmical way of speaking

lil-y *n., pl.* **-ies** any of various plants bearing trumpet-shaped flowers

limb *n.* a large bough of a tree; an animal's appendage used for movement or grasping; an arm or leg

lim-ber *adj.* bending easily; pliable; moving easily; agile

lime *n.* a tropical citrus edible green fruit; calcium oxide

lime-light *n.* a focus of public attention; the center of attention

lim-er-ick *n.* a humorous verse of five lines

lim-it *n.* a boundary; a maximum or a minimum number or amount **limitation** *n.*

limn *v.* to describe; to depict by drawing **limner** *n.*

li-mo-nite *n.* a natural iron oxide used as an ore of iron

lim-ou-sine *n.* a luxurious large vehicle; a small bus used to carry passengers to airports and hotels

limp *v.* to walk lamely *adj.* lacking or having lost rigidity; not firm or strong

lim-pet *n.* any of numerous marine gastropod mollusks having a conical shell and adhering to tidal rocks

lim-pid *adj.* transparently clear **limpidity** *n.*, **limpidly** *adv.*

lin-den *n.* any of various shade trees having heart-shaped leaves

lin-e-age *n.* a direct line of descent from an ancestor

lin-e-a-ment *n.* a contour, shape, or feature of the body and especially of the face

lin-e-ar *adj.* of, pertaining to, or resembling a line; long and narrow

lin-en *n.* thread, yarn, or fabric made of flax; household articles, such as sheets and pillow cases

ling *n.* any of various marine food fishes related to the cod

lin-ger *v.* to be slow in parting or reluctant to leave; to be slow in acting; to procrastinate **-er** *n.*, **-ingly** *adv.*

lin-ge-rie *n.* women's undergarments

lingo *n., pl.* **goes** language that is unfamiliar; a specialized vocabulary

lin-guist *n.* one who is fluent in more than one language

lin-i-ment *n.* a liquid or semiliquid medicine applied to the skin

lin-ing *n.* a material which is used to cover an inside surface

lin-net *n.* a small Old World finch

li-no-le-um *n.* a floor covering

lin-seed *n.* the seed of flax, used in paints and varnishes

lin-tel *n.* a horizontal beam across the top of a door which supports the weight of the structure above it

li-on *n.* a large carnivorous mammal of the cat family, found in Africa and India

li-on-ize *v.* to treat someone as a celebrity

liq-ue-fy *or* **liq-ui-fy** *v.* to make liquid **liquefaction** *n.*

li-queur *n.* a sweet alcoholic beverage; a cordial

liq-ui-date *v.* to settle a debt by payment or other settlement; to close a business by settling accounts and dividing up assets; to get rid of, to kill **liquidation**, **-or** *n.*

liq-uor *n.* a distilled alcoholic beverage

lisle *n.* a fine, tightly twisted cotton thread

lisp *n.* a speech defect or mannerism marked by lisping

list *n.* a series of numbers or words; a tilt to one side

list-less *adj.* lacking energy or

enthusiasm **listlessly** adv.

lit-a-ny n., pl. **-ies** a prayer in which phrases recited by a leader are alternated with answers from a congregation

li-tchi or **li-chee** n. a Chinese tree, bearing edible fruit

lit-er-al adj. conforming to the exact meaning of a word **literally** adv., **-istic** adj.

lit-er-al-ism n. adherence to the explicit sense of a given test; literal portrayal; realism

lit-er-ar-y adj. pertaining to literature; appropriate to or used in literature

lit-er-ate adj. having the ability to read and write **literacy**, **literate** n.

lithe adj. bending easily; supple **lithely** adv., **litheness** n.

lith-i-um n. a silver-white, soft metallic element symbolized by Li

li-thog-ra-phy n. a printing process **lithograph** n. & v.

li-thol-o-gy n. the microscopic study and classification of rocks **lithologist** n.

lit-i-gate v. to conduct a legal contest by judicial process **litigation** n.

lit-ter-bug n. one who litters a public area

lit-to-ral adj. relating to or existing on a shore n. a shore

lit-ur-gy n., pl. **-ies** a prescribed rite or body of rites for public worship

live-li-hood n. a means of support or subsistence

live-ly adj. vigorous **liveliness** n.

liv-er n. the large, very vascular, glandular organ of vertebrates which secretes bile

live-stock n. farm animals raised for human use

live wire n., Slang an energetic person

liv-id adj. discolored from a bruise; very angry

liz-ard n. one of various reptiles, usually with an elongated scaly body

load n. a mass or weight that is lifted or supported; anything, as cargo

loaf n., pl. **loaves** a food, especially bread, that is shaped into a mass v. to spend time in idleness

loam n. soil that consists chiefly of sand, clay, and decayed plant matter

loan n. money lent with interest to be repaid; something borrowed for temporary use v. to lend

loath adj. averse

loathe v. to dislike intensely

loath-ing n. intense dislike

loath-some adj. arousing disgust **-ly** adv., **-ness** n.

lob v. to hit or throw in a high arc

lob-by n., pl. **-ies** a foyer, as in a hotel or theatre; a group of private persons trying to influence legislators

lobe n. a curved or rounded projection or division, as the fleshy lower part of the ear **lobar**, **lobed** adj.

lob-lol-ly n., pl. **-ies** a mudhole; mire

lo-bo n. the gray wolf

lo-bot-o-my n., pl. **-mies** surgical severance of nerve fibers by an incision into the brain

lob-ster n. any of several large, edible marine crustaceans

lob-ule n. a small lobe; a subdivision of a lobe **-ar** adj.

lo-cal adj. pertaining to, being in, or serving a particular area or place **locally** adv.

lo-cale n. a locality where a particular event takes place; the setting or scene, as of a novel

lo-cate v. to determine the place, position, or boundaries of; to look for and find **locator** n.

loch n., Scot. a lake

lock n. a device used, as on a door, to secure or fasten

lock-et n. a small, ornamental case for a keepsake, often a picture, worn as a pendant on a necklace

lock-jaw n. tetanus

lock-smith n. a person who makes or repairs locks

lo-co adj., Slang insane

lo-co-mo-tion n. the act of moving

lo-co-mo-tive n. a self-propelled vehicle that is generally electric or diesel-powered and is used for moving railroad cars

lo-cust n. any of numerous grasshoppers which often travel in swarms and damage vegetation

loft n. one of the upper, generally unpartitioned floors of an industrial buildings

loge n. a small compartment, especially a box in a theatre; a small partitioned area

log-gi-a n. a roofed but open arcade along the front of a building; an open balcony

log-ic n. the science dealing with the principles of reasoning, especially of the method and validity of deductive reasoning

log-i-cal adj. something marked by consistency of reasoning logically adv.

lo-gis-tics pl., n. the methods of procuring, maintaining, and replacing material and personnel logistic adj.

lo-go-type n. identifying symbol for a company or publication

lo-gy adj. something marked by sluggishness logier adj.

loins n. the thighs and groin; the reproductive organs

loi-ter v. to stay for no apparent reason; to dawdle or delay loiterer n.

loll v. to move or act in a lax, lazy or indolent manner

lol-ly-gag v., Slang to fool around

lone adj. single; isolated; sole

lone-ly adj. being without companions loneliness n.

lon-er n. a person who avoids the company of others

long-bow n. a wooden bow that is approximately five to six feet in length

lon-gev-i-ty n. long life; long duration; seniority

lon-gi-tude n. the angular distance that is east and west of the prime meridian at Greenwich, England

lon-gi-tu-di-nal adj. of or relating to the length; relating to longitude

look v. to examine with the eyes; to see; to glance, gaze, or stare at

look-out n. a person positioned to keep watch

loom v. to come into view as a image; to seem to be threatening

loo-ny or **loo-ney** adj. crazy loony n.

loose adj. not fastened; not confined or fitting; free

loot n. goods, usually of significant value, taken in time of war; goods that have been stolen v. to plunder

lope v. to run with a steady gait lope, lopper n.

lop-sid-ed adj. larger or heavier on one side than on the other; tilting to one side -ly adv., -ness n.

lo-qua-cious adj. overly talkative -ly adv., -ity n.

Lord n. God. a man having dominion and power over other people

lore n. traditional fact; knowledge that has been gained through education or experience

lorn n. forlorn

lose v. to mislay; to fail to keep loser n.

loss n. the suffering or damage used by losing; someone or something that is lost losses pl. n. killed, wounded, or captured

lost adj. unable to find one's way

lot n. fate; fortune; a parcel of land having boundaries

lo-tion n. a liquid medicine for external use on the hands and body

lounge v. to move or act in a lazy, relaxed manner n. a

room, as in a hotel or theatre; a couch

lounger n.

louse n., pl. **lice** a small, wingless biting or sucking insect which lives as a parasites on various animals and also on human beings

lous-y adj. lice-infested. Slang mean; poor; inferior

lout n. an awkward, stupid person **loutish** adj.

love n. intense affection for another arising out of kinship or personal ties; a strong feeling of attraction resulting from sexual desire

lov-er n. a person who loves another; a sexual partner

low adj. not high; being below or under normal height, rank, or level; depressed

low-brow n. an uncultured person **lowbrow** adj.

low-down n. the whole truth; all the facts adj. despicable; mean; depressed

low frequency n. a radio-wave frequency between 30 and 300 kilohertz

low-key or **low-keyed** adj. restrained

low-ly adj. low in position or rank **lowliness** n.

low--pres-sure adj. being capable of operation with or under low pressure

low pro-file n. a deliberately inconspicuous life style or posture

low--rise n. having one or two stories in height

low tide n. the tide at its farthest ebb

lox n. smoked salmon; liquid oxygen

loy-al adj. faithful in allegiance to one's country and government; faithful to a person, cause, ideal

loy-al-ist n. one who is or remains loyal to political cause, party, government, or sovereign

lu-au n. a traditional Hawaiian feast

lub-ber n. an awkward, clumsy or stupid person; an inexperienced sailor

lu-bri-cant n. a material, as grease or oil, applied to moving parts to reduce friction

lu-bri-cious adj. smooth, unstable; shifty **lubriciously** adv.

lu-cid adj. easily understood; mentally clear; rational; shining

Lucifer n. the devil; Satan.

lu-cra-tive adj. producing profits or great wealth

lu-cre n. money; profit; monetary gain

lu-cu-brate v. to study or work laboriously

lu-di-crous adj. amusing or laughable through obvious absurdity; ridiculous

luge n. a small sled

lu-gu-bri-ous adj. mournful; dejected; especially exaggeratedly or affectedly so

lull v. to cause to rest or sleep; to cause to have a false sense of security

lul-la-by n., pl. **-bies** a song to lull a child to sleep

lum-ba-go n. painful rheumatic pain of the muscles and tendons of the lumbar region

lum-bar adj. part of the back and sides between the lowest ribs and the pelvis

lum-ber n. timber, sawed or split into boards

lu-mi-nar-y n., pl. **-ies** a celestial body, as the sun; a notable person

lu-mi-nes-cence n. an emission of light without heat, as in fluorescence

lu-mi-nous adj. emitting or reflecting light; bathed in steady light; illuminated

lum-mox n. a clumsy oaf

lump n. a projection; a protuberance; a swelling

lu-na-cy n., pl. **-ies** insanity.

lu-nar adj. of, relating to, caused by the moon

lu-na-tic n. a crazy person.

lunch-eon n. a lunch

lung n. one of the two spongy organs that constitute the basic respiratory organ of air-breathing vertebrates

lunge n. a sudden forward movement **lunge** v.

lu-pus n. a bacterial disease of the skin

lure n. a decoy; something appealing; v. to attract or entice with the prospect of reward or pleasure

lurk v. to lie in concealment, as in an ambush

lus-cious adj. very pleasant to smell or taste; appealing to the senses **lusciously** adv.

lush adj. producing luxuriant growth or vegetation Slang an alcoholic **lushly** adv.

lust n. intense sexual desire; an intense longing; a craving **lustful** adj.

lus-ter or **lus-tre** n. a glow of reflected light; sheen; brilliance or radiance

lust-y adj. vigorous; healthy; robust; lively **lustily** adv.

lute n. a medieval musical stringed instrument

lu-te-ti-um or **lu-te-ci-um** n. a silvery rare-earth metallic element symbolized by Lu

lux-u-ri-ant adj. growing or producing abundantly; lush; plentiful

lux-u-ri-ate v. to enjoy luxury or abundance

lymph node n. a roundish body of lymphoid tissue; lymph gland

lynch v. to execute without authority or the due process of law

lynx n. a wildcat adj. having acute eyesight

lyre n. an ancient Greek stringed instrument related to the harp

lyr-ic adj. concerned with thoughts and feelings; romantic; appropriate for singing in a lyric poem; a lyric composition

ly-ser-gic ac-id di-eth-yl-am-ide n. an organic compound which induces psychotic symptoms similar to those of schizophrenia; LSD

M, m the thirteenth letter of the English alphabet

ma-ca-bre adj. suggesting death and decay; having death for a subject -ly adv.

mac-a-roon n. small cookie made of coconut, eggs, and sugar

ma-caw n. type of tropical American parrots

mac-er-ate v. to make a solid substance soft; to waste away **maceration** n.

ma-chet-e n. a large, heavy type of knife

mach-i-nate v. to plot in an attempt to do harm

ma-chine n. device built to use energy to do work **machinery** n., **-able** adj.

ma-chin-er-y n. a collection of machines as a whole; the mechanism or operating parts of a machine

ma-chin-ist n. the person who operates and repairs machines for others

ma-chis-mo n. an exaggerated sense of masculinity

ma-cho adj. exhibiting machismo in character

mack-er-el n. kind of fish that is found in the Atlantic Ocean

mack-in-tosh n. raincoat

mac-ra-me n. the craft of tying knots

mac-ro-bi-ot-ic adj. being an extremely restricted diet to promote longevity

ma-cron n. the (-) placed over a vowel to indicate a long sound

mac-ro-scop-ic adj. large enough to be seen by the naked eye

mad adj. being angry; insane **madness** n., **madly** adv.

mad-am n. title used to address a married woman

made v. past tense of make

mad-e-moi-selle n. an unmarried French girl

made--to--order adj. to be custom-made

made--up adj. being fabricated; invented

mad-house n. a place of confusion or disorder

mad-ri-gal *n.*, *Music* unaccompanied song **madrigalist** *n.*

mael-strom *n.* any irresistible or dangerous force

maes-tro *n.* a person mastering any art

mag-a-zine *n.* publication; explosives storehouse

ma-gen-ta *n.* a purplish red color or hue

mag-got *n.* the legless larva of insects **maggoty** *adj.*

mag-ic *n.* art of illusions -ically *adv.*, -ical *adj.*

mag-is-trate *n.* civil officer of law **magistratically** *adv.*

mag-ma *n.* the molten rock beneath the earth's surface

mag-nan-i-mous *adj.* being forgiving; generous -ness *n.*, **magnanimously** *adv.*

mag-nate *n.* kind of business tycoon

mag-ne-sia *n.* a light, white powder used in medicine as an antacid

mag-ne-si-um *n.* a light, silvery metallic element which burns with a hot flame

mag-net *n.* body attracting other magnetic material -ically *adv.*, **magnetize** *v.*

mag-net-ic *adj.* pertaining to magnetism or a magnet

mag-net-ite *n.* a black iron oxide in mineral form

mag-net-ize *v.* to have magnetic properties

mag-ne-to *n.* small alternator that uses magnets to operate

mag-nif-i-cent *adj.* beautiful -cence *n.*, -cently *adv.*

mag-ni-fy *v.* increase in size -fication *n.*, -fiable *adj.*

mag-nil-o-quent *adj.* speaking in a lofty manner

mag-ni-tude *n.* the greatness in size

mag-no-lia *n.* flowering tree

mag-num *n.* wine bottle holding two quarts

mag-pie *n.* large, noisy bird

ma-ha-ra-ja *n.* a king or prince who rules an Indian state

ma-ha-ra-ni *n.* the wife of the maharaja

ma-hat-ma *n.* a title of respect

ma-hog-a-ny *n.*, *pl.* -ies trees with hard wood

maid *n.* a young unmarried woman or girl

maid-en *n.* young girl

maid-en-hair *n.* a delicate fern with dark stems and lightgreen, feathery fronds

maid-en name *n.* woman's family name before marriage

mail *n.* printed matter

mailbox *n.*, **mailed** *adj.*

mail order *n.* goods which are ordered and sent by mail

maim *v.* to cripple or disfigure another **maimer** *n.*

main *adj.* being most important part **mainly** *adv.*

main-land *n.* the land part of a country as distinguished from an island

main-line *v.* to inject a drug directly into a vein

main-stream *n.* a main direction or line of thought

main-tain *v.* keep in existence **maintainer** *n.*, -ble *adj.*

maize *n.* type of corn

maj-es-ty *n.* stateliness; one's exalted dignity

ma-jor *adj.* being greater in importance

ma-jor-ette *n.* a young woman who marches and twirls a baton in her hand

ma-jor-i-ty *n.* greater number of something

ma-jor med-i-cal *n.* type of insurance policy

make *v.* create; cause to happen **maker** *n.*, -able *adj.*

make-be-lieve *n.* something pretended; imagined

make-up *n.* composition

mal-a-chite *n.* green basic copper carbonate

mal-a-droit *adj.* lacking skill -ness *n.*, **maladroitly** *adv.*

mal-a-dy *n.*, *pl.* -ies chronic disease or sickness

mal-aise *n.* the vague discomfort sometimes indicating the beginning of an illness

mal-a-prop-ism *n.* foolish misuse of a word

mal-ap-ro-pos *adj.* being not

appropriate in style

ma·lar·i·a n., *Pathol.* disease caused by the bite of mosquitos **malariaious** adj.

ma·lar·key n. foolish or insincere talk

mal·con·tent adj. unhappy with surroundings

mal·de·mer n. seasickness

male adj. being a man

mal·e·dic·tion n. a curse; execration

mal·for·ma·tion n. a defective form of something

mal·func·tion n. the failure to work

mal·ice n. the desire to harm others **maliciously** adv.

ma·lign v. to speak evil of **malignly** adv., **maligner** n.

ma·lig·nant adj., *Pathol.* to be relating to tumors **malignantly** adv., **-cy** n.

ma·lin·ger v. pretend sickness to avoid work

mal·lard n. wild duck

mal·let n. hammer with a short handle

mal·nour·ished adj. being underfed; lacking food

mal·oc·clu·sion n. improper alignment of the teeth

mal·prac·tice n. the mistreatment by a doctor

malt n. grain **malty** adj.

mal·treat v. to treat another unkindly **maltreatment** n.

mam·mal n. the group of animals who suckle their young **mammalian** adj.

mam·mog·ra·phy n. x-ray of the breast for detection of cancer

mam·moth n. extinct form of an elephant

man n. the adult male; the human race

man·a·cle n. handcuffs

man·age v. direct or control **manageable** adj., **-ability** n.

man·ag·er n. one in charge of a situation **managership** n.

man·a·tee n. type of aquatic mammal

man·date n. an order or command

man·da·to·ry adj. required

man·do·lin n. a musical instrument **mandolinist** n.

mane n. long hair on animals neck **maned** adj.

mange n. the skin disease of the dogs

man·ger n. the box for animal feed

man·gle v. to disfigure or to mutilate

man·grove n. tropical tree

man·han·dle v. to handle roughly **manhandled** adj.

man·hole n. sewer drain

ma·ni·a n. the desire for something

man·i·cot·ti n. pasta

man·i·cure n. the care of the fingernails **manicurist** n.

man·i·fest n. the list of cargo a vehicle carries **-ation** n.

man·i·fold adj. having many parts, or types

ma·nip·u·late v. to manage shrewdly **manipulation** n.

man·kind n. human race

man·made adj. not developed naturally

man·ner n. way in which things are done **-less** adj.

man·ner·ly adj. being well-behaved **mannerliness** n.

ma·nom·e·ter n. instrument to measure pressure

man·or n. estate **manorial** adj.

man·slaugh·ter n., *Law* the unlawful killing of another without malice

man·tel n. shelf over a fireplace **mantelpiece** n.

man·til·la n. light scarf

man·u·al adj. operated by the hand **manually** adv.

man·u·fac·ture v. make a product **-er** n., **-able** adj.

ma·nure n. animal dung used for fertilizer

man·u·script n. a typed copy of an article, or book

man·y adj. indefinite number

map n. plane surface of a region **mapper** n.

ma·ple syr·up n. sap of the sugar maple

mar v. deface **marrer** n.

mar·a·thon n. foot race of 26 miles

mar·ble n. the limestone **marbleize** v., **marbling** n.

march *v.* to walk with measured steps -ing*n.*

mare *n.* female of the horse

mar-ga-rine *n.* kind of butter substitute

mar-gin *n.* edge of printed text -al *adj.*, -ally *adv.*

mar-i-jua-na *n.* kind of hallucinogenic drug

ma-ri-na *n.* harbor for boats

mar-i-nade *n.* brine for soaking meat

ma-rine *adj.* to be pertaining to the sea mariner *n.*

mar-i-o-nette *n.* puppet operated by strings

mark *n.* visible impression

mar-ket *n.* public place to purchase or sell goods

marks-man *n.* the skill in the firing of a gun

mar-lin *n.* large marine game fish

ma-roon *v.* to abandon one on the shore

mar-riage *n.* the legal union of two people in wedlock -ability *n.*, -able *adj.*

mar-row *n.* the tissue in bone cavities marrowy *adj.*

marsh *n.* low, wet land; swamp marshy *adj.*, -iness *n.*

mar-shal *n.* military officer

marsh-mal-low *n.* kind of soft confection

mar-su-pi-al *n.* animals with external pouches

mar-tial arts *pl., n.* self-defense, such as karate

mar-ti-ni *n.* cocktail of gin and vermouth

mar-tyr *n.* person who would die for a cause -dom *n.*

mar-zi-pan *n.* paste of almonds, sugar and egg whites made into candy

mar-vel *n.* be in awe marvelous *adj.*, -ously *adv.*

mas-car-a *n.* the cosmetic used for the eyelashes

mas-cot *n.* object to bring good luck

mas-cu-line *adj.* male sex

mash *n.* the mixture to distill alcohol

mask *n.* covering to conceal the face masklike *adj.*

mas-o-chism *n.* the sexual pleasure from pain -istic *adj.*, **masochismist** *n.*

ma-son *n.* brick layer

mas-quer-ade *n.* a costume party or gathering

mass *n.* body of matter with no form

mas-sa-cre *n.* savage killing of human beings massacrer *n.*

mas-sage *n.* rub down of one's body to relieve tension massager *n.*

mas-sive *adj.* of great intensity

mast *n.* pole which supports the sails

mas-ter *n.* person with the control **masterful** *adj.*

mas-ter-piece *n.* work of art

mas-ti-cate *v.* to chew -tor, -tion *n.*, -able *adj.*

mas-to-don *n.* kind of extinct mammal

mas-tur-ba-tion *n.* ones sexual stimulation without intercourse

mat-a-dor *n.* bullfighter

match *n.* identical; piece of wood that ignites -er *n.*

ma-te-ri-al-ize *v.* to take form or shape

ma-te-ri-el *n.* the equipment or the supplies

ma-ter-nal *adj.* relating to mother -ly *adv.*, -istic *adj.*

math-e-mat-ics *n.* the study of form, quantity and magnitude of numbers -cally *adv.*, -cal *adj.*

mat-i-nee *n.* afternoon movie

mat-ri-cide *n.* one who kills his mother

ma-tric-u-late *v.* enroll into a college matriculation *n.*

mat-ri-mo-ny *n.* ceremony of marriage matrimonial *adj.*

ma-tron *n.* married woman

mat-ter *n.* the substance of anything

ma-ture *adj.* completely developed maturity *n.*

mat-zo *n.* flat piece of unleavened bread

maud-lin *adj.* sentimental

maul *n.* heavy hammer

maun-der *v.* talk incoherent

mau-so-le-um *n.* large tomb

mav-er-ick *n.* an unbranded calf

max-i-mum n. greatest possible quantity

may v. permitted or allowed

may-be adv. perhaps

may-on-naise n. the dressing used for salads

may-or n. chief magistrate of a town mayoralty n.

maze n. a complicated network of passages

mead n. alcoholic beverage

mead-ow n. a field of grassland

mea-ger adj. thin; lean in quantity meagerness n., meagerly adv.

mean v. purpose or intent; bad tempered meanness n.

me-an-der v. wander about -ingly adv., -drous adj.

mea-sles n. kind of contagious disease

mea-sly adj. very small

meas-ure n. the dimension of anything measurer n.

meat n. flesh of an animal used as food

me-chan-ic n. person skilled with tools mechanical adj.

mech-a-nism n. the parts of a machine

med-al n. an award medalist n.

med-dle v. to interfere in other's affairs or business meddlesome adj., meddler n.

me-di-al adj. being situated in the middle

me-di-ate v. to help settle or decide a dispute

med-ic n. intern; corpsman

med-i-cal adj. the study of medicine medically adv.

med-i-cine n. the treatment of diseases

me-di-o-cre adj. being common; plain mediocrity n.

med-i-tate v. in contemplative thought -tor n., -tive adj.

me-di-um n. the middle; intermediary professing to give messages from the dead

med-ley n. a jumble; musical composition

meek adj. to be lacking in spirit meekness n.

meet v. to come upon

meg-a-ton n. weight equal to one million tons

mel-an-chol-y adj. gloomy or sad melancholiness n., melancholically adv.

mel-a-no-ma n., pl. -mas or -mata malignant mole

mel-io-rate v. to improve meliorator n., -able adj.

mel-lif-er-ous adj. to be producing honey

mel-o-dra-ma n. type of dramatic presentation -tic adj., melodramatics n.

mel-on n. the fruit of the gourd family

melt v. change from solid to liquid -er n., -able adj.

melt-down n. melting of a nuclear reactor core

mem-ber n. a person belonging to a club membership n., -less adj.

mem-brane n. thin layer of skin membranous adj.

me-men-to n. keepsake

mem-oir n. an autobiography of a person

mem-o-ra-ble adj. worth remembering -bly adv.

mem-o-rize v. to commit to one's memory -zation n., memozable adj.

men-ace n. a threatening person menacingly adv.

me-nar-che n. beginning of menstruation

me-ni-al adj. requiring little skill menially adv.

men-o-pause n., Physiol. time of final menstruation menopausal adj.

men-tal adj. of the mind

men-tal re-tar-da-tion n. a mental deficiency

men-tion v. refer to briefly mentioner n., -able adj.

men-u n. the list of the food at a restaurant

mer-can-tile adj. to be relating to commerce

mer-ce-nar-y n. a greedy person mercenarily adv.

mer-cer-ize v. to treat cotton yarn

mer-chan-dise n. goods bought and sold -er n.

mer-chant n. person who operates a retail business

mer-cu-ry n. the silvery liquid found in thermometers

mer-cy *n.*, *pl.* -ies kind treatment **merciless** *adj.*, **mercifully** *adv.*

mere *adj.* no more than is stated **merely** *adv.*

merge *v.* to unite as one **mergence** *n.*

mer-it *n.* act worthy of praise **meritedly** *adv.*, **-less** *adj.*

mer-maid *n.* an imaginary sea creature

mer-ry-go-round *n.* kind of carrousel

me-sa *n.* flat-topped hill

mesh *n.* open spaces in wire

mes-mer-ize *v.* to put into a trance **mersmerizer** *n.*

mess *n.*, *pl.* messes disorderly confused heap

mes-sage *n.* the information which is sent from one person to another

mes-sen-ger *n.* one who does errands for another

mess-y *adj.* untidy; dirty

me-tab-o-lism *n.* chemical changes in living cells

met-a-gal-ax-y *n.* the universe

met-a-mor-pho-sis *n.* change in the structure and formation of animals

me-te-or *n.* moving particle in the solar system

me-te-or-ol-o-gy *n.* the science of weather forecasting **meteorological** *adj.*

meth-a-done *n.* man-made narcotic used to treat heroin addiction

meth-od *n.* the manner of doing something

me-tic-u-lous *adj.* very precise **meticulously** *adv.*

met-ro *n.* subway system

met-ro-nome *n.* instrument designed to mark musical time **metronomic** *adj.*

me-trop-o-lis *n.* large capital city

mew *n.* hideaway

mez-za-nine *n.* the lowest balcony

mi-crobe *n.* minute living organism **microbial** *adj.*

mi-cro-com-put-er *n.* type of computer using a microprocessor

mi-cro-film *n.* film used to record reduced printed material

mi-cro-phone *n.* instrument which amplifies sound

mi-cro-proc-es-sor *n.* semiconductor processing unit

mi-cro-scope *n.* device to magnify small objects

mi-cro-scop-ic *adj.* very small; minute **-cally** *adv.*

mi-cro-wave *n.* electromagnetic wave

mi-cro-wave o-ven *n.* the oven using microwaves to heat food quickly

mid-day *n.* noon

mid-dle *adj.* the center

midg-et *n.* very small person

mid-night *n.* 12 o'clock p.m.

mid-point *n.* near the middle

mid-riff *n.* midsection of the human torso

mid-ship-man *n.* person who is in training at the U.S. Naval Academy

mid-term *n.* the middle of academic term

miff *n.* a displeasure

might *n.* a force

mighty *adj.*, **mightily** *adv.*

mi-graine *n.* kind of severe headaches

mi-grant *n.* person moving to find work

mi-grate *v.* move from place to place **migratory** *adj.*, **migration** *n.*

mild *adj.* gentle in manner **mildness** *n.*, **mildly** *adv.*

mile *n.* 5,280 feet

mil-i-ta-rize *v.* train for war

mi-li-tia *n.* armed forces used in an emergency

Milk-y Way *n.* luminous galaxy in the solar system

mil-li-ner *n.* one who sells women's hats

mil-lion *n.* number equal to 1,000 x 1,000

mim-e-o-graph *n.* kind of duplicating machine

mim-ic *v.* imitate another person **mimical** *adj.*

mince *v.* to chop something into small pieces **mincing** *adj.*, **mincer** *n.*

mind *n.* organ for thought **mindful** *adj.*, **mindfulness** *n.*

mine n. underground excavation; belongs to me

min-er-al n. an inorganic kind of substance

min-e-stro-ne n. kind of thick vegetable soup

min-gle v. to mix together

min-i-a-ture n. copy greatly reduced in size

mini-disk n. 5.25 inch floppy disk used for storing data

min-i-mum n. least amount

min-is-ter n. pastor of a church ministerial adj.

mink n. an animal with valuable fur

min-now n. small, fresh water fish

mi-nor adj. not of legal age

mi-nor-i-ty n., pl. -ies smaller in number

min-u-et n. kind of slow, stately dance

mi-nus prep., Math. reduced, by subtraction

min-ute n. 60 seconds in time; small in size

mir-a-cle n. kind of supernatural event

mi-rage n. optical illusion

mir-ror n. a glass which reflects images

mirth n. a merriment or a joyousness
mirthfulness n., mirthful adj.

mis-an-thrope n. the hatred of mankind

mis-ap-pro-pri-ate v. to embezzle money
misappropriation n.

mis-car-riage n. premature birth of a fetus

mis-cel-la-ne-ous adj. mixed variety of parts, etc.

mis-chief n. a behavior causing harm or damage

mis-con-ceive v. to misunderstand the meaning

mis-de-mean-or n., Law a crime less serious than a felony

mi-ser n. person who hoards money -ly adj., -liness n.

mis-er-a-ble adj. very unhappy -bly adv., -ness n.

mis-er-ly n. the state of great unhappiness

mis-fire v. fail to explode

mis-fit n. one not adjusted to his environment

mis-for-tune n. bad luck

mis-giv-ing n. the feeling of doubt

mis-han-dle v. to manage inefficiently

mis-hap n. an unfortunate accident

mish-mash n. jumble or hodgepodge

mis-in-ter-pret v. understand incorrectly -er n.

mis-judge v. make a mistake in judgment misjudgement n.

mis-lay v. lose something

mis-lead v. to deceive misleader n., misleading adj.

mis-no-mer n. an inappropriate name

mis-pro-nounce v. to pronounce incorrectly

mi-sog-a-my n. the hatred of the marriage

mi-sog-y-ny n. the hatred of women

Miss n. the title for unmarried girl

mis-sile n. object that is shot at a target

mis-sion n. kind of task to be carried out

mis-take n. wrong decision

mis-tle-toe n. parasitic plant

mis-tress n. a woman in authority

mis-trust v. have doubt mistrustingly adv., -ful adj.

mite n. very small insect

mit-i-gate v. to make less painful mitigator n., -tive adj.

mitt n. a hand warmer; baseball glove

mix v. blend; combine; unite -able adj., -ability n.

mix-up n. state of confusion

moan n. dull sound of pain

moat n. kind of trench around a castle

mob n. an unruly crowd or group of people

mock-up n. a model used for demonstration

mode n. a method of doing something

mod-el n. clothing displayer

mod-er-ate adj. not excessive -ness n., moderately adv.

mod-ern adj. up-to-date

mod-ern-ize v. to improve on something modernization n.

mod-est adj. shy; reserved modesty n., modestly adv.,

mod-i-fy v. make different in form -fier n., -fiable adj.

mod-ule n. a series of standardized components modular adj.

mod-us op-er-an-di n. the method of operating

moist adj. slightly wet; damp moisten v., moistly adv.,

mois-ture n. dampness moisturize v., -izer n.

mo-lar n. the grinding tooth

mo-las-ses n. the syrup produced from sugar

mold n. growth produced on damp organic matter; pattern moldy adj., molder n.

mole n. spot on the human skin; kind of small burrowing mammal

mol-e-cule n. smallest part retaining its identity

mo-lest v. to accost someone sexually molestation n.

mol-li-fy v. make less angry -fier n., -fiable adj.

molt v. to cast off or shed feathers molter n.

mol-ten adj. transform to liquid form by heat -ly adv.

mo-men-tous adj. being of a great importance

mo-men-tum n., pl. -ta or -tums increasing force; body in motion

mon-arch n. one who reigns an empire

mon-as-ter-y n., pl. -ies the place where monks work and live

mon-e-tar-y adj. to be relating to money monetarily adv.

mon-ey n. the medium of exchange

mon-grel n. the mixed breed animal

mo-ni-tion n. the caution or warning about something

monk n. a member of a religious order -ishness n., -ishly adv.

mon-key n., pl. -keys member of the primates, excluding man

mon-o-cle n. the eyeglass used for one eye

mo-nog-a-my n. sexual relationship with only one person

mon-o-logue n. speech by one person monologuist n.

mon-o-ma-ni-a n. mental disorder monomaniac adj.

mon-o-nu-cle-o-sis n. kind of infectious disease

mo-nop-o-ly n., pl. -ies the exclusive ownership

mon-o-rail n. train traveling on a single rail

mon-o-the-ism n. the belief there is just one God

mon-o-tone n. the sounds uttered in a single unvarying tone monotoneic adj.

mon-ot-o-nous adj. lacking variety -ness n., -ly adv.

mon-ox-ide n. oxide containing one oxygen atom per molecule

mon-soon n. periodic wind

mon-ster n. animal having abnormal form

mon-tage n. the composite picture of something

month-ly adj. being payable each month

mon-u-ment n. the object in memory of a person monumental adj., -ally adv.

mooch v. Slang acquire by begging moocher n.

mood n. the temporary state of one's mind

mood-y adj. being gloomy moodiness n., moodily adv.

moon n. earth's only satellite moony adj., mooniness n.

moon-lit adj. lighted by the moon

moor v. fasten with anchors

moose n. very large deer

moot v. debate; argue

mope v. to be dejected; to be quietly unhappy moper n., moping v.

mo-ped n. motorbike

mor-al adj. referring to conduct of right or wrong

mo-rale n. an individual's state of mind

mor-a-to-ri-um n. temporary

pause

mor-bid *adj.* gruesome; gloomy -ness *n.*, -ly *adv.*

more *adj.* being of greater number or degree

more-o-ver *adv.* furthermore

mo-res *n. pl.* moral customs of a social group

morgue *n.* place to keep dead bodies

morn-ing *n.* the early part of the day

mo-roc-co *n.* soft leather made of goatskin

mo-ron *n.* an adult with a low intelligence level

moronism *n.*, moronic *adj.*

mor-ose *adj.* marked by gloom moroseity *n.*, morosely *adv.*

mor-phine *n.* a highly addictive narcotic, derived from opium

mor-sel *n.* a small quantity of food

mor-tal *adj.* to having caused death; about to cause death

mort-gage *n.* conveyance as security for the repayment of a debt

mor-ti-cian *n.* undertaker

mo-sa-ic *n.* decorative inlaid design of tile

moss *n.* small green plants

most *adj.* majority of; greatest in quantity

mo-tel *n.* roadside dwellings for travelers

moth *n.* nocturnal insect

moth-er *n.* female parent

mo-tif *n.* the main element or theme of something

mo-tile *adj.* being capable of moving alone

mo-tion *n.* the act of changing position

mo-tive *n.* the need or the desire to act

mo-tor *n.* the device which develops energy for motion

mot-tle *v.* marked with spots or streaks of colors

mot-to *n.* phrase, or word expressing purpose

mound *n.* small hill of earth

mourn *v.* to express one's grief or sorrow

mov-ie *n.* motion picture

mow *v.* to cut down

much *adj.* being of great amount or quantity

muck *n.* moist, sticky soil

mu-cus *n.* the liquid secreted by glands

mud *n.* the mixture of water and earth

muf-fle *v.* to suppress; to deaden sound

mug *n.* large drinking cup

mug-gy *adj.* being humid and being sultry

mul-ber-ry *n.* trees having an edible fruit

mulch *n.* protective covering of compost or wood chips

mull *v.* ponder; think over

multi- *prefix* multiple; two or more

mul-ti-far-i-ous *adj.* having great variety

mul-ti-ple *adj.* to be consisting of more than one individual or part

mul-ti-ply *v.* increase in amount or number

mul-ti-tude *n.* large amount or number of something

mum *adj.* not speaking

mum-ble *v.* to speak in a confused manner

mum-my *n., pl.* -ies body embalmed for burial -ify *v.*

mumps *pl. n.* contagious viral disease

munch *v.* chew noisily

mun-dane *adj.* relating to the world mundanely *adv.*

mu-nic-i-pal *adj.* relating to local affairs

mu-ral *n.* kind of painting created on a wall

mur-der *n.* the crime of killing a person

mur-mur *n.* a low sound

mus-cle *n.* bodily tissue which produces strength

mus-cu-lar *adj.* brawny

mu-sic *n.* the organized tones in sequences

mu-si-cian *n.* a performer of music

mus-lin *n.* a sheer, or coarse fabric

muss *v.* to mess up

mus-sel *n.* a type of freshwater bivalve mollusk

must *v.* to be forced to; to be

obligated

mus-tache *n.* hair growing on the human upper lip

mus-tang *n.* wild horse

mus-tard *n.* from the seeds of the mustard plant

mus-ter *v.* to come or bring things together

mustn't *contr.* must not

mute *adj.* unable to speak

mu-ti-late *v.* maim or cripple

mu-ti-ny *n., pl.* -ies revolt against lawful authority

mutt *n., Slang* a dog that is of a mixed breed

mut-ter *v.* to speak or utter in a low voice

mut-ton *n.* the flesh of a fully grown sheep

mu-tu-al *adj.* having the same relationship mutuality *n.*

my *adj.* of myself *interj.* to express surprise, dismay, or pleasure

my-ce-li-um *n., pl.* -lia the mass of filaments which form the main structure of a fungus

my-col-o-gy *n.* scientific study of fungi mycologist *n.*

my-e-li-tis *n.* the inflammation of the spinal cord or the bone marrow

my-elo-ma *n.* the tumor of the bone marrow

myo-car-dio-graph *n.* recording tool which traces the action of the heart muscles

myo-car-di-um *n.* muscular layer of the heart, located in the heart wall

my-o-pia *n.* a visual defect; nearsightedness

myr-i-ad *adj.* having large, indefinite aspects

myr-mi-don *n.* loyal follower

myr-tle *n.* evergreen shrub

my-self *pron.* one identical with me

mys-ter-y *n., pl.* -ies something that is not understood

mys-tic *n.* person practicing or believing in mysticism mystical *adj.,* mystically *adv.*

mys-ti-cism *n.* the spiritual discipline of communion with God

mys-ti-fy *v.* to perplex

N, n. the fourteenth letter of the English alphabet

nab *v., Slang* to seize

na-bob *n.* man having great prominence or money

na-celle *n.* a shelter which is enclosed and used for aircraft

nag *v.* to bother by scolding or constant complaining. *n.* A worthless horse nagger *n.*

na-iad *n.* a nymph in mythology giving life to rivers and to lakes

na-ked *adj.* without clothes on the body; nude; exposed; uncovered

nakedly *adv.,* nakedness *n.*

nam-by--pam-by *adj.* weak; indecisive; lacking in substance

name *n.* a title or word by which something or someone is known *v.* to give a name nameable *adj.*

nape *n.* the back of the neck

nap-kin *n.* a cloth or soft paper, used at the dinner table for wiping the lips and fingers

nar-cis-sus *n.* a widely grown type of bulbous plant

nar-co-sis *n.* a deep drug-induced state of stupor or unconsciousness

nar-cot-ic *n.* a drug which dulls the senses, relieves pain, and induces a deep sleep; if abused, it can become habit-forming and cause convulsions or comas

nar-rate *v.* to tell a story or give a description in detail narration *n.,* narrator *v.*

nar-row *adj.* slender or small in width narrowly *adj.*

narrow--mind-ed *adj.* lacking sympathy or tolerance

nar-whal *n.* an aquatic mammal of the Arctic regions, closely related to the white whale

na-sal *adj.* of or pertaining to the nose

na-stur-tium *n.* a five-petaled garden plant usually having red, yellow, or orange flowers

nas-ty adj. dirty, filthy, or indecent **nastily** adv., **nastiness** n.

na-tal adj. pertaining to or associated with birth

na-tion n. a group of people made up of one or more nationalities under one government **national** adj., **nationally** adv.

na-tion-al-ism n. devotion to or concern for one's nation

na-tion-al-i-ty n. the fact or condition of belonging to a nation

na-tion-al-ize v. to place a nation's resources and industries under the control of the state

na-tive n. a person born in a country or place adj. belonging to one by nature or birth

na-tiv-i-ty n. birth, circumstances, or conditions; the birth of Christ

nat-u-ral adj. produced or existing by nature; not artificial. Mus. A note that is not sharp or flat **naturalness** n., **naturally** adv.

natural child-birth n. childbirth with little stress or pain; childbirth requiring training for the mother and father and medical supervision, but without the use of drugs, anesthesia, or surgery

nat-u-ral-ize v. to confer the privileges and rights of full citizenship **-tion** n.

na-ture n. the universe and its phenomena; kind, sort, or type **natured** adj.

naught n. nothing; the number zero

naugh-ty adj. unruly; not proper **-ily** adv., **-iness** n.

nau-se-a n. an upset stomach with a feeling that one needs to vomit **nauseous** adj.

nau-ti-cal adj. pertaining to ships or seamanship **nautically** adv.

na-val adj. of or relating to ships

na-vel n. a small mark or scar on the abdomen where the umbilical cord was attached

nav-i-ga-ble adj. sufficiently deep and wide enough to allow ships to pass

nav-i-gate v. to plan the course of a ship or aircraft; to steer a course **navigation, navigator** n.

na-vy n. one of a nation's organizations for defense; a nation's fleet of ships; a very dark blue

Ne-an-der-thal adj. suggesting a caveman in behavior or appearance; primitive or crude **Neanderthal** n.

neap tide n. a tide in the minimum range which occurs twice a month

near adv. at, to, or within a short time or distance adj. closely or intimately related **nearness** n.

near-by adj. & adv. adjacent

near-sight-ed adj. able to see clearly at short distances only

neat adj. tidy and clean; free from disorder and dirt **neatly** adv., **neatness** n.

neb-u-lous adj. confused or vague

nec-es-sar-y adj. unavoidable **necessarily** adv.

ne-ces-si-tate v. to make necessary; to oblige; to require

ne-ces-si-ty n., pl. **-ies** the condition of being necessary

neck n. the part of the body which connects the head and trunk; a narrow part or projection, as of land, a stringed instrument, or bottle v. to caress and kiss

neck-tie n. a narrow strip of material worn around the neck

nec-tar n. a good-tasting beverage; a sweet fluid in various flowers, gathered by bees to help make honey **nectarous** adj.

nee n. born; the surname a woman was born with

need n. the lack of something desirable, useful, or necessary

nee-dle n. a slender, pointed steel implement which contains an eye through which thread is passed

needle-point n. decorative stitching done on canvas

need-n't contr. need not

ne-far-i-ous adj. extremely wicked

ne-gate v. to nullify; to deny; to rule out negation n.

neg-a-tive adj. expressing denial or disapproval; not positive negatively adv., negativeness n.

neglect v. to ignore; to pay no attention to neglectful adj.

neg-li-gee n. a woman's loose-fitting dressing gown

neg-li-gent adj. to neglect what needs to be done; neglectful

ne-go-ti-ate v. to confer with another person to reach an agreement negotiation, negotiator n.

ne-groid adj. of or relating to the Black race negroid n.

neigh-bor n. one who lives near another; fellowman

neighbor-hood n. a section or small region that possesses a specific quality

nei-ther adj. not one or the other pron. not the one or the other conj. not either; also not

neo prefix recent; new

neo-dym-i-um n. a metallic element of the rare-earth group, symbolized by Nd

ne-on n. an inert gaseous element used in lighting fixtures, symbolized by Ne

ne-o-nate n. a newborn child less than a month old

ne-o-na-tol-o-gy n. the medical study of the first 60 days of a baby's life

neo-phyte n. a novice; a beginner

ne-o-plasm n. a tumor tissue serving no physiologic function neoplastic adj.

neph-ew n. the son of one's sister, brother, sister-in-law, or brother-in-law

ne-phrit-ic adj. relating to the kidneys

nep-o-tism n. the act of showing favoritism to relatives or friends in the work force nepotist n.

nep-tu-ni-um n. a radioactive metallic element, symbolized by Np

nerve n. the bundles of fibers which convey sensation and originate motion through the body

nerv-ous adj. affecting the nerves or the nervous system nervously adv., -ness n.

nervous system n., Physiol. the body system that coordinates, regulates, and controls the various internal functions and responses to stimuli

nest n. a shelter, or home built by a bird to hold its eggs and young

nest egg n. a supply of money accumulated or saved for future use

nes-tle v. to settle snugly; to lie close to nestler n.

net n. a meshed fabric made of cords, ropes, threads, or other material knotted or woven together; the profit, weight, or price which remains after all additions, subtractions, or adjustments have been made

neth-er adj. situated below or beneath

net-tle n. a plant having toothed leaves covered with stinging hairs

net-work n. a system of interlacing tracks, channels, or lines

neu-ral adj. relating to a nerve or the nervous system

neu-ral-gia n. pain that occurs along the course of a nerve

neu-ri-tis n. an inflammation of a nerve which causes pain, the loss of reflexes, and muscular decline neurotic adj.

neu-rol-o-gy n. the medical and scientific study of the nervous system and its disorders neurological adj.,

neurologist n.

neu-ron or **neu-rone** n., Anat. a granular cell nerve which is the main functional unit of the nervous system

neu-ro-sis n. any one of various functional disorders of the mind or emotions having no physical cause **neurotic** adj., **neurotically** adv.

neu-ter adj. neither feminine nor masculine n. a castrated animal **neuter** v.

neu-tral adj. not supporting either side of a debate, quarrel, or party; a color which does not contain a decided hue Chem. neither alkaline nor acid **-ity** n., **neutrally** adv.

neu-tral-ize v. to make or declare neutral

neu-tron n. an uncharged particle in the nucleus of an atom

nev-er adv. not ever

nev-er-the-less adv. nonetheless

new adj. not used before; unaccustomed; unfamiliar

news n., pl. current information and happenings

news-cast n. a television or radio news broadcast

news-pa-per n. a weekly or daily publication which contains recent news and information

news-print n. an inexpensive machinefinished paper made from wood pulp and used chiefly for newspapers and some paperback books

New Testament n. the second part of the Christian Bible containing the Gospels, Acts, Epistles, and the Book of Revelation

next adj. immediately following or proceeding

nib-ble v. to bite a little at a time **nibble**, **nibbler** n.

nice adj. pleasing; enjoyable **nicely** adv., **niceness** n.

niche n. a recess or alcove in a wall, usually used for displays

nick n. a small chip or cut on a surface; the final critical moment

nick-el n. a hard, silver, metallic element used in alloys and symbolized by Ni; a United States coin worth five cents

nick-el-o-de-on n. a movie theatre which charged five cents for admission; a coin-operated juke box

nick-name n. the familiar form of a proper name, expressed in a shortened form **nickname** v.

nic-o-tine or **nicotin** n. a poisonous alkaloid found in tobacco and used in insecticides and medicine

niece n. a daughter of one's sister or brother or one's sister-in-law or brother-in-law

nigh adv. near in relationship, time, or space

night n. the time between dusk and dawn or the hours of darkness

nightcap n. an alcoholic drink usually taken before retiring for the night

night-in-gale n. a songbird with brownish plumage, noted for the sweet, nocturnal song of the male

night-mare n. a frightening and horrible dream

nim-ble adj. marked by a quick, light movement; quick-witted **nimbleness** n., **nimbly** adv.

nin-com-poop n. a silly or stupid person

nine n. the cardinal number that is equal to $8 + 1$ **nine** adj., pron.

ni-o-bi-um n. a gray, metallic element used in alloys, symbolized by Nb

nip v. to pinch, bite, or grab something **nipper** n.

nip-ple n. the small projection of a mammary gland through which milk passes

ni-tro-gen n. a nonmetallic gaseous element which is essential to life, symbolized by N

ni-tro-glyc-er-in *n.* a highly flammable, explosive liquid, used to make dynamite and, in medicine, to dilate blood vessels

no *adv.* used to express rejection

no-bel-i-um *n.* a radioactive element, symbolized by No

Nobel prize *n.* an award given to people with achievements in literature, economics, medicine, and other fields, established by the last will and testament of Alfred Nobel

no-bil-i-ty *n., pl.* -ies the state or quality of being noble

no-ble *adj.* morally good; superior in character or nature -ness *n.*, -y *adv.*

no-bod-y *pron.* not anybody

noc-tur-nal *adj.* pertaining to or occurring during the night; active at night and quiet during the daylight hours   nocturnally *adv.*

nod *n.* a quick downward motion of the head as one falls off to sleep; a downward motion of the head indicating acceptance or approval

node *n.* a swollen or thickened enlargement

no-el *n.* a Christmas carol

noise *n.* a sound which is disagreeable or loud; in computer science, unwanted data in an electronic signal   noisy *adj.*, noisily *adv.*

no-mad *n.* a member of a group of people who wander from place to place   nomadic *adj.*, nomadism *n.*

no-men-cla-ture *n.* the set of names used to describe the elements of art, science, and other fields

nom-i-nal *adj.* of or relating to something that is in name or form only   nominally *adv.*

nom-i-nate *v.* to select a candidate for an elective office; to appoint or designate to a position -tion, -tor *n.*

nom-i-nee *n.* a person nominated for a position or office

non- *prefix* not

non-a-ge-nar-i-an *adj.* a person between the ages of 90 and 100 years

non-cha-lant *adj.* giving an effect of casual unconcern -ance *n.*, -ly *adv.*

non com-pos men-tis *adj.* mentally unbalanced; not of sound mind

non-con-form-ist *n.* a person who does not feel compelled to follow or accept his community's customs or traditions

none *pron.* not any; not one

non-sec-tar-i-an *adj.* not associated with or restricted to one religion, faction, or sect

non-sense *n.* something that seems senseless or foolish; something which is very unimportant -ical *adj.*

non se-qui-tur *n.* an inference that does not follow as the logical result of what has preceded it

non-sex-ist *adj.* not discriminating on the basis of gender

noo-dle *n.* a flat strip of dried dough made with eggs and flour *Slang* the head

nook *n.* a corner, recess, or secluded place

noon *n.* the middle of the day; 12:00 o'clock

noose *n.* a loop of rope secured by a slipknot, allowing it to decrease in size as the rope is pulled

nor *conj.* not either; or not

norm *n.* a rule, model, or pattern typical for a particular group

nor-mal *adj.* ordinary, average, usual; having average intelligence; standard   normalcy, -lity *n.*, -lly *adv.*

north *n.* the direction to a person's left while facing east

nose *n.* the facial feature containing the nostrils; the sense of smell

nose-dive *n.* a sudden plunge as

made by an aircraft

nos-tal-gia n. a yearning to return to the past **nostalgic** adj.

nos-tril n. the external openings of the nose

nos-y or **nos-ey** adj. snoopy; inquisitive; prying

not adv. in no manner; used to express refusal or denial

no-ta-ble adj. remarkable; distinguished n. a person or thing which is notable **notably** adv.

no-ta-rize v. to acknowledge and certify as a notary public

notary public n. a person who is legally authorized as a public officer to witness and certify documents

no-ta-tion n. a process or system of figures or symbols used in specialized fields to represent quantities, numbers, or values

notch n. a v-shaped indentation or cut **notch** v.

note n. a record or information in short form. Mus. A tone or written character **note** v.

not-ed adj. famous; well-known

noth-ing n. not any thing; no part or portion adv. in no way; not at all

no-tice n. an announcement; a notification v. to give notice; to become aware of **noticeable** adj., **-ably** adv.

no-ti-fy v. to give notice of; to announce **notifier**, **notification** n.

no-tion n. an opinion; a general concept; an idea **notions** pl., n. small useful articles, as thread or buttons

no-to-ri-ous adj. having a widely known and usually bad reputation

not-with-stand-ing prep. in spite of adv. nevertheless; anyway conj. although

noun n. a word which names a person, place, or thing

nour-ish v. to furnish with the nutriment and other substances needed for growth and life **nourishing** adj.,

nourishment n.

nou-veau riche n. a person who has recently become rich

no-va n., pl. **-vae** or **-vas** a star which flares up and fades away after a few years or months

nov-el n. an inventive narrative dealing with human experiences; a book

nov-el-ty n., pl. **-ies** something unusual or new

nov-ice n. a person who is new and unfamiliar with an activity or business

now adv. at the present time

no-where adv. not in or at any place

nox-ious adj. harmful; obnoxious

noz-zle n. a projecting spout or vent of something

nu-ance n. a slight variation

nub n. a knob; a small piece or lump

nu-bile adj. suitable or ready for marriage

nu-cle-ar adj. pertaining to and resembling a nucleus

nu-cle-us n., pl. **-clei** or **-cleuses** a central element around which other elements are grouped; the starting point

nude adj. unclothed; naked; uncovered **nudity**, **nudist** n.

nudge v. to poke or push gently **nudge** n.

nug-get n. a lump, as of precious metal

nui-sance n. a source of annoyance; something that is harmful

null adj. invalid; having no value or consequence; void **nullification** n.

nul-li-fy v. to counteract

numb adj. lacking physical sensation; paralyzed or stunned; insensible **numbness** n.

num-ber n. a word or symbol which is used in counting or which indicates how many or which one is in a series

number-less adj. too many to be counted; innumerable

nu·mer·al *n.* a symbol, figure, letter, word, or a group of these which represents a number

nu·mer·a·tor *n.* the term in mathematics indicating how many parts are to the term; the number in a fraction which appears above the line

nu·mer·ous *adj.* consisting or made up of many units

nun *n.* a woman who has joined a religious group and has taken vows to give up worldly goods and never to marry

nup·tial *adj.* of or pertaining to a wedding **nuptials** *pl., n.* a wedding

nurse *n.* a person who is specially trained to care for disabled or sick persons *v.* to feed a baby from a mother's breast; to provide care to a sick or disabled person

nurs·er·y *n., pl.* **-ies** a room reserved for the special use of infants or small children; a business or place where trees, shrubs, and flowers are raised and sold

nur·ture *n.* the upbringing, care, or training of a child **nurture** *v.,* **nurturer** *n.*

nut *n.* a hard-shelled fruit or seed which contains an inner, often edible kernal *Slang* a person who does crazy or silly things

nu·tri·ent *n.* a substance which nourishes

nu·tri·tion *n.* the process by which a living being takes in food and uses it to live and grow **nutritive, nutritional** *adj.,* **-ally** *adv.*

nut·meg *n.* an aromatic spice used be baking

nuts *adj., Slang* foolish, crazy

nuz·zle *v.* to gently rub against something with the nose; to cuddle

ny·lon *n.* a strong, elastic material; yarn or fabric made from nylon **nylons** stockings made of nylon

O, o the fifteenth letter of the English alphabet

oaf *n.* stupid person **oafishly** *adv.,* **oafish** *adj.*

oak *n.* large tree with durable wood **oaken** *adj.*

oak-moss *n.* lichens that grown on aok trees and yield resin that is used in perfume

oar *n.* pole with a broad blade used to propel boats

oasis *n.* part of the desert that contains water

oath *n.* solemn promise

ob·du·rate *adj.* stubborn **-ness** *n.,* **obdurately** *adv.*

o·be·di·ent *adj.* to be obeying others

o·bese *adj.* very fat **obeseness** *n.,* **obesely** *adv.*

o·bey *v.* to carry out instructions **obeyer** *n.*

o·bit·u·ar·y *n.* announcement indicating that a person has died

ob·ject *v.* to voice disapproval

ob·li·ga·tion *n.* the responsibility one has

o·blige *v.* to do a favor for someone **obliger** *n.,* **-ed** *adj.*

o·blique *adj.* being inclined; being slanted **obliqueness** *n.*

o·blit·er·ate *v.* to wipe out **-tive** *adj.,* **obliteration** *n.*

ob·liv·i·ous *adj.* unmindful

ob·nox·ious *adj.* unpleasant

o·boe *n.* woodwind instrument

ob·scene *adj.* to be indecent

ob·scure *adj.* being remote; not being clear

ob·serve *v.* to pay attention

ob·sess *v.* to preoccupy the mind with something

ob·so·lete *adj.* no longer in use

ob·sta·cle *n.* an obstruction

ob·ste·tri·cian *n.* physician who delivers babies

ob·sti·nate *adj.* stubborn **obstinateness** *n.*

ob·struct *v.* to block

ob·tain *v.* to acquire possession of something

ob·tuse *adj.* insensitive **obtuseness** *n.,* **obtusely** *adv.*

ob·vi·ous *adj.* to be easily seen by others **obviousness** *n.*

oc·ca·sion *n.* a celebration **occasional** *adj.,* **-lly** *adv.*

oc-cult adj. being concealed
occultness n., occultly adv.

oc-cu-pa-tion n. a profession or job

oc-cur v. to suggest; to happen occurent adj.

o-cean n. body of salt water

o-ce-lot n. large spotted cat

oc-ta-gon n. a polygon with eight sides

odd adj. being unusual oddness n., oddly adv.

odds n. betting difference

o-dor n. a smell odorless adj., odored adj.

off adv. no longer on

of-fend v. to make someone or thing angry offender n.

of-fense n. the act of attacking someone offenseless adj.

of-fer v. to propose an idea or something offer n.

of-fice n. the place for conducting business

of-fi-cer n. the position of authority

of-fi-cial adj. having proper authority officially adv.

off-spring n. descendants

oil v. to lubricate

oint-ment n. a medication

old adj. to have existed for a long time oldish adj.

om-i-nous adj. threatening ominousness n., -ly adv.

o-mit v. to leave an idea or something out omitter n.

om-nip-o-tent adj. having unlimited authority

om-nis-cient adj. to be knowing all or everything

om-niv-or-ous adj. to be absorbing everything

on prep. positioned upon

once adv. a single time

one adj. being a single thing

on-ly adj. sole

on-ward adv. moving forward

o-pal n. translucent mineral

o-pen adj. having no barrier

op-er-ate v. to function; to perform surgery

oph-thal-mol-o-gy n. the science dealing with the eye

o-pin-ion n. a suggestion

op-po-nent n. an adversary

op-por-tune adj. occurring at the right time

op-por-tu-ni-ty n. chance for advancement of something

op-pose v. to resist

op-press v. to worry the mind

op-ti-mum n. a most favorable or wanted result

op-tion n. act of choosing

or conj. alternative

o-ral adj. being spoken

orb n. a globe or a sphere

or-bit v. to circle something

or-chard n. the land used for growing fruit trees

or-ches-tra n. a group of musicians

or-chid n. tropical plant

or-deal n. a severe test of one's character

or-der n. instructions

or-di-nance n. a command

or-di-nar-y adj. to be normal

ore n. type of underground substance

or-gan n. musical instrument

or-gan-ic adj. to be pertaining to life

or-gan-ize v. to put in an orderly manner

or-i-gin n. a beginning place

o-rig-i-nal n. first of a kind

or-tho-dox adj. following established traditions

or-tho-pe-dics n. the bone surgery

os-cil-late v. to swing

os-mo-sis n. passage of fluid through membrane

os-tra-cize v. to shut out

oth-er adj. additional; being different from what is implied or thought

ought v. to be advisable

ounce n. measurement that is equal to 1/16 of a pound

our adj. to be relating to us; ourselves

out adv. away from the inside

out-cast n. the one who is excluded or kicked out

out-do v. to excel in achievement

out-fit n. a person's clothes

out-law n. a criminal

out-let n. an exit

out-line n. the outward line of a figure or shape

out-look n. point of view

out-rage n. an act of violence

out-right adj. to be free from reservations

out-spo-ken adj. being without reserve

out-stand-ing adj. excellent

out-ward adj. to be pertaining to the outside

o-val adj. shape of an egg

o-va-ry n. the female reproductive glands

o-va-tion n. an applause

ov-en n. an enclosed chamber used for baking or for heating

o-ver-all adj. to be covering everything

o-ver-bear v. crush by force

o-ver-cast adj. to be gloomy

o-ver-haul v. to make all the needed repairs

o-ver-seas adv. abroad, across the seas

o-ver-see v. to supervise

o-ver-sexed adj. having an overactive interest in sex

o-ver-sight n. the mistake made inadvertently

o-ver-size adj. being larger than the average size

o-vert adj. open to view

o-ver-throw v. remove from power by force; to bring about destruction

o-ver-time n. the amount of time worked beyond the specified hours

o-ver-whelm v. to overcome completely

o-void adj. having the shape of an egg

o-vu-late n. discharge eggs from an ovary

o-vum n. the female reproductive cell

owe v. to be in debt

own adj. to be belonging to oneself **ownship** n.

ox n. kind of bovine animal

ox-ide n. the compound of oxygen and another element

ox-y-gen n. the colorless, tasteless gaseous element, essential to all life

oys-ter n. kind of edible marine mollusk

o-zone n. pale-blue gas formed of oxygen with an odor like chlorine

P, p the sixteenth letter of the English alphabet

pace n. length of a person's step **paced** adj.

pace-mak-er n. the surgically implanted electronic instrument to stabilize the heartbeat

pac-i-fy v. to quiet or soothe anger **pacifistic** adj.

pack n. bundle; band of animals **-ing** n., **-able** adj.

pack-age n. something tied or bound together **packager** n.

pact n. the agreement between nations

pad n. a cushion; writing tablet **padding** n.

pad-dle n. implement used to propel a boat **paddler** n.

pad-dy wag-on n., Slang type of police vehicle

pad-lock n. lock with u-shaped hasp **padlocked** adj.

pa-dre n. title for a priest

pa-gan n. a heathen **paganism** n., **paganish** adj.

page n. person who runs errands; leaf of a book

pag-eant n. a spectacular parade **pageantry** n.

paid v. past tense of pay

pail n. a type of cylindrical container **painful** adj.

pain n. an unpleasant feeling from an injury **-fully** adv., **-lessness** n.

paint n. the coloring pigments **painter** n.

pair n., pl. pairs or pair two things that are similar

pa-ja-mas pl., n. garment used for sleeping

pal-ace n. royal residence

pal-at-a-ble adj. pleasant tasting **-bly** adv., **-ness** n.

pale adj. deficient in color **paley** adv., **paleness** n.

pal-ette n. artist's board for mixing colors

pall n. the cloth used to cover a coffin

pall-bear-er n. the person who carries a coffin

pal-lid adj. deficient in color **pallidness** n., **pallidly** adv.

palm n. the inner area of the hand

pal·sy *n., pl.* **-ies** the loss of control of one's movements

pam·phlet *n.* kind of brief publication of information

pan·a·ce·a *n.* the remedy for all diseases

pan·cre·as *n., Anat.* gland that produces insulin

pan·da *n.* a large black and white bear

pan·el *n.* a wooden surface; a jury

pan·ic *n.* an unreasonable fear **panicky** *adj.*

pan·o·ram·a *n.* unlimited view **-ically** *adv.,* **-ic** *adj.*

pan·sy *n.* garden plant

pant *v.* to breathe in short gasps **panting** *n.*

pan·ther *n.* black leopard

pan·to·mime *n.* gesture without speaking

pants *pl, n.* the trousers

pa·per *n.* a substance made from wood

pa·pri·ka *n.* kind of red seasoning powder

par·a·ble *n.* short story with a moral

par·a·chute *n.* folded fabric to assure safe landing from airplane **parachutist** *n.*

par·a·dise *n.* the place of beauty; heaven

par·a·dox *n.* statement which contradicts itself **-ical** *adj.*

par·a·gon *n.* the model of perfection

par·a·graph *n.* composition dealing with a single idea **-ical** *adj.,* **paragrapher** *n.*

par·a·keet *n.* small parrot

par·al·lel *adj.* moving in the same direction

pa·ral·y·sis *n., pl.* **-ses** the loss of the ability to feel or to move

par·a·mount *adj.* above all others **-ly** *adv.,* **-ship** *n.*

par·a·noi·a *n.* mental delusions of grandeur

par·a·pher·na·lia *n.* the personal effects

par·a·phrase *v.* to express in other words

par·a·site *n.* the one that lives off another **-ically** *adv.,*

parasitic *adj.*

par·a·sol *n.* small umbrella

par·boil *v.* to precook something

par·cel *n.* package

parch *v.* to become very dry **parched** *adj.*

parch·ment *n.* the sheepskin used for writing

par·don *v.* to forgive; excuse **-able** *adj.,* **pardonably** *adv.*

pare *v.* to remove the outer surface

par·ent *n.* mother or father **parenthood** *n.,* **parental** *adj.*

pa·ren·the·sis *n., pl.* **-ses** curved lines to enclose qualifying remark

par·ish *n.* district under a priest **parishioner** *n.*

park *n.* a recreation area **parker** *n.*

par·ka *n.* a hooded coat

par·lia·ment *n.* the lawmaking body of various countries

pa·ro·chi·al *adj.* belonging to a parish

par·o·dy *n., pl.* **-ies** a song, or a poem which mimics another **-ist** *n.,* **parodic** *adj.*

pa·role *n.* early release of a prisoner **parolee** *n.*

par·ri·cide *n.* the act of a person who murders his parents

par·rot *n.* kind of semitropical bird which can be taught to talk **parrot** *adj.*

parse *v.* to identify the parts of speech

par·si·mo·ny *n.* reluctance to spend one's money **-iously** *adv.,* **-ious** *adj.*

pars·ley *n.* an herb used for seasoning foods

par·son *n.* a clergyman **parsonage** *n.,* **parsonical** *adj.*

part *n.* division of a whole

par·take *v.* to have a share or part **partaker** *n.*

par·tial *adj.* to be incomplete **partially** *adv.*

par·tic·i·pate *v.* to join in **participation** *n.*

par·ti·cle *n.* very small piece

par·tic·u·lar *adj.* having to do with a specific person or thing **particularist** n.

part-ing n. separation

part-ner n. an associate in business **partnership** n.

par-tridge n. game bird

par-ty n., pl. **-ies** people who gather for pleasure

pass v. to proceed; to move in an direction **passer** n.

pas-sen-ger n. one who travels in a vehicle

pas-sion n. powerful feeling; sexual desire **passionless** adj.

pas-sive adj. inactive **passiveness** n., **passively** adv.

pass-port n. official permission to travel to foreign countries

pass-word n. the secret word to enter a place

paste n. mixture for holding things together

pas-tor n. the clergyman of a church **pastorship** n.

pas-try n. the dessert which is made of dough

pas-ture n. an area used for grazing animals **pastured** n.

pat v. tap lightly

patch n. the repair for a torn garment

pat-ent n. inventors copyright to an invention

pa-ter-nal adj. being inherited from a father **paternally** adv., **-ism** n.

path n. track or route

pa-thet-ic adj. to be arousing pity from another **-ally** adv.

pa-thol-o-gy n. the science dealing with diseases **-gically** adv., **-gical** adj.

pa-tience n. the ability to be calm

pa-tient adj. person under medical care

pa-ti-o n. an area attached to a house

pa-tri-arch n. leader of a family; revered man

pa-tri-ot n. the one who defends his country **patriotism** n., **-ically** adv.

pa-trol n. guard to keep an area secure **patroler** n.

pa-tron n. a person who supports a cause; a customer

pat-tern n. a guide; a sample **patterned** adj.

pau-per n. very poor person

pause v. to linger or to hesitate **pauser** n.

pave v. to surface a road with asphalt or other material

pa-vil-ion n. sheltered area

paw n. the foot of an animal

pawn n. the security placed for a loan; chess piece **pawnable** adj.

pay-roll n. the money which is paid to employees

peace n. state of mental serenity **peaceable** adj.

peach n. kind of sweet, juicy fruit

peak n. the summit of a mountain

peal n. ringing of bells

pear n. edible fruit

pearl n. white gem from the oyster

peas-ant n. person of low class **peasantry** n.

peat moss n. the plant food and mulch

peb-ble n. the small, smooth stone

peck v. to strike with the beak

pe-cu-liar adj. being strange in character

ped-al n. lever worked by the foot

ped-dle v. to sell merchandise **peddler** n.

ped-es-tal n. the base used for a statue

pe-des-tri-an n. person on foot

pe-di-at-rics n. branch of medicine dealing with children and infants

ped-i-gree n. the line of ancestors

peek v. look shyly or quickly

peel n. the outside protective covering of fruit **peeling** n.

peer v. look searchingly

peg n. a small pin

pei-gnoir n. kind of woman's dressing gown

pelt n. skin of an animal **peltry** n.

pen n. instrument for writing

pen-al-ty n. the legal punishment for crime

pen-ance n. one's repentance for sin

pend-ing adj. being not yet decided

pen-e-trate v. to force a way into

pen-i-cil-lin n. an antibiotic derived from mold used to treat infections

pen-in-su-la n. piece of land that projects into water

pe-nis n. male sex organ

pen-i-tent adj. sorry

pen-ny n., pl. -ies U.S. coin worth one cent ($.01)

pen-sion n. money received after retirement

pen-sive adj. quiet, serious thought

pen-ta-gon n. an object having five sides

pe-on n. a servant

peo-ple n., pl. peo-ple human beings

pep-per n. strong aromatic condiment   pepperish adj.

per an-num adv. occurring each year

per-cale n. cotton fabric

per-ceive v. to become aware of

per-cent-age n. the rate per hundred of something

per-cept n. the mental impression   perceptible adj.

per-en-ni-al adj. from year to year   perennially adv.

per-fect adj. flawless; accurate

per-form v. to carry out an action

per-fume n. a type of sweet fragrance

per-haps adv. maybe

per-il n. source of danger

pe-ri-od n. an interval or amount of time periodic adj.

per-ish v. to ruin or to spoil; an untimely death   perishable adj.

per-jure v. to lie while under oath

per-me-ate v. to spread through

per-mit v. to consent to; allow to happen

per-ni-cious adj. harmful

per-pen-dic-u-lar adj. at right angles to the horizon

per-pe-trate v. to commit a crime   perpetrator n.

per-pet-u-al adj. to be lasting forever   perpetually adv.

per-plex v. to confuse

per-se-cute v. to harass or to annoy someone

per-se-vere v. to persist in any purpose or idea

per-sist v. to continue despite obstacles   persistence n.

per-son n. human being

per-son-i-fy v. to represent; be a symbol of   personifier n.

per-son-nel n. the people working for a business

per-spec-tive n. drawing technique which seems to give depth

per-spi-ra-tion n. fluid excreted from the glands

per-suade v. to convince by means of reasoning persuader n., -able adj.

per-tain v. relate to; refer to

per-ti-na-cious adj. being stubbornly persistent

per-ti-nent adj. being relating to the matter being discussed   pertinently adv.

per-turb v. to disturb; make uneasy   perturbable adj.

per-vade v. spread through every part   pervader n.

per-ver-sion n. deviant form of sexual behavior

pes-si-mism n. gloomy view of a situation

pest n. an annoying person; an insect

pes-ter v. harass; bother

pes-ti-cide n. chemical used to destroy insects

pes-ti-lence n. widespread often infectious disease

pe-tite adj. being small in size

pet-it four n. small dessert cakes

pe-ti-tion n. solemn request petitioner n.

pet-ri-fy v. to convert into a stony mass

pet-ti-coat n. undergarment for women

pet-ty adj. having little importance   pettiness n.

pet-ty cash n. cash on hand

pew n. a long bench in a

church

phan-tasm *n.* a fantasy; a phantom

phamtasmal *adj.*

phar-ma-ceu-ti-cal *adj.* relating to a pharmacy

phar-ma-cy *n.* a drugstore

phase *n.* stage in development

phe-nom-e-non *n.* a rare occurrence of some event

phi-lat-e-ly *n.* the collecting of postage stamps

phi-los-o-phy *n.*, *pl.* -ies the study of human knowledge or human values

pho-bi-a *n.* compulsive fear of a situation

phon-ic *adj.* pertaining to sounds in speech

pho-no-graph *n.* a record player

phos-phate *n.*, *Chem.* acid which contains phosphorus and oxygen

pho-to-cop-y *v.* to reproduce printed material

pho-to-graph *n.* image recorded by a camera

phrase *n.*, *Gram.* words forming part of a sentence

phy-si-cian *n.* one licensed to practice medicine

phys-ics *n.* the scientific study of energy

pi-an-o *n.* musical instrument with a keyboard

pi-ca *n.* printer's type size

pic-co-lo *n.* small flute

pick-pock-et *n.* person who steals from another

pic-nic *n.* an outdoor social gathering

piece *n.* part of a whole

piece-meal *adv.* in small amounts; gradually

pier *n.* dock to provide access to vessels

pierce *v.* to penetrate

pi-geon *n.* a bird

pig-ment *n.* coloring matter

pig-skin *n.* strong leather used for footballs and saddles

pile *n.* anything that is thrown in a heap

pil-fer *v.* to steal

pil-grim *n.* a traveler to a holy place

pill *n.* small medicated tablet

pil-lar *n.* column

pil-low *n.* a soft cushion

pi-lot *n.* person licensed to operate an airplane

pi-men-to *n.* sweet pepper

pim-ple *n.* a small eruption of the skin

pin-a-fore *n.* a sleeveless garment

pinch *v.* to squeeze between a finger and thumb

pine *n.*, *Bot.* evergreen trees

pine-ap-ple *n.* tropical fruit

pin-na-cle *n.* peak

pi-noch-le *n.* card game

pint *n.* measure equal to half of a quart; two cups

pi-o-neer *n.* first settlers

pi-ous *adj.* devout -ness *n.*

pique *n.* the feeling of resentment

pi-rate *n.* robber on the high seas

pis-ta-chi-o *n.* nut

pis-til *n.* seed-producing organ of a flower

pit *n.* the manmade hole in the ground

pitch *n.* residue of coal tar

pitch-er *n.* baseball player; container for liquids

pit-fall *n.* a trap

pith *n.*, *Bot.* the center part of stem

pit-y *n.*, *pl.* -ies. the feeling of sorrow

piz-za *n.* Italian food covered with tomato sauce, and toppings

pla-cate *v.* appease; satisfy

place *n.* region; area

pla-cen-ta *n.*, *pl.* -tas or -tae *Anat.* organ which supplies a fetus with the nourishment

plac-id *adj.* peaceful; calm

plaid *n.* checkered design

plain *adj.* being flat; open, as in view

plain-tiff *n.* a person who brings suit against another

plan *n.* an arrangement; the scheme one has

plane *n.* the tool for smoothing wood

plan-et *n.*, *astron.* type of celestial body

plank *n.* a kind of broad piece

of wood

plant n. living organism

plaque n. an engraved tablet for mounting

plas-ter-board n. kind of building material

plas-tic n. synthetically made material

plas-tic sur-ger-y n. the restoration of destroyed or damaged body parts

plate n. dish which is used for serving food

plat-form n. elevated stage

pla-toon n. military unit

plat-ter n. large serving dish

plau-si-ble adj. probable; seeming to be true

play v. amuse oneself

pla-za n. an open air marketplace

plea n. urgent request

plea bar-gain-ing v. making a pretrial agreement

pleas-ant adj. to giving pleasure to

please v. make happy

pleas-ure n. the satisfaction; the enjoyment

pleat n. fold in a cloth

plebe n. freshman at the U.S. Naval Academy

pledge n. solemn promise

plen-ty n. ample amount

pli-a-ble adj. flexible; being easy to bend

pli-ers pl., n. implement used for an oject

plight n. a distressing situation

plot n. small piece of ground

plow n. implement for turning soil

plug n. hole stopper

plum-age n. the feathers of a bird

plumb n. lead weight to test the perpendicular line of something

plumb-er n. a person who repairs or who installs plumbing

plume n. feather

plu-ral adj. containing more than one

plus prep. symbol (+) indicates addition

ply v. mold or bend; thickness

of yarn, etc.

ply-wood n. kind of building material for structures

pneu-mo-ni-a n. the inflammation of the lungs

poach v. cook in a liquid; steal wild game **poacher** n.

pock-et n. the small pouch in a garment

po-di-um n. a small raised platform

po-em n. a composition in verse

po-et n. the person who writes or creates poetry

point n. tapered end of something **pointed** adj.

point blank adj. direct

poise v. to hold one's balance; self-confidence

poi-son n. the substance which kills **poisonous** adj.

poke v. to push or prod

pok-er n. card game

pole n. the two ends of the earth axis

pol-i-o-my-e-li-tis n. inflammation of the spinal cord; also known as polio

po-lice-man n. law officer

pol-i-cy n., pl. -ies plan which guides decision making

po-lite adj. mannerly

poll n. the votes in an election; survey

pol-lute v. to contaminate something **pollution** n.

po-lo n. game played on horseback

pol-ter-geist n. a mischievous ghost

pol-y-es-ter n. type of synthetic material

pol-y-graph n. lie detector machine

pomp-ous adj. having an appearance of importance **pompousness** n., **-ly** adv.

pond n. body of still water

pon-der v. to weigh or think about

pon-der-ous adj. massive **ponderousness** n., **-ly** adv.

pon-tiff n. the pope

po-ny n., pl. -ies small horse

pool n. small body of water

poor adj. to be lacking money

pop v. to cause to burst Slang

Soda

pope *n.* the head of the Catholic Church

pop-u-lar *adj.* widely liked **popularly** *adv.,* **popularity** *n.*

pop-u-la-tion *n.* total people in a given area

porch *n.* covered entrance

pore *v.* ponder **pored** *adj.*

por-nog-ra-phy *n.* pictures that arouse sexual excitement

po-rous *adj.* full of tiny holes **porousness** *n.,* **porously** *adv.*

port *n.* the city with a harbor; kind of wine

port-a-ble *adj.* movable **portably** *adv.,* **-bility** *n.*

por-ter *n.* one who carries baggage

port-fo-li-o *n.* carrying case

por-tion *n.* part of a whole; share of **portionless** *adj.*

por-tray *v.* to represent by drawing something

pose *v.* place, as for a picture; assume a specific position

po-si-tion *n.* spot where something is placed; a job **positioner** *n.*

pos-i-tive *adj.* absolutely certain

pos-se *n.* deputized group to assist the sheriff

pos-ses-sive *adj.* not wanting to share **-ness** *n.,* **-ly** *adv.*

pos-si-ble *adj.* capable of happening **possibility** *n.*

post *n.* an upright piece of wood or board

post-age *n.* fee for mailing something

pos-te-ri-or *adj.* in the back

post-mor-tem *adj.* following death

post-pone *v.* put off; defer **-er,** **-ment** *n.,* **-able** *adj.*

pos-ture *n.* the carriage of the body

pot *n.* deep container for cooking; marijuana

po-ta-to *n.,* *pl.* **-toes** edible, tuber vegetable

po-tent *adj.* to be powerful **potently** *adv.*

po-ten-tial *adj.* being possible

pot-pour-ri *n.* dried sweet-smelling flower petals

pouch *n.* small bag

poul-try *n.* a type of fowl for eggs or meat

pound *n.* weight equal to sixteen ounces

pov-er-ty *n.* the state of someone being poor

pow-der *n.* finely ground substance

pow-er-ful *adj.* to be possessing great force

prac-ti-cal *adj.* serving a purpose **-ness** *n.,* **-ly** *adv.*

prai-rie *n.* wide area of rolling land with out

praise *v.* to express approval for something **praiser** *n.*

prank *n.* mischievous trick

pray *v.* to address prayers to God

prayer *n.* devout request

pre- *pref* prior to something

preach *v.* to deliver a sermon to a group of people **-er** *n.*

pre-cau-tion *n.* care taken in advance **precautionary** *adj.*

pre-cede *v.* go before in time

pre-cept *n.* rule to guide one's conduct

pre-cinct *n.* electoral district

pre-cious *adj.* having great value **preciousness** *n.*

pre-cip-i-ta-tion *n.* snow, rain, sleet, etc.

pre-cip-i-tous *adj.* very steep **precipitousness** *n.*

pre-cise *adj.* exact; strictly following rules

pre-clude *v.* shut out; prevent

pre-co-cious *adj.* to be developing skills early in life

pre-con-ceive *v.* to form an opinion beforehand

pred-a-tor *n.* person who survives by stealing

pre-des-ti-na-tion *n.* one's destiny; one's fate

pred-i-cate *n.* *Gram.* word that says something about the subject in a sentence

pre-dict *v.* to tell something beforehand **predictable** *adj.*

pree-mie *n.* *Slang* baby born before it has completely developed

pre-empt *v.* to claim before hand

pre-fab-ri-cate *v.* built in sections **prefabrication** *n.*

pref-ace *n.* introduction in the front of a book

pre-fer *v.* being the favorite **preferability** *n.*

pre-fix *v.* to put at the beginning of a word

preg-nant *adj.* being with child

prej-u-dice *n.* a biased opinion

prel-ude *n.* an introductory action

pre-ma-ture *adj.* born before the natural or proper time **prematurity** *n.*

pre-med-i-tate *v.* to plan something in advance

pre-mi-um *n.* an object that is offered free

pre-na-tal *adj.* prior to birth

pre-pare *v.* to make ready

pre-pay *v.* pay for in advance

prep-o-si-tion *n.* a word, as for, by, or with, used before a noun or pronoun that shows relation to some other word in the sentence

pre-pos-ter-ous *adj.* being ridiculous; impossible

pres-age *n.* an omen; feeling of danger

pre-scribe *v.* to impose as a guide for something

pres-ent *adj.* to be current; not past

pres-en-ta-tion *n.* a kind of formal introduction

pre-serve *v.* keep or save

pre-side *v.* be in charge

pres-i-dent *n.* the chief executive of a country or company

press *v.* to exert steady pressure; to squeeze

pres-sure *n.* constraining moral force; burden

pres-tige *n.* importance based on achievements

pre-sume *v.* take for granted **presumably** *adv.*

pre-tend *v.* to make believe

pre-text *n.* hidden purpose

pret-ty *adj.* to be attractive

pre-vail *v.* win control over

pre-vent *v.* to keep from happening or occurring

pre-vi-ous *adj.* to be occurring earlier **previously** *adv.*

price *n.* the set amount of money

prick *n.* puncture

pride *n.* the sense of personal dignity

priest *n.* clergyman

pri-ma-ry *adj.* first in origin

prim-i-tive *adj.* being of the earliest time

prince *n.* son of a king

prin-cess *n.* the daughter of a king

prin-ci-pal *adj.* most important; *n.* the headmaster of a school

prin-ci-ple *n.* moral standard

print *n.* an impression made with ink **printable** *adv.*

print-out *n.* the output of a computer

pri-or *adj.* previous in time

pris-on *n.* the place of confinement; a jail

pri-vate *adj.* being secluded; to be secret

priv-i-lege *n.* special right

prize *n.* an award given to winner

pro *n.* in favor of something

prob-a-ble *adj.* likely to take place **probability** *n.*

pro-ba-tion *n.* period to test qualifications

prob-lem *n.* a perplexing situation

pro-ce-dure *n.* method of doing something

pro-ceed *v.* carry on

pro-cess *n.* the course toward a result

pro-ces-sion *n.* group moving in a formal manner

pro-ces-sor *n.* central unit of a computer

pro-claim *v.* to announce publicly

pro-cras-ti-nate *v.* put off **procrastination** *n.*

pro-cure *v.* to acquire

prod *v.* to poke

prod-i-gal *adj.* being wasteful of money

pro-duce *v.* to bring forth; to manufacture

pro-fane *adj.* vulgar

pro-fess *v.* admit openly

pro-fes-sor *n.* the faculty member of a college

pro-fi-cient *adj.* being highly

skilled

pro-file *n.* outline of a person's face or figure

prof-it *n.* financial return after expenses

pro-found *adj.* deeply felt

pro-fuse *adj.* overflowing

prog-e-ny *n., pl.* -ies an offspring

pro-gram *n.* the prearranged plan

prog-ress *n.* advancement to a higher goal

pro-hib-it *v.* to forbid

pro-ject *n.* plan of action **projectivity** *n.*

pro-jec-tile *n.* anything hurled through the air

pro-lif-er-ate *v.* to grow with great speed

pro-logue *n.* an introductory statement of a song or play

pro-long *v.* extend in time

prom-e-nade *n.* an unhurried walk

prom-i-nent *adj.* widely known **prominence** *n.*

pro-mis-cu-ous *adj.* lacking discrimination

prom-ise *n.* agreement; pledge **promissory** *adj.*

pro-mote *v.* raise to a higher rank **promotion** *n.*

prompt *adj.* on time; punctual **promptly** *n.*

pro-noun *n., gram.* word used in the place of a noun

proof *n.* establishment of fact by evidence

proof-read *v.* to read in order to detect errors in printer's proof

prop *n.* support

prop-er *adj.* appropriate

prop-er-ty *n., pl.* -ies piece of land

proph-et *n.* one who foretells the future

pro-pi-ti-ate *v.* to win the goodwill of

pro-por-tion *n.* relation of one thing to another

pro-pose *v.* make an offer

prop-o-si-tion *n.* scheme or plan offered for consideration

pro-pri-e-ty *n.* the state of being proper in accordance with recognized principles

pro-pul-sion *n.* the act or process of propelling

pro-rate *v.* divide proportionately

pro-scribe *v.* outlaw

prose *n.* ordinary language, speech, or writing which is not poetry

pros-e-cute *v.* to bring suit against; to seek enforcement for legal process

pros-pect *n.* something that has the possibility of future success

pros-per *v.* be successful; to achieve success

pros-ti-tute *n.* harlot

pros-trate *adj.* to be lying face down to the ground

prot-ac-tin-i-um *n.* a radioactive metallic element symbolized by Pa

pro-tect *v.* to guard against injury

pro-test *v.* to make a strong objection; to object to

pro-to-col *n.* the rules of state etiquette

pro-ton *n.* a unit of positive charge equal in magnitude to an electron

pro-tract *v.* to extend in space; to protrude

pro-trude *v.* thrust outward; to extend out; to protract

proud *adj.* have a feeling of satisfaction; self-respect

prove *v.* show evidence that something is true

prov-erb *n.* old saying which illustrates a truth

pro-vide *v.* furnish what is needed

pro-vi-sion *n.* a supply of food or needed equipment

pro-voke *v.* incite to anger

prox-i-mate *adj.* near; close; direct; immediate

prox-y *n.* the authority to act for another

prude *n.* a person who is very modest, especially in matters related to sex

pru-dent *adj.* cautious; discreet; managing something very carefully

prune *n.* the dried fruit of a

plum **pruner** n.

psalm n. sacred hymn

pso-ri-a-sis n. noncontagious, inflammatory skin disease characterized by itching

psych v. to prepare oneself mentally for something

psy-chi-a-try n. treatment of mental disorders

psy-chic n. person who communicates with the spirit world

psy-chol-o-gy n. the science of emotions, behavior, and the mind of a person

psy-cho-path n. mental disorder with antisocial and aggressive behavior

pu-ber-ty n. beginning of sexual development

pub-lic adj. for everyone's use

pub-lic do-main n. public property

pub-li-ca-tion n. the business of publishing

pub-lic-i-ty n. the state of being known to the public

pub-lish v. to print and to distribute the printed matter **publisher** n.

puck n. hard disk used in the game of hockey

pud-dle n. a small pool of water, usually after it rains

puff n. a brief discharge of air or of smoke

pull v. apply force **puller** n.

pulp n. the soft juicy part of a fruit; a soft moist mass

pul-pit n. elevated platform lectern used in a church

pul-sate v. beat rhythmically **pulsation** n., **pulsator** n.

pulse n., physiol. beating of the heart, felt in the arteries

pul-ver-ize v. reduced to dust **-zation** n., **-zable** adj.

pump n. mechanical device for moving liquid

pump-kin n. edible yellow-orange fruit

punch n. tool for piercing

punc-tu-al adj. arriving on time

punc-tu-ate v. give or show emphasis **punctuation** n.

punc-ture v. to prick or to pierce **punctureable** adj.

pun-gent adj. sharp in smell or taste **pungency** n.

pun-ish v. to subject a person to confinement or impose a penalty for a crime

pun-ish-ment n. penalty for a crime

punk n., Slang bizarre style of clothing

punt n. flatbottomed boat; kick a football

pup n. young dog

pu-pil n. person attending school

pup-pet n. the figure which is manipulated by strings **puppetry, puppeteer** n.

pur-chase v. to obtain by money; buy **purchaser** n.

pure adj. free from contaminates **pureness** n.

purge v. make clean; free from guilt or sin

pu-ri-fy v. to make clean or pure in character

pu-ri-ty n. the quality of being pure; freedom from sin

pur-ple n. a color between red and violet

pur-port v. imply, with the intent to deceive **-ed** adj.

pur-pose n. desired goal purposely adv., **-less** adj.

purse n. handbag; pocketbook

pur-sue v. chase; follow; to seek to achieve something

pur-vey v. supply provisions

pus n. secretion from infected tissue

push v. exert force; sell illegal drugs **pusher** n.

put v. place in a location

pu-ta-tive adj. being commonly supposed

pu-tre-fy v. decay

putt n. the light stroke in the game of golf **putter** n.

puz-zle v. to confuse puzzling adj.

py-or-rhe-a n., pathol. the inflammation of the gums

pyr-a-mid n. structure with square base and triangular sides which meet at a point

py-ro-ma-ni-a n. a person's compulsion to set fires

py-thon n. kind of large nonvenomous snake

Q, q the seventeenth letter of the English alphabet

qat n. a small plant found in Africa, the fresh leaf is chewed for a stimulating effect

Qa-tar n. country located on the western coast of the Persian Gulf

qi-vi-ut n. yarn spun from the fine, soft hair of the musk ox

quack n. the harsh, croaking cry of a duck **quack** v., **quackery** n.

quack grass n. a type of European grass

quad-ran-gle n., Math a plane figure with four sides and four angles

quad-rant n. a quarter section of a circle, subtending or enclosing a central angle of 90 degrees; an instrument which is used to measure altitudes

qua-draph-o-ny n. the recording of sound using four transmission channels

quad-rat n. rectangular area used for population studies

quad-rate adj. being square or almost square

qua-drat-ics n. a branch of algebra concerned with equations

quad-ra-ture n. an arrangement of two celestial bodies with a separation of 90 degrees

quad-ri-ceps n. the muscle located in the front of the thigh

qua-dri-ga n. a chariot pulled by a team of four horses

qua-drille n. a square dance with five or six figures executed by four couples

quad-ril-lion n. a thousand trillions; one followed by fifteen zeros

quad-ru-ped n. any animal having four feet

quad-ru-ple adj. consisting of four parts; multiplied by four

quaff v. to drink with abundance

quag-mire n. an area of soft muddy land that gives away underfoot; a marsh

quail n., pl. a small game bird

quaint adj. pleasing in an old-fashioned, unusual way

quake v. to shake or tremble voilently

Quak-er n. the religious sect called the Society of Friends

qual-i-fi-ca-tion n. an act of qualifying; the ability, skill, or quality which makes something suitable for a given position

qual-i-fy v. to prove something able; restrict; limit; modify

qual-i-ty n., pl., -ties a distinguishing character which makes something such as it is

qualm n. a sudden feeling of sickness

quan-da-ry n. a state of perplexity

quan-ti-ty n. number; amount

quan-tum n., pl., quanta an amount or quantity

quar-an-tine n. a period of enforced isolation for a specified period of time

quar-rel n. an unfriendly or angry disagreement

quar-ry n., pl. quarries an animal hunted for food; an open pit or excavation from which limestone or other material is being extracted

quart n. a unit of measurement equaling four cups

quar-ter n. one of four equal parts into which anything may be divided; a place of lodging

quar-ter-back n., Football the offensive player who directs the plays for his team

quar-ter-mas-ter n. the officer in charge of supplies for army troops

quar-tet n. a musical composition for four voices or instruments

quartz n. a hard, transparent crystallized mineral

qua-sar n. one of the most distant and brightest bodies in the universe

quea-sy adj. nauseated; sick

queasiness n.

queen n. the wife of a king; a woman sovereign or monarch; in chess, the most powerful piece on the board

queer adj. strange; unusual; different from the normal Slang homosexual

quell v. to put down with force

quench v. to extinguish or put out; to cool metal by thrusting into water

quer-u-lous adj. complaining or fretting; expressing complaints

que-ry n. an injury; a question

quest n. a search; pursuit

ques-tion n. an expression of inquiry which requires an answer

question mark n. a mark of punctuation, (?), used in writing to indicate a question

ques-tion-naire n. a written series of questions

queue n., Computer Science a sequence of stored programs or data on hold for processing

quib-ble v. to raise trivial objection

quibble, quibbler n.

quiche n. unsweetened custard baked in a pastry shell

quick adj. moving swiftly; occurring in a short time

quickly adv., **quickness** n.

quick-sand n. a bog of very fine, wet sand of considerable depth

quid n. a small portion of tobacco; a cow's cud

qui-es-cent adj. being in a state of quiet repose

qui-et adj. silent; making very little sound; still; tranquil; calm

quill n. a strong bird feather; a spine from a porcupine

quilt n. a bed coverlet made of two layers of cloth with a soft substance between and held in place by lines of stitching

qui-nine n., Chem. a very bitter, colorless, crystalline powder used in the treatment of malaria

quin-sy n., Pathol. a severe inflammation of the tonsils

quin-tes-sence n. the most essential and purest form of anything

quin-tet n. a musical composition written for five people

quin-tu-ple adj. increased five times

quip n. a sarcastic remark

quipster n.

quire n. twenty-five sheets of paper removed from a complete ream of paper

quirk n. a sudden, sharp bend or twist; a personal mannerism

quis-ling n. a person who is a traitor, working against his own country from within

quit v. to cease; to give up; to depart; to abandon

quite adv. to the fullest degree; really; actually

quiv-er v. to shake with a trembling motion. n. the arrows used in archery

quix-ot-ic adj. extravagantly romantic; impractical

quiz v. to question, as with an informal oral or written examination **quiz, quizzer** n.

quoin n. the external corner or angle of a building

quoit n. a game in which a metal ring connected to a rope is thrown in an attempt to encircle a stake

quo-rum n. the number of members needed in order to validate a meeting

quo-ta n. an allotment or proportional share

quo-ta-tion n. the exact quoting of words as a passage

quo-ta-tion mark n. the mark of punctuation (" ") showing a direct quote

quote v. to repeat exactly what someone else has previously stated

quo-tid-i-an adj. occurring or recurring daily

quo-tient n., Math the amount or number which results when one number is divided by another

r the eighteenth letter of the English alphabet

a-ba-to n. a collar made of lace and worn in 17th century

b-bet n. recess or groove on the edge of a piece of wood

b-bet joint n. the joint which is formed by two rabbeted boards

b-bi n. the ordained leader of Jews

b-bin-ate n. the body of rabbis

b-bin-ism n. the rabbinic traditiions

b-bit n. kind of burrowing mammal related to the hare and having large ears

b-bit brush n. type of low branching shrubwith yellow flowers and linear leaves

b-bit-eye n. type of blueberry found in southeastern U.S.

b-bit-ry n. the place where rabbits are kept

b-ble n. disorderly crowd; disorganized collection of items or things

b-id adj. affected with rabies; mad; furious

a-bies n. the disease of the nervous system

c-coon n., pl. -coons, -coon a nocturnal mammal with a black, mask-like face

ce n. the division of the human population having common origin and traits; a type of contest

-cial adj. being characteristic of a race

c-ism n. belief that a particular race is superior

ck n. the framework used for displaying or holding something

ck-et n. lightweight bat-like object used in tennis

c-y adj. having a spirited or strongly marked quality **aciness** n.

-dar n. device for detection of aircraft or other objects

-di-al adj. pertaining to a ray or radius

-di-ant adj. emitting rays of heat or light

ra-di-a-tion n. energy radiated from nuclear particles

rad-i-cal adj. making extreme changes in views, or habits

ra-di-o n. technique of communicating by radio waves

ra-di-o-ac-tiv-i-ty n., Physics a spontaneous emission of electromagnetic radiation

rad-ish n. the edible root of the radish plant

ra-di-um n. the radioactive metallic element that is symbolized by Ra

ra-di-us n. line from the center of a circle to its surface

ra-don n. a radioactive gaseous element symbolized by Rn

raf-fi-a n. a fiber from an African palm tree for making baskets, hats, etc.

raf-fle n. the game of chance; the lottery

raft n. structure made from logs or planks and used for water transportation

raf-ter n. the beam that supports a roof

rag n. waste piece of clothing

rag-ged adj. being unkempt; having an irregular edge

rage n. violent anger

raid n. sudden invasion

rail n. a horizontal bar of metal forming a track on the railroad

rain n. the water from atmospheric vapor

rain-bow n. the rays of light appearing in the sky after a rain

rain-check n. the stub for merchandise which is out of stock

raise v. to cause to move upward; to rear as children

rai-sin n. grapes which are dried for eating

rake n. tool with a long handle and teeth for gathering the leaves of a tree

ral-ly v. to call together a group for a purpose

ram n. a male sheep; implement used to crush something by impact

RAM abbr. random access

memory

ram-ble v. stroll or walk aimlessly; talk in a long winded fashion -**blingly** adv.

ram-bunc-tious adj. being rough or boisterous

ramp n. an incline which connects two different levels

ram-page n. a course of destruction or of a violent behavior

ram-pant adj. out of control; wild in actions

ram-rod n. metal rod used for cleaning barrels of a rifle or other firearm

ram-shack-le adj. to be falling apart due to poor construction or maintenance

ranch n. large establishment for raising livestock or crops

ran-cid adj. to be sour-smelling from spoilage

ran-cor n. a malice; a kind of deep resentment

ran-dom adj. done without a purpose or direction

R & R abbr. rest and relaxation

rang v. past tense of ring

range n. cooking stove; tract of land on which animals can graze; a row, especially of the mountains

rank n. degree of official position or status

rank adj. strong and disagreeable odor, smell, or taste

ran-sack v. plunder through every part of something

ran-som n. the money demanded or paid to free a kidnaped person

rant v. to talk in a wild, loud way or manner

rap v. to strike something with a blow; knock slang converse; talk

ra-pa-cious adj. living on prey seized alive; plundering -**ly** adv., -**ness** n.

rape n. the crime of forcible sexual intercourse

rap-id adj. to be having great speed **rapidness** n.

ra-pi-er n. a kind of long slender straight sword with two edges

rap-ine n. the forcible taking of another's property

rap-port n. a harmonious relationship

rapt adj. deeply absorbed o engrossed with something

rap-ture n. the state of extrem ecstasy

rare adj. scarce; infrequent c far apart; not fully cooked

rare-bit n. the dish which is made with cheese

rare-ly adv. seldom

ras-cal n. a person full of mischief; a person who is not honest

rash adj. acting without consideration or caution n. a skin irritation

rasp n. a coarse file v. scrape with a coarse file **rasper** n.

rasp-berry n. a small edible fruit, red or black in color

rat n. a rodent similar to the mouse, but having a longe tail; the one who betrays hi friends

ratch-et n. the mechanism consisting of a pawl that al lows movement in one dir ection only

rate n. the fixed ratio or price on something

rath-er adv. preferably; mo accurate or precise

rat-i-fy v. to approve some thing in an official way ratification n.

ra-tio n. the relationship be tween two things in amount size, or degree

ra-tion n. a fixed portion or share allowed rationing n.

ra-tio-nal adj. having the faculty of reasoning; being of sound mind -**ity** n.

ra-tion-al-ize v. explain or jus tify in a logical manner

rat-tan n. the palm whose stems are used to make wickerworks

rat-tle v. make a series of rapi noises in quick succession to talk rapidly; chatter

rat-tler n. slang a venomou snake; a rattlesnake

rau-cous adj. being loud an rowdy; having a rough hoarse sound

raun-chy *adj.* lewd; slovenly

rav-age *v.* to bring on heavy destruction; devastate

rave *v.* to speak incoherently; to speak with enthusiasm

rav-el *v.* to separate fibers or threads; to unravel

ra-ven *n.* a large bird, with shiny black feathers

rav-en-ous *adj.* starved

ra-vine *n.* long narrow valley

ra-vi-o-li *n.* the dough enclosing meat or cheese and served in sauce

rav-ish *v.* seize and carry off with violence

rav-ish-ing *adj.* entrancing

raw *adj.* not fully cooked; sore; lacking refinement

raw-hide *n.* the untanned skin of cattle

ray *n.* thin line of light

ray-on *n.* synthetic fiber

ra-zor *n.* sharp-edged instrument used for shaving beards, etc.

reach *v.* to extend the outstretched hand so as to touch something or one

re-ac-tion *n.* reversed action toward a previous condition

re-ac-ti-vate *v.* to become effective again

read *v.* understand the meaning of something written or printed

read-er *n.* schoolbook for instruction in reading

re-adjust *v.* put in order again

ready *adj.* prepared for action

re-al *adj.* to be genuine; true; existing as fact

re-al-ize *v.* understand clearly

realm *n.* a kingdom; a domain or a scope

ream *n.* 500 sheets of paper

reap *v.* to harvest a crop with a sickle

re-ap-pear *v.* to appear anew or again

rear *n.* opposite side of the front; background

rea-son *n.* the motive or explanation one has

re-bate *n.* a discount

re-bel *v.* refuse allegiance

re-bel-lion *n.* organized uprising to change or overthrow an existing authority

re-birth *n.* the revival or renaissance

re-bound *v.* spring back

re-buff *n.* refuse

re-buke *v.* reprimand

re-call *v.* to order or summon to return something

re-cant *v.* public confession

re-cede *v.* move back

re-ceipt *n.* proof of purchase

re-ceive *v.* to take or to obtain something

re-cent *adj.* fresh; newer

re-cep-ta-cle *n.* an electrical outlet

re-cep-tion *n.* formal entertainment for guests

re-cess *n.* rest period

rec-i-pe *n.* the directions and a list of ingredients for preparing food

re-cip-ro-cate *v.* give in return

re-cite *v.* repeat from memory; give an account of something in detail

reck-on *v.* calculate

re-claim *v.* to redeem

re-cline *v.* to assume a supine position

rec-og-nize *v.* to experience or identify something or someone **recognizable** *adj.*

rec-ol-lect *v.* to remember

rec-om-mend *v.* to suggest to another as desirable; to advise **-ation** *n.*

rec-on-cile *v.* to restore a friendship with another

re-con-sid-er *v.* to think about again with a view to changing it

re-cord *v.* to preserve sound on a tape or disk for replay

re-coup *v.* to be reimbursed for something; to recover

re-course *n.* a turning to or an appeal for help

re-cover *v.* to regain something which was lost; to be restored to good health

rec-re-a-tion *n.* a diversion; an amusement

re-cruit *v.* to enlist for military duty

rec-tan-gle *n.* parallelogram with all right angles

rec-ti-fy *v.* to make correct

rec-tum *n.* connecting the colon and anus

re-cu-per-ate *v.* regain strength

re-deem *v.* buy back; recover

re-doubt *n.* small fortification

re-duce *v.* make less; diminish in quantity or size

reef *n.* the coral near the surface of water

reek *v.* to emit a strong and unpleasant odor

re-fer *v.* to direct someone for help referral *n.*

ref-er-ee *n.* official in football; one who settles a dispute

re-fine *v.* to make pure; free from impurities

re-fin-ish *v.* apply a new surface on wood, etc.

re-flex *n.* involuntary reaction

re-for-ma-to-ry *n.* a jail-like institution

re-frac-to-ry *adj.* unmanageable; obstinate

re-frain *v.* hold back

re-frig-er-ate *v.* chill or cool

ref-uge *n.* a protection from harm

ref-u-gee *n.* the one who flees to find safety

re-fund *v.* pay back; reimburse

re-fur-bish *v.* to make clean; to renovate

re-gain *v.* to recover

re-gale *v.* entertain or delight

re-gard *v.* to look upon something with esteem

re-gat-ta *n.* boat race

re-gen-er-ate *v.* reform morally

re-gent *n.* the one who acts as a ruler

regiment *n.* military unit; regulated course of exercise, etc.

re-gion *n.* geographical area

re-gis-ter *n.* book containing names and accounts, etc.

reg-is-trar *n.* keeper of records

re-gress *v.* to return to previous the state

re-gret *v.* feel sorry about

reg-u-la-tion *n.* governing rule

re-hash *v.* to rework or go over old material

re-hears-al *n.* the act of practicing for a performance

re-im-burse *v.* pay back

reign *n.* time a monarch rules a country

rein-deer *n.* a large deer found in northern regions

re-in-force *v.* support

re-in-state *v.* to restore something to its former condition

re-it-er-ate *v.* to do something over and over again

re-ject *v.* to refuse; to discard as useless

re-joice *v.* fill with joy

re-ju-ve-nate *v.* to restore to youthful appearance or vigor

re-lapse *v.* fall back

re-lent *v.* to slacken

re-late *v.* to tell the events of; to narrate

rel-a-tive *adj.* considered in comparison or relationship to other *n.* a member of one's family

re-lax *v.* to make loose or lax; to become less formal or less reserved relaxation *n.*

re-lease *v.* to set free from confinement; to unfasten

rel-e-vant *adj.* relating to matters at hand

rel-ic *n.* ancient remains

re-lig-ion *n.* system of worship

re-luc-tant *adj.* unwilling

re-mains *pl., n.* what is left after all other parts have been taken away

re-mark *n.* the brief expression or comment

re-mark-able *adj.* extraordinary remarkably *adv.*

re-mem-ber *v.* to bring back or recall to the mind

re-mind *v.* to cause or to help to remember

rem-i-nis-cence *n.* the practice or process of recalling the past reminiscent *adj.*

re-miss *adj.* negligent

re-mit *v.* to send money as payment

re-morse *n.* regret for past misdeeds

re-mote *adj.* distant in time

ren-ais-sance *n.* revival or rebirth; revival of classical art, literature, etc. in Europe

ren-der *v.* to submit or give

ren-dez-vous *n.* a prearranged

meeting

ren-e-gade *n.* an outlaw; a traitor

re-nown *n.* widely honored

rent *n.* payment made for the use of another's property

rep-ar-tee *n.* quick reply

re-pay *v.* pay back money

re-peal *v.* withdraw officially

re-peat *v.* to say or to perform again **repeatable** *adj.*

re-pel *v.* to drive back or force away

re-pent *v.* change ways

re-per-cus-sion *n.* unforeseen effect by an action

rep-er-toire *n.* the artistic achievements

rep-e-ti-tion *n.* act of repeating; something done a second time **-tious** *adj.*

re-plen-ish *v.* to supply again; to restock

rep-li-ca *n.* a reproduction of an original

re-ply *v.* answer; respond

re-port *v.* bring back or relate an account of facts

re-pose *n.* at rest

rep-re-hend *v.* to express disapproval; to censure

rep-re-sent *v.* act on behalf of

re-press *v.* restrain

re-prieve *v.* delay punishment

rep-ri-mand *v.* to censure something severely

re-pri-sal *n.* inflect injury

re-proach *v.* to blame

re-pu-di-ate *v.* to reject or disown

re-pug-nant *adj.* distasteful

re-pulse *v.* repel or drive back

re-pul-sive *adj.* being distasteful or disgusting

rep-u-ta-tion *n.* evaluation of one's character

re-quest *n.* expression of desire for something to be granted

re-quire-ment *n.* something that is necessary

req-ui-site *adj.* being absolutely needed

re-scind *v.* repeal; to void

res-cue *v.* to free from danger or evil

re-sent *v.* show ill feeling

re-serve *v.* to save for use at a later time

res-er-voir *n.* body of water

re-side *v.* occupy a residence

res-i-due *n.* something which remains behind

re-sign *v.* give up

re-sil-ient *adj.* springing back; buoyant **resiliently** *adv.*

res-in *n.* substance from plants used in making plastics

re-sist *v.* to withstand; to oppose something **resister** *n.*

re-sist-ance *n.* act of resisting

re-sis-tor *n.* conducting body

res-o-lute *adj.* coming from determination **-ness** *n.*

re-solve *v.* to make a firm decision on something

re-sound *v.* echo loudly

re-source *n.* assistance

res-pi-ra-tion *n.* an act of breathing

re-spite *n.* the temporary postponement

re-splend-ent *adj.* magnificent

re-spond *v.* answer; react

re-sponse *n.* a reply; a reaction

re-spon-si-ble *adj.* to be trustworthy **-bility** *n.*

res-tau-rant *n.* public building serving food and beverages

res-ti-tu-tion *n.* compensation for damage, or loss

res-tive *adj.* impatient

re-store *v.* bring back to a former condition **restorer** *n.*

re-strain *v.* hold back

re-strict *v.* to limit confine within the bounds

re-sume *v.* to start again after an interruption

re-sur-gent *adj.* rising again

re-tail *v.* to sell to the public

re-tain *v.* keep possession of

re-tain-er *n.* fee paid to secure services

re-take *v.* recapture

re-tal-i-ate *v.* repay; return like for like **-ation** *n.*

re-tard *v.* delay the progress

re-ten-tion *n.* the power of memory

ret-i-cent *adj.* reserved

ret-i-na *n.* part of the eyeball

re-tire *v.* withdraw; retreat from action

re-tir-ing *adj.* reserved

re-tort *v.* reply quickly

re-trace *v.* to track back; to go

over again

re-tract v. to take back something   retractor n.

re-treat n. a withdrawal from danger

re-trench v. economize

ret-ri-bu-tion n. punishment for a wrong doing

re-trieve v. recover; to rescue or save

ret-ro-ac-tive adj. to be affecting things past -ly adj.

ret-ro-gress v. to move backward; to revert

ret-ro-spect n. review of things in the past

re-turn v. to give back; to restore; to repay

re-un-ion n. gathering together again

rev n. revolution v., Informal increase the speed of

re-veal v. to make known; to open to view

rev-eil-le n. signal at daybreak to awaken soldiers

rev-el v. to take great pleasure in something   reveler n.

rev-e-la-tion n. disclosure

re-venge v. to inflict injury on someone

rev-e-nue n. income

re-ver-ber-ate v. to reflect; to return as sound

re-vere v. to regard with respect; to venerate

rev-er-end n. clergyman

rev-er-ie n. the irregular train of thought

re-verse v. to turn in an opposite direction

re-vert v. to return to former belief

re-view v. examine again; study critically; critique

re-vile v. speak evil of

re-vise v. change and amend

re-vi-sion n. reexamination of something for correction

re-vive v. refresh; activate again; gain vigor

re-voke v. make void by recalling; cancel

re-volt n. fill with disgust

rev-o-lu-tion n. a sudden change in a system

re-volve v. to rotate; to travel in an orbit; ponder

re-ward v. compensate for a good deed

rhap-so-dy n. the outward display of enthusiasm; a musical composition

rhe-ni-um n. kind of metallic element, Re.

rhet-o-ric n. the effective use of the language

rhet-o-ric n. kind of persuasive oratory   rhetorical adj.

rheum n. watery matter

rheu-mat-ic adj. being affected with rheumatism

rheu-mat-ic fe-ver n. a severe infectious disease

rheu-ma-tism n. the painful inflammation of the muscles and the joints

rhi-noc-er-os n. very large mammal having its horns on the snout

rho-di-um n. silver-white metallic element, Rh.

rho-do-den-dron n. evergreen shrubs with showy flowers

rhu-barb n. garden plant having edible stalks

rhyme n. word having a sound similar to another; meter

rhythm n. a movement with a beat or music

rib n. curved bones around the chest; a cut of meat; something riblike

rib-ald adj. being vulgar in one's speech; abusive

rib-bon n. narrow band of silk

rice n. starchy grain

rich adj. being wealthy; to be productive; sweet

rich-es n., pl. wealth

rick n. stack of corn or hay

rick-ets n. kind of bone softening disease

rick-et-y adj. shaky; irregular

ric-o-chet n. glancing rebound off a flat surface

rid v. free; deliver

rid-dle n. a large sieve; a puzzling question

ride v. to sit on and manage; to be borne along

rid-er n. passenger; clause added to bill

ridge n. crest of something; chain of hills   ridged v.

rid-i-cule v. to make fun of

ri-dic-u-lous *adj.* absurd; laughable **-ly** *adv.*

rife *adj.* prevalent; abundant

riff-raff *n.* rabble

ri-fle *n.* the gun that is carried over the shoulder

rift *n.* a fault; crack; fissure; geological fault in the ground; an estrangement

right *adj.* to be just or good; correct; sound or normal; most fitting

right-eous *adj.* virtuous; acting within the dictates of morality **righteousness** *n.*

right-ful *adj.* to be legitimate

right-ism *n.* advocacy of political conservatism

rig-id *adj.* inflexible; rigorous; strict in opinion **-ity** *n.*

rig-or *n.* an austerity; a strictness **rigorous** *adj.*

rile *v.* anger; irritate

rim *n.* the edge of an object that is circular

rind *n.* the firm outward covering of fruits

ring *n.* circular band of material; circle; sound of a bell **ringing** *v.*

ring-lead-er *n.* leader of a circus performance

ring-let *n.* curl

rink *n.* smooth area for skating

rinse *v.* wash lightly

ri-ot *n.* public disturbance of a violent nature

rip *v.* tear; cut open

ripe *adj.* being ready for reaping; matured

rip-ple *v.* form small waves; agitate lightly

rise *v.* to get up; to become active; to appear

rite *n.* formal custom

rit-u-al *n.* religious act; any solemn ceremony

ri-val *n.* competitor

river *n.* natural stream of flowing water

ri-vet *n.* short metal pin with a head for joining metal, pants, etc.

road *n.* highway; route

roam *v.* to wander or rove

roar *v.* to howl

roast *v.* to cook by exposure to heat; dry and parch

rob *v.* to steal someone's possessions

robe *n.* kind of woman's long flowing gown

ro-bot *n.* mechanical device resembling man

ro-bust *adj.* vigorous; possessing great strength

rock *n.* large mass of stone

rock-et *n.* vehicle orbited into space; firecracker

ro-dent *n.* a mammal, such as a rat or mouse

ro-de-o *n.* show of cowboy skills, bronco riding, etc.

roe *n.* eggs of a female fish

rogue *n.* dishonest person

roll *v.* to move by turning; flow; take the shape of a ball

ro-mance *n.* tale of chivalric love; love affair

roof *n.* cover of a building

room *n.* place of lodging; amount of space

room-mate *n.* the one who shares a room or rooms with another person

room-y *adj.* spacious

roos-ter *n.* male of the domestic chicken

root *n.* part of a plant which is below the surface of the earth; foundation

rope *n.* a cord made of twisted fibers **roped** *v.*

ro-sa-ry *n.* a series of prayers; rose garden

rose *n.* attractive flower; pinkish color

ros-ter *n.* list of names

ros-trum *n.* a speaker's platform from which a speech is given to the public

ro-tate *v.* revolve or move around the center

ro-tis-ser-ie *n.* the container with a rotating spit used for roasting food

rot-ten *adj.* decaying; corrupt

ro-tund *adj.* being rounded; plump; resonant

ro-tun-da *n.* kind of round building with a dome

rouge *n.* the kind of cosmetic for the cheeks

rough *adj.* not smooth; uneven; unruly; stormy; rebellious; crude; not perfected

rou-lette *n.* a game of chance

round *adj.* spherical; having a curved form; plump

rouse *v.* wake from sleep; excite to action

rout *n.* a disorder and confusion; an uproar

route *n.* course taken; regular line of travel

rou-tine *n.* the schedule followed regularly

rove *v.* to wander or walk over a wide area

row *n.* a number of things positioned next to each other

row-boat *n.* small boat propelled with oars

row-house *n.* group of houses joined by a common wall

roy-al *adj.* to be relating to the king or queen

rub *v.* to move back or forth on a surface

rub-ber *n.* a resinous elastic material obtained from the sap of tropical plants or produced synthetically

rub-bish *n.* debris; trash

ru-bid-i-um *n.* a silvery element symbolized by Rb

ru-by *n.* a kind of deepred precious stone

ruck-us *n.* uproar; disturbance

rud-der *n.* the steering or guiding part of a boat

rude *adj.* discourteous; impolite **rudeness** *n.*

ru-di-ment *n.* in an underdeveloped state **-ary** *adj.*

rue *v.* to regret; to have compassion for

ruff *n.* stiff, pleated collar

ruf-fi-an *n.* rowdy person

ruf-fle *n.* a pleated strip or frill

rug *n.* a heavy textile fabric used to cover the floor

rug-ged *adj.* having a rough uneven surface

ru-in *n.* destruction; downfall

ru-in-a-tion *n.* destruction

rule *n.* control; custom; point of law *v.* govern; control

rul-er *n.* a straight edge used for measuring length; one who rules

rul-ing *a* predominant *n.* the decision settle by a court or by a judge

ru-mi-nate *v.* chew a cud

rum-mage *v.* to ransack

rum-my *n.* a card game in which each player tries to get rid of his hand in sequences of three cards or more of the same suit

ru-mor *n.* uncertain truth which is circulated from one person to another

ru-mor-mon-ger *n.* one who spreads malicious rumors

rump *n.* the buttocks

rum-ple *v.* wrinkle; crease

rum-pus *n.* disturbance; a riot; loud noise

run *v.* hurry busily from one place to another

run-a-round *n.* evasive action

run-a-way *n.* someone or something that runs away

run-down *n.* pursue; overtake; *adj.* tired; dilapidated

rung *n.* step of a ladder

run-in *n.* altercation

run-ner *n.* racer; messenger; that on which something runs or sides

run-ning *adj.* moving rapidly; functioning

run-ny *adj.* tending to drop

run-of-the--mill *adj.* average

runt *n.* the smallest animal in a litter, such as with dogs

run--through *n.* cursory review; rapid rehearsal

run-way *n.* clear pathway used by airplanes for taking off and for landing

rup-ture *n.* the act of bursting or breaking; a hernia

ru-ral *adj.* to be pertaining to the country life

rush *v.* to move quickly; to hurry with speed *n.* a kind of grass-like herb

rus-set *n.* reddish or yellowish brown color

rust *n.* coating which forms on iron when exposed to air and moisture

rus-tic *n.* simple person

rut *n.* a habitual pattern of one's behavior

ru-the-ni-um *n.* metallic element symbolized by Ru.

ruth-less *adj.* merciless; cruel

Rx. *n.* the prescription for a medicine

S, s the nineteenth letter of the English alphabet

Sab-bath *n.* the seventh day of the week

sa-ber *n.* sword

sa-ble *n.* carnivorous mammal

sab-o-tage *n.* a willful destruction of something

sac-cha-rin *n.* type of non-caloric sugar substitute

sa-chet *n.* bag of sweet-smelling powder

sack *n.* large bag used to hold and carry items **sacking** *n.*

sac-ra-ment *n.* the religious ceremony such as the baptism **sacramentally** *adv.*

sa-cred *adj.* being dedicated to worship

sac-ri-fice *v.* give up something of value **-fical** *adj.*

sad *adj.* to be unhappy, sorrowful **sadly** *adv.*

sad-dle *n.* seat for a rider on a horse **saddler** *n.*

sa-dism *n.* pleasure from inflicting cruelty on others

sa-fa-ri *n.* the wild animal hunting trip

safe *adj.* to be secure from harm **safety** *n.*

sa-ga *n.* long heroic story

saint *n.* a kind of holy person **saintly** *adj.*

sake *n.* the motive for doing something

sa-la-ry *n.* set compensation for work done

sa-li-ent *adj.* conspicuous

sa-li-va *n.* the fluid secreted in the mouth

salm-on *n.* large game fish

sa-lon *n.* large drawing room

sa-loon *n.* the place where alcohol is sold

salt *n.* sodium chloride

sa-lute *v.* show honor to a superior officer

sal-vage *v.* to save from destruction

salve *n.* medicated ointment

sam-ple *n.* example; try something **sampler** *n.*

san-a-to-ri-um *n.* institution for insane people

sanc-tu-ar-y *n.* holy place

sand *n.* fine grains of disintegrated rock

san-dal *n.* flat soled shoe

sane *adj.* to be of a healthy, sound mind

san-i-tar-y *adj.* free from bacteria or filth **-tarium** *n.*

sap *n.* liquid from tree or plant

sa-pi-ent *adj.* being wise

sap-phire *n.* deep-blue gem

sar-casm *n.* insulting remark

sar-dine *n.* small edible fish

sar-don-ic *adj.* scornful

sat-el-lite *n.* man-made object which orbits a celestial body

sat-is-fac-tion *n.* the fulfillment of a desire

sat-u-rate *v.* to make something completely wet

sauce *n.* the liquid topping used for food

sau-na *n.* steam bath

sau-sage *n.* kind of seasoned, chopped meat

sav-age *adj.* being wild; being uncivilized **savageness** *n.*

save *v.* rescue from danger

sav-ior *n.* one who saves

sa-voir-faire *n.* social skill

saw *p.t.* of see

saw-horse *n.* the frame on which wood rests when it is being sawed

saw-mill *n.* factory where logs are cut into lumber

sax-o-phone *n.* type of brass wind instrument

say *v.* speak aloud **saying** *n.*

scaf-fold *n.* temporary platform for workers

scaf-fold *n.* platform built as support for workmen, tools and materials

scald *v.* burn with hot liquid

scale *n.* weighing device; covering on a fish

scal-lop *n.* marine shellfish

scalp *n.* the skin located on the top of the head

scamper *v.* to run hurriedly

scan *v.* look at quickly

scan-dal *n.* the public gossip about another **-ous** *adj.*

scant *adj.* not plentiful; small in amount **scantling** *n.*

scar *n.* the permanent mark from an injury

scarce *adj.* rare; difficult to get

scat-ter *v.* spread around

scav-en-ger *n.* wild animal

sce-nar-i-o n. synopsis of a dramatic plot

scent n. odor **scentless** adj.

sched-ule n. routine

scheme n. the plan of action one has **schemer** n.

schol-ar n. an intelligent student **scholarly** adj.

school n. place for learning

sci-ence n. the study of the natural phenomena

scis-sors pl., n. cutting tool

scold v. accuse harshly

scope n. range of one's actions

scorch v. parch with heat

scorn n. contempt **-ful** adj.

scoun-drel n. a wicked person

scout v. observe activities

scowl v. make an angry look

scrape v. rub off roughly

scratch v. to mark one with the fingernails

screech v. make a harsh noise

screen n. surface used for showing a movie

screw n. nail-shaped piece of metal with winding threads used for fastening together

scribe n. person who writes

scru-ple n. principle

scuff v. drag feet while walking

scuf-fle v. struggle in a confused manner

scur-ry v. to move quickly

scut-tle n. small opening in the hull of a ship

sea n. large body of salt water

seal n. a tight closure; kind of aquatic mammal

sea lev-el n. used as the starting point in measuring height land

sear v. dry up; burn slightly

sea-son n. spring, summer, fall and winter; flavor enhancer

se-cede v. to withdraw from a group

se-clude v. isolate

se-cret n. the knowledge which is kept from others

sec-re-tary n. the head of a governmental department **secretarial** adj.

se-crete v. to discharge

sec-tion n. the division of something

sec-u-lar adj. relating to something worldly

se-cure adj. sturdy or strong

se-date adj. being serene and composed

see v. power of sight

seed n. fertilized plant ovule

seek v. search for

seem v. appear to be **-ly** adj.

seg-ment n. a portion

seg-re-gate v. to isolate one from others

seize v. take possession forcibly

sel-dom adv. not often

sell v. to exchange a product for money

se-man-tics n. the study of word meanings

sem-i-an-nu-al adj. to be occurring twice a year

sem-i-nar n. convention on a certain subject

sen-ate n. the upper house of a legislature

se-nile adj. having mental deterioration

sen-ior adj. being the older of two people

sen-sa-tion n. feelings

sense n. sensation **-less** adj.

sen-si-ble adj. good judgment

sen-si-tive adj. having intense feelings **sensitively** adv.

sen-tence n. the written complete thought

sen-ti-men-tal adj. very special; emotional

sen-ti-nel n. one who guards

sep-a-rate v. to keep people or things apart **-tor** n.

se-quence n. set arrangement

se-rene adj. being calm

serf n. a slave during the Middle Ages

ser-geant n. officer who ranks above a corporal

se-ries n. one after another

se-ri-ous adj. important

ser-mon n. religious lecture

se-rum n. fluid of the blood which remains after clotting

ser-vant n. one employed to care for someone

serv-ice n. the help which is given to others **-able** adj.

ses-sion n. series of meetings

set-tle v. to arrange or put something in order

sev-en *n.* the cardinal number 7, after 6

sev-en-teen *n.* the cardinal number 17, after 16

sev-en-ty *n.* the cardinal number 70, after 69

sev-er *v.* cut off or separate

sev-er-al *adj.* being more than one or two

se-vere *adj.* strict; stern

sew-er *n.* drain pipe to carry away waste

sex *n.* the divisions, such as in male and female

shad-ow *n.* a shaded area

shaft *n.* ray of light

shake *v.* to tremble

shal-low *adj.* not deep

shame *n.* the feeling of embarrassment

sham-poo *n.* liquid soap to cleanse the hair

shape *n.* the configuration of something

share *v.* divide among others

shark *n.* large marine fish

shat-ter *v.* burst into pieces

shave *v.* remove a thin layer

shear *v.* trim, cut, or remove

sheath *n.* cover for a blade

sheen *n.* a luster or shine

sheep *n.* wool producing, cud-chewing mammal

sheer *adj.* very thin

sheet *n.* cloth for covering a bed; piece of paper

shell *n.* outer covering of certain organisms

shel-ter *n.* the place giving protection

shelve *v.* put aside

shep-herd *n.* the person who tends to sheep

sher-iff *n.* the law enforcement officer

shield *n.* protective device

shim-mer *v.* to shine with a sparkle

shin *n.* front part of the leg

ship *n.* vessel used for deep-water travel

shiv-er *v.* tremble or shake

shock *n.* sudden violent impact

shoot *v.* wound with a firearm

shore *n.* land bordering a body of water

shot *n.* discharging of a gun

shoul-der *n.* place where arm is attached to the body

show *v.* put within sight

show-er *n.* short period of rain

shrap-nel *n.* fragments of an exploded shell

shriek *n.* loud, sharp scream

shrill *adj.* high-pitched sound

shrine *n.* the place used for sacred relics

shrink *v.* make smaller

shroud *n.* a cover

shrug *v.* to raise the shoulders briefly

shuck *n.* outer husk of corn

shud-der *v.* to tremble uncontrollably

shuf-fle *v.* drag the feet

shun *v.* avoid deliberately

sib-ling *n.* children from the same parents

siege *n.* prolonged sickness

sieve *n.* strainer

sigh *v.* exhale a long breath

sight *n.* the ability to see with the eyes

sign *n.* the symbol used instead of words

sig-nal *n.* sign of warning

sig-na-ture *n.* name of a person, written by that person

sig-nif-i-cance *n.* the quality of being important

silent *adj.* making no sound

sil-hou-ette *n.* outline of something seen against light

sil-ver *n.* a white metallic element

sim-i-lar *adj.* almost the same

sim-ple *adj.* easy to do

sim-pli-fy *v.* make easy

sim-u-late *v.* have form

simulator *n.*

si-mul-ta-ne-ous *adj.* occurring at the same time

sin *n.* the breaking of a religious law

since *adv.* time before the present

sin-cere *adj.* being honest

sing *v.* use the voice to make musical tones

sin-gle *adj.* being one

sink *v.* to go down slowly

si-nus *n.* opening in the skull above the nose

si-ren *n.* loud noise, as a warning or signal

sit-u-ate *v.* to give a place to; to fix permanently

six *n.* the cardinal number 6, after five

six-teen *n.* the cardinal number 16, after fifteen

six-ty *n.* cardinal number 60, after fifty nine

size *n.* the measurement of something

skein *n.* quantity of yarn wound in loose loops

skel-e-ton *n.* the framework of one's bones

skep-tic *n.* the one who doubts something **skepticism** *n.*

sketch *n.* rough drawing

skid *v.* to slide to the side of the road

skill *n.* expertise; ability **skillful** *adj.*

skim *v.* to remove the top layer off a liquid **skimming** *n.*

skin *n.* outside covering of man

skip *v.* leap or jump lightly from the ground

skirt *n.* woman's garment worn below the waist

skull *n.* bony part of the head

sky *n.* upper atmosphere above the earth

sky-light *n.* window in the roof to admit light

slack *adj.* not taut or tense **slacken** *v.*

slan-der *n.* a false statement about another **-ous** *adj.*

slang *n.* informal language

slant *v.* to slope; lean

slap *n.* sharp blow with an open hand

slash *v.* reduce or limit greatly

slaugh-ter *v.* to kill the livestock for food

slave *n.* person made to work for another

slaw *n.* a chopped cabbage with dressing

sled *n.* vehicle mounted on runners for snow

sleek *adj.* smooth and shiny

sleep *n.* the natural state of one's rest **sleepiness** *n.*

sleet *n.* frozen rain

sleigh *n.* the vehicle mounted on runners

slen-der *adj.* being slim; being thin or narrow

slice *n.* thin cut

slide *v.* move smoothly across a surface

slight *adj.* being minor in degree **slightly** *adv.*

slim *adj.* being slender in one's shape **slimness** *n.*

slip *v.* loss one's balance

slith-er *v.* to slide along a surface

slo-gan *n.* motto

slope *v.* to slant upward or downward

slot *n.* thin opening **slotted** *v.*

slouch *n.* sagging in posture **sloucher** *n.*

slug-gish *v.* inactive; having little motion

slum *n.* neighborhood marked by poverty

slum-ber *v.* sleep

slump *v.* to decline or to fall suddenly

slur *v.* to insult

slurp *v.* to eat or to drink with noisy sounds

slush *n.* melting snow **-iness** *n.*

sly *adj.* being sneaky

smack *v.* to slap; loud kiss

small *adj.* little in size

small-pox *n.* kind of contagious disease

smart *adj.* intelligent

smash *v.* to break something into small pieces

smear *v.* to smudge **-er** *n.*

smell *v.* notice of scent; odor

smile *v.* express amusement by movement of the mouth

smock *n.* kind of loose-fitting outer garment

smog *n.* the mixture of smoke and fog

smoke *n.* cloudy mass from something burning

smolder *v.* burn slowly without a flame

smooth *adj.* flat

smor-gas-bord *n.* buffet meal with a variety of foods

smother *n.* suffocate

smudge *v.* smear with dirt

smug *adj.* to be self-satisfied

smug-gle *v.* to import goods into an area illegally

snag n. pull in a piece of fabric

snake n. a kind of scaly, long-bodied reptile

snap v. break suddenly

snare n. anything that entangles something

snarl v. to speak in an angry way **snarler** n.

snatch v. make a sudden move to grab something

sneak v. to move in a quiet, sly way or manner

sneer v. express scorn by the look on one's face

sneeze v. to expel the air from the nose

snick-er v. laugh partially under the breath

snor-kel n. device for breathing under water

snow n. frozen crystals of rain

snub v. treat with neglect

snug adj. being comfortable and safe **snugly** adv.

snug-gle v. lie closely for warmth or comfort

soak v. to become saturated with water

soar v. rise higher than usual

sob v. to weep deeply

so-ber adj. not intoxicated

so-cia-ble adj. enjoying the company of others **sociableness** n.

so-ci-e-ty n. working together for a purpose

so-ci-ol-o-gy n. study of society

sock n. short knitted covering for the foot

so-da n. kind of flavored, carbonated drink

soft-ware n. programs for computers

sog-gy adj. damp and wet

so-journ v. to make a temporary stay

sol-ace n. the comfort in time of grief

so-lar adj. relating to the sun

soldier n. person who serves in the military

sole n. single, the only one

sol-emn adj. being very serious in nature **-ness** n.

so-lic-it v. to try to obtain

sol-id adj. definite form, shape and volume

sol-id-ify v. to make solid; to unite firmly

sol-i-taire n. single gemstone

sol-i-tude n. isolation

so-lo n. musical performed by one person

sol-u-ble adj. being able to be solved **-ness** n.

solve v. to find the answer

som-ber adj. being dark; gloomy **somberness** n.

some adj. being of an indefinite number or amount

song n. the music adapted for singing

son n. male offspring

son-ic adj. pertaining to sound

son-net n. kind of poem of fourteen lines

soot n. black residue from fuel

soothe v. make comfortable

so-phis-ti-cat-ed adj. being worldly; subtle

soph-o-more n. second year high school student

so-pran-o n. highest female singing voice

sor-cery n. the supernatural powers one has

sor-did adj. very dirty

sore adj. a wound which is tender to the touch

sor-row n. mental suffering **sorrowfully** adv.

sor-ry adj. feeling sympathy

soul n. spirit in man

sound n. that which is heard

sour adj. being sharp to the taste **sourness** n.

source n. any point of origin

south n. the direction opposite of north

south-paw n. the left-handed person

sou-ve-nir n. item kept as a remembrance

sov-er-eign n. a ruler with supreme power

spa-cious adj. being large and roomy; vast

space n. unlimited area

spa-ghet-ti n. pasta made in long, thin pieces

span n. the space located between two objects

spank v. strike with the hand on the buttocks

spar v. fight; box

spare *n.* an extra

spar-kle *v.* reflect light

sparse *adj.* scant; few **sparseness** *n.*

spasm *n.* muscle contraction

spat-ter *v.* splash a liquid

spat-u-la *n.* the instrument used in cooking

spawn *n.* eggs of water animals

speak *v.* utter words **-able** *adj.*

spear *n.* weapon with a pointed head

spear-mint *n.* mint plant

spe-cial-ize *v.* to study a particular subject

spec-i-men *n.* sample

spec-ta-tor *n.* one who watches or observes

spec-trum *n.* band of colors

spec-u-late *v.* to think deeply about something **-lation** *n.*

speed *n.* rate of movement

spell *v.* to form words with proper letters

sphere *n.* round object

spice *n.* kind of pungently aromatic plant

spic-y *adj.* highly seasoned

spig-ot *n.* faucet

spi-der *n.* eight-legged insect

spike *n.* large, thick nail

spill *v.* allow something to run out of something

spin-ach *n.* widely cultivated leafy plant

spine *n.* the backbone

spir-it *n.* vital essence of man

spir-it-ed *adj.* being lively; full of energy

spite *n.* malicious bitterness

splash *v.* spatter a liquid

splash-down *n.* landing of a missile in the ocean

splen-did *adj.* being magnificent; wonderful

split *v.* part or separate

spoil *v.* destroy the value

spokes-man *n.* one who speaks on behalf of another

sponge *n.* skeleton of a sea animal that is used for absorbing liquid

spon-ta-ne-ous *adj.* to be done on an impulse

spoof *n.* a deception

spool *n.* a cylinder used for holding tape

spoon *n.* kind of eating and cooking utensil

spo-rad-ic *adj.* to be occurring occasionally

sport *n.* physical activity with set rules

spouse *n.* a person's husband or wife

spout *v.* cause to shoot forth

sprain *n.* twisting of a muscle

spray *n.* liquid dispersed in a fine mist

spread *v.* unfold or open fully

spright-ly *adj.* being vivacious, lively **sprightlyness** *n.*

sprin-kle *v.* to scatter something in small drops

sprint *n.* short, fast race

spruce *n.* evergreen tree

spry *adj.* quick; lively

spur *n.* sharp device worn on a rider's boot

spy *n.* the secret agent who obtains information

squab-ble *v.* petty argument

squad *n.* a small group of policemen

squall *n.* the sudden violent gust of wind

squan-der *v.* spend wastefully

square *n.* parallelogram with four equal sides

squash *n.* edible vegetable; game played with rackets

squat *v.* sit back on the heels

squaw *n.* an American Indian woman

squea-mish *adj.* being easily shocked **squeamishness** *n.*

squeeze *v.* press together

squelch *v.* to suppress completely; silence

squint *v.* close eyes partially

squir-rel *n.* rodent with gray-brown fur

squirt *v.* to eject in a thin stream **squirter** *n.*

stab *v.* to pierce something with a pointed weapon

sta-bi-lize *v.* to keep from changing

sta-ble *n.* place for lodging farm animals

stack *n.* the large pile of something **stacker** *n.*

sta-di-um *n.* large structure for holding sporting events

staff *n.* people employed to assist in business

stag *n.* adult male of animals

stag-ger *v.* to walk about unsteadily **staggering** *adj.*

stag-nant *adj.* to be standing still **stagnancy** *n.*

stain *n.* the discoloration from dirt, etc.

stair *n.* step or a series of steps

stake *n.* pointed rod; money put up as a wager

stale *adj.* having lost freshness

stalk *n.* the supporting stem of a plant

stall *n.* the place to confine animals

stal-wart *adj.* being large in frame; muscular

stamp *v.* to put one's foot down with force

stand *v.* to be in an upright position

stand-ard *n.* model which stands for comparison

stand-ing *n.* a reputation, or an achievement

sta-ple *n.* piece of metal for holding papers, etc.

star *n.* celestial bodies seen at night in the sky

starch *n.* the nutrient carbohydrates

stare *v.* to look with a direct gaze **starer** *n.*

stark *adj.* utter; desolate

star-let *n.* young actress

star-tle *v.* sudden surprise

starve *v.* to suffer from not having food

stash *v.* to hide or to store for safekeeping

state *n.* a nation; *v.* make known verbally

stat-ic *adj.* not moving

sta-tion *n.* the scheduled stopping place

sta-tis-tic *n.* the numerical data **statistical** *adj.*

stat-ue *n.* carved figure

stay *v.* to remain

stead *n.* position of another

stead-fast *adj.* not changing

stead-y *adj.* firmly placed

steal *v.* to take another person's property

steam *n.* the water in the form of vapor **steaminess** *n.*

steel *n.* various mixtures of iron, and carbon

steer *v.* to guide the course of something

stem *n.* main stalk of a plant

sten-cil *n.* form cut into a sheet of material **stenciling** *n.*

ste-nog-ra-phy *n.* a writing in shorthand

step *n.* move one foot at a time

ste-reo-phon-ic *adj.* three-dimensional effect of auditory perspective

ster-e-o-type *n.* conventional opinion or belief

ster-ile *adj.* being sanitary; unable to reproduce

stern *n.* rear of a boat or ship

steth-o-scope *n.* instrument used to listen to the internal sounds of a body

stew-ard *n.* one who manages another's property **-ship** *n.*

stick *n.* small branch of a tree; cause to adhere

stiff *adj.* not flexible **-ness** *n.*

sti-fle *v.* to suffocate

stig-ma *n.* the mark of a disgrace **stigmatize** *v.*

still *adj.* silent; motionless

still-birth *n.* the birth of a fetus that has no life

stim-u-late *v.* to increase one's vital energy

stim-u-lus *n.* something that excites to action

sting *v.* cause sharp pain

stin-gy *adj.* not giving freely **stinginess** *n.*

stink *v.* give off a foul odor

stip-u-late *v.* settle something by agreement

stir *v.* to mix a substance by moving it round and round **stirring** *adj.*

stir-rup *n.* support for the foot on a saddle

stitch *n.* work done by sewing

stock *n.* supply of goods kept on hand

stock-ade *n.* the barrier for protection

stock-y *adj.* being short and plump **stockiness** *n.*

stole *n.* long, narrow scarf

stom-ach *n.* digestive organ

stone *n.* small rock

stool n. three or four leg seat without a back

stop v. bring to a standstill

stor-age n. act of storing

store n. business offering merchandise for sale

storm n. violent wind with rain, snow, etc.

story n. fictitious tale

stout adj. being strong; being sturdy **stoutness** n.

stove n. device for cooking

stow v. pack or put away

strad-dle v. to spread legs wide apart

straight adj. being without curves or bends

strain v. stretch beyond a proper limit

strait n. the passageway which connects two bodies of water

strand n. land that borders a body of water; run aground

strange adj. being odd; peculiar **strangeness** n.

stran-gle v. kill by choking

strat-e-gy n. skillful planning

stray v. to roam or wander

streak n. narrow line or stripe

stream n. the small body of flowing water

street n. a type of thoroughfare in a city

strength n. power in general **strengthened** adj.

stren-u-ous adj. being of a vigorous effort **-ly** adv.

stress n. special significance

stretch v. extend fully

strew v. scatter about

strick-en adj. to be suffering, as from illness

strict adj. holding to rules exactly **strictly** adv.

strike v. hit with the hand; means of protest

strin-gent adj. having strict requirements

stroke n. movement of striking

stroll v. to walk in an unhurried way

stroll-er n. baby carriage

strong adj. physical power

struc-ture n. the manner of building

strug-gle v. put forth effort

strych-nine n. extremely poisonous substance

stub n. short, projecting part

stub-born adj. difficult to control or handle **-ness** n.

stud n. upright post, as in a building frame

stud-y n. applying the mind to acquire knowledge

stun v. knock senseless **stunningly** adv.

stunt n. the unusual performance of skill

stu-pid adj. mentally slow

stu-pen-dous adj. to be astonishing **stupendousness** n.

stur-dy adj. strongly built

stut-ter v. speak with repetitions of sound

sty n. inflammation of the edge of an eyelid; the pen for swine

style n. manner, type

suave adj. being smoothly pleasant in manner

sub-con-scious adj. to be not fully conscious

sub-di-vide v. to divide something into parts

sub-due v. bring under control

sub-ject n. the control over another

sub-ma-rine n. kind of underwater vessel

sub-merge v. to go under water

sub-mit v. surrender to another's authority

sub-or-di-nate adj. being of lower class

sub-se-quent adj. to be following in order

sub-side v. become less intense

sub-sid-i-ar-y adj. being one that helps

sub-si-dy n. financial aid

sub-sist v. continued existence

sub-stance n. matter of which anything consists

sub-stan-tial adj. of considerable size

sub-sti-tute n. that which takes the place of another

sub-ter-ra-ne-an adj. to be located underground

sub-tle adj. cunning

sub-tract v. take away from

sub-urb n. community near a large city

sub-way n. railway beneath the surface of the street

suc-ceed v. to gain a favorable accomplishment

suc-cess n. the achievement of something

suc-ces-sive adj. to be following in order

such adj. of that kind or thing

sud-den adj. without notice; unexpected

sue v. seek justice by legal processes

suede n. soft leather

suf-fer v. to feel pain or distress **suffering** n.

suf-fi-cient adj. as much that is needed or desired

suf-fix n. form added to the end of a word

suf-fo-cate v. stop breathing due to lack of oxygen

sug-gest v. to give an idea for action

su-i-cide n. the act of taking one's own life

suite n. the connected series of rooms

sulk v. be sullenly silent

sul-len adj. ill-humored; depressing **sullenness** n.

sul-try adj. being hot and humid; to be muggy

sum n. the result that is obtained by adding

sum-ma-ry n. giving the sum; expressed in few words

sum-mit n. the top and highest level of something

sum-mons n. order to appear

sun n. star around which other planets orbit

su-per adj. excellent

su-per-fi-cial adj. pertaining to a surface

su-per-in-tend-ent n. person who oversees

su-pe-ri-or adj. of higher rank

su-per-la-tive adj. highest degree of excellence

su-per-sede v. to take the place of **superseder** n.

su-per-son-ic adj. speed greater than sound

su-per-sti-tion n. belief from faith in chance

su-per-vise v. to direct and to control

sup-ple adj. bending easily without breaking

sup-ple-ment n. part that compensates for what is lacking

sup-pli-ant adj. entreating or begging earnestly

sup-ply v. to provide with what is needed

sup-port v. to hold the weight of something

sup-pose v. to assume something as true **-edly** adv.

sup-press v. to end something by force

su-preme adj. being of the highest authority

sure adj. impossible to doubt

surf-board n. bouyant board used to ride incoming waves

sur-face n. the external layer of something

surge v. increase suddenly

sur-geon n. physician who practices surgery

sur-ly adj. rude; rough

sur-mise v. to guess

sur-mount v. to overcome something

sur-name n. family's last name

sur-pass v. to be greater than **surpassable** adj.

sur-plus n. amount beyond what is needed

sur-prise v. to come upon one unexpectedly; to cause to feel amazed or astonished **surpriser** n., **-ingly** adv.

sur-ren-der v. cease resistance; to give up or to yield possession of something

sur-rey n. a four-wheeled, horse-driven carriage

sur-ro-gate n. a person acting in place of another

sur-round v. to extend around all the edges; to enclose or to shut something in

sur-veil-lance n. kind of close observation kept over one, especially as a suspect

sur-vey v. examine in detail; to determine boundries or the position of something

sur-vive v. continue to exist;

outlast something

sus-cep-ti-ble *adj.* capable of emotional impression

su-shi *n.* a Japanese dish of thin slices of fresh, raw fish

sus-pect *v.* distrust; have doubt; have a suspicion

sus-pend *v.* cause to hang; temporary relief of a position

sus-pense *n.* the feeling of being uncertain

sus-pi-cion *n.* the instance of suspecting something is wrong without proof **-ous** *adj.*, **-ously** *adv.*

sus-tain *v.* hold up and keep from falling

su-ture *n.* stitching together of an incision

swab *n.* mop for cleaning floors, decks, etc.

swad-dle *v.* to wrap closely, using a long strip of flannel

swag-ger *v.* to walk with a proud or conceited air

swal-low *v.* cause food to pass from the mouth to the stomach **swallower** *n.*

swamp *n.* low marshy ground saturated with water

swap *v.* trade something for something in return

swarm *n.* the large number of insects, as bees; a large group of people or things

swat *v.* to hit something with a violent blow

swatch *n.* strip of cloth cut off a larger piece

swath *n.* the area of grass cut by a machine

swathe *v.* to bind or to wrap with a bandage

sway *v.* to move or swing from right to left or side by side

sway-back *n.* the unnatural sagging of the back

swear *v.* make an affirmation under oath

sweat *n.* secrete moisture from the pores of the skin

sweat-er *n.* a knitted or crocheted garment with or without sleeves attached

sweat gland *n.* gland that secretes sweat

sweep *v.* clean with a broom

sweet *adj.* having a sugary flavor or taste **sweetness** *n.*

swell *v.* increase in size or bulk

swel-ter *v.* to suffer from extreme heat

swerve *v.* turn aside from the regular course

swin-dle *v.* to practice fraud **swindler** *n.*

swine *n.* kind of domesticated hog or pig

swing *v.* to move freely back and forth

swirl *n.* a whirling motion, such as of water

switch *n.* to exchange **-er** *n.*

sword *n.* kind of weapon with a long blade

syl-la-ble *n.* pronouncing division of a word

sym-bol *n.* the representation of something

sym-pa-thy *n.* affection during a time of sadness

sym-pho-ny *n.* concert by a large orchestra

symp-tom *n.* sign of change in body functions

syn-chro-nize *v.* to take place at the same time

syn-co-pate *adj.* modify, as a piece of music

syn-di-cate *n.* a unit of companies

syn-drome *n.* symptoms that indicate a disorder

syn-o-nym *n.* the word that means the same

syn-op-sis *n.* shortened statement or narrative

sy-ringe *n.* instrument that is used to inject or draw fluids from the body

sys-tem *n.* the method of doing something

sys-tem-at-ic *adj.* formulated or presented as a system systematically *adv.*, **-ness** *n.*

sys-tem-atism *n.* the practice of organizing or forming intellectual systems

sys-tem-atize *v.* to arrange in accordance with a definite scheme or plan

sys-to-le *n.* contraction of the heart that pumps blood through the aorta and pulmonary artery

T, t the twentieth letter of the English alphabet

tab *n.* strip, flap, or small loop that projects from something *slang* bill or total, as for a meal

ta-ba-nid *n.* member of large bloodsucking insects such as the horse fly

tab-ard *n.* a cape; the tunic worn by a knight

tab-by *n.* type of domestic cat having a striped coat

tab-er-na-cle *n.* portable shelter or structure used by the Jews during their journey out of Egypt

ta-bes dor-sa-lis *n.* disease of the spinal cord

ta-bla *n.* hand drums used for Hindu music

tab-la-ture *n.* a tabular surface or structure

ta-ble *n.* article of furniture
v. put off something until another time

tab-leau *n.* a striking picture representation

ta-ble-cloth *n.* the cloth placed over the table before eating

ta-ble-land *n.* braod flat land; a plateau

ta-ble-spoon *n.* the large spoon usually for serving

ta-ble-spoon-ful *n.* amount large enough to fill a tablespoon

tab-let *n.* pad used for writing

ta-ble ten-nis *n.* a game of hitting a plastic ball on a table

ta-ble-ware *n.* the eating utinsils for the table

tab-loid *n.* small newspaper

ta-boo *n.* custom or rule against doing, using, or mentioning something

tab-o-ret *n.* portable stand; a stool without arms

tab-u-lar *adj.* pertaining to or arranged in a table or list
tabularly *adv.*

tab-u-late *v.* to place into tabular formation
tabulation *n.*

tab-u-la-tor *n.* a machine or person who tabulates items

tach-i-nid *n., adj.* type of fly whose larva is used for insect control

ta-chis-to-scope *n.* instrument for testing visual perception
-ically *adv.,* -ic *adj.*

ta-chom-e-ter *n.* an instrument for measuring velocity and speed

tach-y-car-di-a *adj.* rapid heart movement or action

ta-chyg-ra-phy *n.* the art of shorthand; stenography
-ic, -ical *adj.*

tac-it *adj.* understood; expressed or implied nonverbally; implicit

tac-i-turn *adj.* speaking infrequently taciurnity *n.*

tack-le *n.* equipment used for fishing or other sports or occupations tackled *v.*

tacky *adj.* being slightly sticky; shabby; to be lacking style or good taste
-iness *n.,* -ily *adv.*

ta-co *n., pl.* -cos type of Mexican or Spanish food made of a tortilla

tact *n.* having the ability to avoid what would disturb or offend someone

tac-tic *n.* way or method of working toward a goal

tad *n.* small boy; an insignificant degree or amount

tae-ni-a-sis *n.* a sickness due to the presence of tapeworms

taf-fe-ta *n.* stiff, smooth fabric of rayon, nylon, or silk
taffetized *adj.*

taff-rail *n.* rail around the stern of a boat or ship

taf-fy *n.* candy made from sugar, butter and flavoring

taf-fy pull *n.* an informal party where guest make and pull taffy

tag *n.* piece of plastic, metal, paper, or other material that is attached to something in order to identify it; children's game tagger *n.*

tag-board *n.* very sturdy cardboard used to make posters, and signs

tail *n.* posterior extremity, extending from the end or back of an animal Tails opposite side of a coin from heads

tai·lor n. one whose profession is making, mending, and altering clothing v. adapt for a specific purpose

taint v. spoil, contaminate, or pollute n. blemish or stain

take v. seize or capture; to get possession of; to move to a different place; to choose

talc n. soft, fine-grained, smooth mineral used in making talcum powder

tale n. story or recital of relating events that may or may not be true

tal·ent n. aptitude, or ability of a person **talented** adj.

talk v. communicate by words or speech; to engage in chatter or gossip

tall adj. greater than average height; of a designated or specified height; imaginary, as a tall tale **tallness** n.

tal·low n. hard fat rendered from sheep or cattle, used to make candles, lubricants, and soap **tallow** adj.

tal·ly n., pl. **-ies** record or counting of money, amounts, or scores

tal·on n. long, curved claw found on birds or animals

tam·bou·rine n. percussion instrument made of a small drum with jingling metal disks around the rim

tame adj. not wild or ferocious; domesticated or manageable v. make docile or calm **tamely** adv., **tamer**, **tameness** n.

tam·per v. change, meddle, or alter something; to use corrupt measures; to scheme **-proof** adj., **-er** n.

tan·dem n. any arrangement that involves two or more things, animals, or persons arranged one behind the other

tang n. sharp, distinct taste, smell, or quality

tan·gent n. line that touches a curved line but does not intersect or cross it; a sudden change from one course to another **tangency** n., **tangential** adj.

tan·ger·ine n. small citrus fruit

tan·gi·ble adj. capable of being appreciated or felt by the sense of touch **tangibly** adv.

tan·gle v. mix, twist, or unite in a confused manner making separation difficult **tangle**, **tanglement** n.

tank n. large container for holding or storing a gas or liquid **tankful** n.

tan·ta·lize v. tease or tempt by holding or keeping something just out of one's reach **tantalizer** n.

tan·ta·lum n. metallic element symbolized by Ta

tan·trum n. fit; an outburst or a rage of bad temper

tap v. strike repeatedly, usually while making a small noise; to strike or touch gently

tape n. narrow strip of woven fabric **tape** v.

ta·per n. very slender candle v. become gradually smaller or thinner at one end

tap·es·try n., pl. **-ies** thick fabric woven with designs and figures

tap·i·o·ca n. bead-like substance used for thickening and for puddings

taps n. pl. Mil. bugle call that signals lights out, also sounded at memorial and funeral services

tar·dy adj. late; not on time **tardily** adv., **tardiness** n.

tar·get n. object marked to shoot at; an aim or goal

tar·iff n. duty or tax on merchandise coming into or going out of a country

tar·nish v. become discolored or dull; to lose luster; to spoil **tarnishable** adj.

tar·ot n. set of 22 cards used for fortune-telling, each card showing a virtue, an elemental force, or a vice

tar·pau·lin n. sheet of waterproof canvas used as a protective covering

tar·ry v. linger, or delay

tart adj. sharp; sour; cutting,

biting in tone or meaning

tartly adv., **tartness** n.

task n. bit of work, usually assigned by another; a job

tas-sel n. ornamental decoration made from a bunch of string or thread

taste n. ability to sense or determine flavor in the mouth; a personal liking or dislike **tasteful**, **tasteless** adj., **taster** n.

tat-tle v. reveal the secrets of another by gossiping

tattle-tale n. one who betrays secrets concerning others; a person, usually a child, who informs on others

tat-too n. permanent design or mark made on the skin by pricking and inserting an indelible dye **tattooer** n.

taught v. past tense of teach

taut adj. tight; emotionally strained **-ly** adv., **-ness** n.

tau-tol-o-gy n., pl. **-ies** redundancy; a statement which is an unnecessary repetition of the same idea

tav-ern n. inn; an establishment or business licensed to sell alcoholic beverages **taverner** n.

tax n. payment imposed and collected from individuals or businesses by the government v. strain

tax--ex-empt adj. exempted from tax

tax-i v. move along the ground or water surface on its own power before taking off

taxi-cab n. vehicle for carrying passengers for money

tax-i-der-my n. art or profession of preparing, stuffing, and mounting animal skins **taxidermist** n.

tea n. small tree or bush which grows where the climate is very hot and damp; a drink made by steeping the dried leaves of this shrub in boiling water

teach v. communicate skill or knowledge; to give instruction **-ing** n., **-able** adj.

teach-er n. person who teaches; one who instructs

team n. two or more players on one side in a game; a group of people trained to work together; two or more animals harnessed to the same implement

tear v. become divided into pieces; to separate; to rip into parts or pieces

tear n. fluid secreted by the eye to moisten and cleanse v. to cry **teary** adj.

tease v. make fun of; to bother; to annoy

tech-ne-tium n. metallic element symbolized by Tc

tech-ni-cal adj. expert; derived or relating to technique; related to industry or mechanics **technically** adv.

tech-nique n. technical procedure or method of doing something

tech-nol-o-gy n., pl. **-ies** application of scientific knowledge to serve man in industry, commerce, medicine and other fields

te-di-ous adj. boring; taking a long time **tediously** adv.

teem v. swarm or crowd; to abound; to be full of

teens pl., n. ages between 13 and 19; the years of one's life between 13 and 19

teeth pl., n. plural of tooth

tel-e-cast n. television broadcast **telecast** v.

tel-e-gram n. message sent or received by telegraph

tel-e-graph n. system for communicating; a transmission sent by wire or radio

te-lep-a-thy n. communication by means of mental processes rather than ordinary means **-ic** adj., **-ist** n.

tel-e-phone n. system or device for transmitting conversations by wire **telephoner** n.

tel-e-pho-to adj. relating to a camera lens which produces a large image of a distant object **-graph** n.

tel-e-scope n. instrument which contains a lens system which makes distant objects appear larger and nearer

telescopic adj.

tel-e-thon n. long telecast used to raise money for a worthy cause

tel-ex n. teletype communications by means of automatic exchanges

tell v. relate or describe; to command or order

tem-per n. state of one's feelings **temperable** adj.

tem-per-a-ment n. personality; a characteristic way of thinking, reacting **temperamental** adj.

tem-per-ance n. moderation; restraint from drinking alcoholic beverages

tem-per-ate adj. avoiding extremes; moderate **-ly** adv.

tem-per-a-ture n. measure of heat or cold in relation to the body or environment; an elevation in body temperature above the normal 98.6

tem-pest n. severe storm, with snow, hail, rain, or sleet

tem-ple n. place of worship

tem-po n., pl. **-pos** or **-pi** Mus. rate of speed at which a musical composition is to be played

tem-po-rar-y adj. lasting for a limited amount of time

tempt n. encourage or draw into a foolish or wrong course of action

te-na-cious adj. persistent; stubborn **tenaciously** adv., **tenaciousness** n.

ten-ant n. person who pays rent to occupy another's property **tenantable** adj.

Ten Commandments n. ten rules of moral behavior which were given to Moses by God

tend v. to be inclined or disposed; to look after

ten-den-cy n., pl. **-ies** disposition to act or behave in a particular way

ten-der adj. fragile; soft; not hard or tough; painful or sore when touched

ten-don n. band of tough, fibrous tissues that connect a muscle and bone

ten-nis n. sport played with a ball and racket by 2 or 4 people

ten-or n. adult male singing voice, above a baritone

tense adj. taut or stretched tightly; nervous **tense** v.

ten-sion n. condition of stretching or the state of being stretched **-less** adj.

tent n. portable shelter made by stretching material over a supporting framework

ten-ta-cle n. long, unjointed, flexible body part that projects from certain invertebrates, as the octopus

ten-ta-tive adj. experimental; not definite **-ly** adv.

ten-ure n. the right, state, or period of holding something, as an office or property **-ed, -ial** adj.

tep-id adj. lukewarm

ter-cen-ten-a-ry n., pl. **-ries** time span of 300 years

term n. phrase or word; a limited time or duration

ter-mi-nal adj. of, forming, or located at the end; final

ter-mi-nate v. bring to a conclusion or end **-ion** n.

ter-mite n. winged or wingless insect which lives in large colonies feeding on wood

ter-race n. open balcony or porch

ter-ra cot-ta n. hard, baked clay used in ceramic pottery

ter-rain n. surface of an area, as land

ter-ra-pin n. edible turtle of North America

ter-res-tri-al adj. something earthly; not heavenly

ter-ri-ble adj. causing fear or terror; intense; extreme; horrid **-ly** adv., **-ness** n.

ter-rif-ic adj. terrifying Informal excellent; causing amazement **-ally** adv.

ter-ri-fy v. fill with fear or terror; to frighten; to menace **terrified, terrifying** adj.

ter-ri-to-ry n., pl. **-ies** area, usually of great size, which is controlled by a particular government -ial adj.

ter-ror n. extreme fear

ter-ror-ism n. the use of intimidation to attain one's goals or to advance one's cause

terse adj. brief; using as few words as possible without loss of force or clearness

tersely adj., terseness n.

test n. examination to determine one's knowledge, skill, intelligence or other qualities tester n.

tes-ta-ment n. legal document which states how one's personal property is to be distributed upon his death

Testament n. one of the two sections of the Bible

testamentary adj.

tes-tate adj. having left a valid will

tes-ti-fy v. give evidence while under oath testifier n.

tes-ti-mo-ni-al n. formal statement; a gift, dinner, reception, or other sign of appreciation given to a person as a token of esteem

tes-ti-mo-ny n., pl. -ies a solemn affirmation made under oath

tes-tis n., pl. testes sperm producing gland of the male

teth-er n. rope or chain which fastens an animal to something

text n. actual wording of an author's work; the main part of a book textual adj.

text-book n. book used by students to prepare their lessons

tex-tile n. cloth made by weaving; yarn or fiber for making cloth textile adj.

tex-ture n. look, surface, or feel of something

thal-li-um n. metallic element resembling lead, symbolized by Tl

than conj. in comparison with or to something

thank v. express one's gratitude; to credit

thank-ful adj. feeling or showing gratitude

thanks pl., n. expression of one's gratitude

that adj., pl. those person or thing present or being mentioned

thaw v. change from a frozen state to a liquid or soft state; to melt thaw n.

the-a-tre or the-a-ter n. building adapted to present dramas, motion pictures, plays, or other performances

the-at-ri-cal adj. extravagant; designed for show, display, or effect theatricals n.

theft n. act or crime of stealing; larceny

their adj. & pron. possessive case of they

the-ism n. belief in the existence of God theist n., theistic adj.

them pron. objective case of they

theme n. topic or subject of something thematic adj.

them-selves pron. them or they; a form of the third person plural pronoun

then adv. at that time; soon or immediately

adj. being or acting in or belonging to or at that time

thence adv. from that place

thence-forth adv. from that time on

the-oc-ra-cy n., pl. -ies government by God or by clergymen who think of themselves as representatives of God -tic adj., -tically adv.

the-ol-o-gy n., pl. -ies religious study of the nature of God, beliefs theologian n.

the-o-rize v. analyze theories

the-o-ry n., pl. -ies general principle or explanation which covers the known facts

ther-a-peu-tics n. medical treatment of disease therapeutist n.

ther-a-py n., pl. -ies treatment of certain diseases -ist n.

there adv. in, at, or about that place; toward, into, or to

thereabouts, thereafter, thereby, therefore, therefrom, therein adv.

ther-mal adj. having to do with or producing heat

ther-mo-plas-tic adj. pliable and soft when heated or warm but hard when cooled **thermoplastic** n.

ther-mo-stat n. device that automatically responds to temperature changes and activates equipment to adjust the temperature to correspond with the setting on the device **-ic** adj.

the-sau-rus n., pl. **-ruses** or **-ri** book which contains synonyms and antonyms

these pron. plural of this

the-sis n., pl. **-ses** formal argument or idea; a paper written by a student that develops an idea

they pron. two or more beings just mentioned

they'd contr. they had

they'll contr. they will

they're contr. they are

they've contr. they have

thick adj. having a heavy or dense consistency

thief n., pl. **thieves** person who steals

thieve v. take by theft **thievery** n.

thigh n. part of the leg between the hip and the knee of man

thin adj. having very little depth or extent from one side or surface to the other; not fat; slender **thinly** adv.

thing n. something not recognized or named; an idea, or conception

things n. one's belongings

think v. exercise thought; to use the mind **-able** adj.

third n. next to the second in time or place; the last in a series of three

thirst n. uncomfortably dry feeling in the throat and mouth; a desire for liquids

this pron., pl. **these** person or thing that is near, present, or just mentioned

this-tle n. prickly plant usually producing a purplish or yellowish flower

thith-er adv. to that place; there

thong n. narrow strip of leather used for binding

tho-rax n., pl. **-raxes** or **-races** section or part of the human body between the neck and abdomen

tho-ri-um n. radioactive metallic element symbolized by Th

thorn n. sharp, pointed, woody projection on a plant stem **thorny** adj.

thor-ough adj. complete; intensive **thoroughly** adv.

thor-ough-bred adj. being of a pure breed of stock

thor-ough-fare n. public highway, road or street

those adj. & pron. plural of that

though adv. nevertheless; in spite of

thought n. process, act, or power of thinking; an idea **thoughtful, thoughtless** adj.

thrash v. to beat or strike with a whip; to move violently about; to defeat **-er** n.

threat n. expression or warning of intent to do harm

thresh v. to separate seed from a harvested plant mechanically

thresh-old n. horizontal piece of wood or other material which forms a doorsill

threw v. past tense of throw

thrice adv. three times

thrift n. careful use of money and other resources

thrill n. feeling of sudden intense excitement, fear, or joy **-ing** adj., **-ingly** adv.

thrive v. to prosper; to be healthy; to do well in a position

throat n. front section or part of the neck containing passages for food and air

throb v. to beat, move, or vibrate in a pulsating way

throm-bo-sis n., pl. **-ses** development of a blood clot in a blood vessel or in the heart cavity

throng n. large group or crowd
v. to crowd around or into

throt-tle n. valve which controls the flow of fuel to an engine

through prep. from the beginning to the end

through-out prep. in every place; everywhere; at all times

throw v. to toss or fling through the air with a motion of the arm

thru prep., adv. & adj. through

thrush n. small songbird having a brownish upper body and spotted breast

thrust v. to push; to shove with sudden or vigorous force

thru-way or **throughway** n. major highway; an expressway

thud n. dull thumping sound

thug n. tough or violent gangster **thuggish** adj.

thumb n. short first digit of the hand

thump n. blow with something blunt or heavy

thun-der n. loud explosive sound made as air is suddenly expanded by heat and then quickly contracted again

thus adv. in this or that way

thwack v. strike hard, using something flat

thwart v. prevent from happening

thy adj. pertaining to oneself

thyme n. an aromatic mint herb whose leaves are used in cooking

thy-roid adj. Anat. pertaining to the thyroid gland

thy-rox-ine n. hormone secreted by the thyroid gland

ti-ar-a n. bejeweled crown

tick n. one of a series of rhythmical tapping sounds made by a clock; a small bloodsucking parasite

tick-et n. printed slip of paper or cardboard allowing its holder to enter a specified event or to enjoy a privilege

tick-le v. to stroke lightly so as to cause laughter; to amuse or delight **tickler** n.

tid-bit n. choice bit of food, news, or gossip

tide n. rise and fall of the surface level of the ocean

tid-ings pl., n. news; information about events

ti-dy adj. well arranged; neat; orderly **tidiness** n.

tie v. to secure or bind with a rope or other similar material; to make a bow or knot in; to match an opponent's score

tier n. layer or row placed one above the other **-ed** adj.

ti-ger n. large carnivorous cat having tawny fur with black stripes

tiger-eye n. yellow-brown gemstone

tight adj. set closely together; bound or securely firm; not loose adv. firmly

tight-en v. to become or make tighter **tightener** n.

tights pl., n. skintight stretchable garment

till prep. & conj. until; unless or before v. to cultivate; to plow.

til-er n. machine or person that tills land

tilt v. to tip, as by raising one end

tim-ber n. wood prepared for building

timber line n. height on a mountain beyond which trees cannot grow

time n. continuous period measured by clocks, watches, and calendars
adj. of or pertaining to time

tim-id adj. shy

tin n. white, soft, malleable metallic element, symbolized by Sn

tinc-ture n. tinge of color; an alcohol solution of some medicinal substance

tin-der n. readily combustible substance or material

tine n. narrow pointed spike or prong, as of a fork or antler

tinge v. to impart a faint trace

of color n. trace of color

tin-gle v. to feel a stinging or prickling sensation

tin-kle v. to produce a slight, sharp series of metallic ringing sounds **tinkle** n.

tin-ny adj. pertaining to or composed of tin

tin-sel n. thin strips of glittering material used for decorations **tinsel** adj.

tint n. slight amount or trace of color v. to color

ti-ny adj. minute; very small

tip-ple v. drink an alcoholic beverage to excess

tip-sy adj. partially intoxicated

ti-rade n. long, violent speech

tire v. become or make weary n. outer covering for a wheel, usually made of rubber, serving to absorb shock and to provide traction

tis-sue n., Biol. similar cells and their products developed by plants and animals

ti-ta-ni-um n. metallic element symbolized by Ti

tithe n. income given voluntarily for the support of a church **tithe** v., **tither** n.

tit-il-late v. excite or stimulate in a pleasurable way

ti-tle n. identifying name of a book, poem, play, or other creative work; a name or mark of distinction indicating a rank or an office

to prep. toward, opposite or near; in contact with; as far as; used as a function word indicating an action, movement, or condition suggestive of movement; indicating correspondence, dissimilarity, similarity, or proportion

toad n. tailless amphibian

toaster n. device for toasting bread

to-bac-co n. plant widely cultivated for its leaves

to-bog-gan n. long sled-like vehicle without runners

to-day adv. on or during the present day

tod-dle v. walk unsteadily

toddler n. small child

tod-dy n., pl. -ies drink made with hot water, sugar, spices, and liquor

toe n. one of the extensions from the front part of a foot; the part of a stocking, boot or shoe

tof-fee n. chewy candy made of butter and brown sugar

to-geth-er adv. in or into one group, mass, or body; regarded jointly

toil v. to labor very hard and continuously **toilsome** adj.

toi-let n. porcelain apparatus with a flushing device, used as a means of disposing body wastes

toi-lette n. act of washing, dressing, or grooming oneself

tol-er-ate v. to put up with; to endure; to suffer

toll v. fixed charge for travel across a bridge or along a road v. to sound a bell in repeated single, slow tones

tom n. male turkey or cat

tom-a-hawk n. ax used as a weapon or tool by North American Indians

to-ma-to n., pl. -toes garden plant cultivated for its edible fruit; the fruit of such a plant

tomb n. vault for burying the dead; a grave

tomb-stone n. stone used to mark a grave

to-mor-row n. day after the present day

ton n. measurement of weight equal to 2,000 pounds

tone n. vocal or musical sound that has a distinct pitch v. to change or soften the color

tongs pl., n. implement with two long arms joined at one end

tongue n. muscular organ attached to the floor of the mouth, used in tasting, chewing, and speaking

ton-ic n. medicine or other agent used to restore health

to-night n. this night; the night that is coming

ton-sil n. one of a pair of tissue

similar to lymph nodes, found on either side of the throat

ton-sil-lec-to-my *n.* surgical removal of tonsils

too *adv.* also; as well; more than is needed

tool *n.* implement used to perform a task **tooling** *n.*

tooth *n., pl.* **teeth** one of the hard, white structures rooted in the jaw and used for chewing and biting; the small, notched, projecting part of any object, such as a gear, comb or saw

toothed, toothless *adj.*

top *n.* highest part or surface of anything; a covering or lid; the highest degree

to-paz *n.* gemstone

top-coat *n.* outer coat

top-ic *n.* subject discussed in an essay, thesis, speech or other discourse; the theme

top-most *adj.* uppermost

to-pog-ra-phy *n., pl.* **-ies** detailed description of a region or place

top-ple *v.* to fall; to overturn

To-rah *n.* body of law and wisdom contained in Jewish Scripture and oral tradition; a parchment scroll that contains the first five books of the Old Testament

torch *n.* stick of resinous wood which is burned to give light *Slang* to set fire to

tor-ment *n.* extreme mental anguish or physical pain *v.* to cause terrible pain; to pester, harass, or annoy **-ingly** *adv.,* **-or** *n.*

tor-na-do *n., pl.* **-does** *or* **-dos** whirling, violent windstorm accompanied by a funnel-shaped cloud that travels a narrow path over land

tor-pe-do *n., pl.* **-oes** large, self-propelled, underwater missile launched from a ship, containing an explosive charge

tor-pid *adj.* having lost the power of motion or feeling; dormant **-ity** *n.,* **-ly** *adv.*

tor-rent *n.* swift, violent

stream **torrential** *adj.*

tor-rid *adj.* parched and dried by the heat **torridly** *adv.*

tor-sion *n.* act or result of twisting **torsional** *adj.*

tor-so *n., pl.* **-sos** *or* **-si** trunk of the human body

tort *n., Law* wrongful act requiring compensation for damages

tor-toise *n.* turtle that lives on the land

tor-tu-ous *adj.* marked by repeated bends, turns, or twists; devious **-ness** *n.*

tor-ture *n.* infliction of intense pain as punishment

toss *v.* fling or throw about continuously; to throw up in the air *n.* a throw

tot *n.* young child; a toddler

to-tal *n.* whole amount or sum; the entire quantity *adj.* absolute; complete

to-tal-i-tar-i-an *adj.* characteristic of a government controlled completely by one party **totalitarian** *n.*

tote *v.* carry something on one's arm or back

to-tem *n.* animal or plant regarded as having a close relationship to some family clan or group

tot-ter *v.* walk unsteadily

tou-can *n.* brightly colored tropical bird having a very large thin bill

touch *v.* allow a part of the body, as the hands, to feel or come into contact with; join; to come next to; to have an effect on; to move emotionally **touchable** *adj.*

tough *adj.* resilient and strong enough to withstand great strain without breaking or tearing; difficult to cut or chew **n.** unruly person; a thug **toughness** *n.*

tou-pee *n.* wig worn to cover a bald spot on one's head

tour *n.* trip with visits to points of interest; a journey **tourism, tourist** *n.*

tour-na-ment *n.* contest involving a number of competitors for a title or championship

tour-ni-quet *n.* device used to temporarily stop the flow of blood through an artery

tou-sle *v.* to mess up

tout *v.* to solicit customers

tow *v.* drag or pull, as by a chain or rope

to-ward or towards *prep.* in the direction of; just before; somewhat before; regarding

tow-el *n.* absorbent piece of cloth used for drying or wiping **towel** *v.*

tow-er *n.* very tall building or structure; a skyscraper **towering** *adj.*

town *n.* collection of houses and other buildings larger than a village and smaller than a city

tox-e-mi-a *n., Pathol.* blood poisoning; a condition in which the blood contains toxins

tox-ic *adj.* relating to a toxin; destructive, deadly, or harmful

tox-in *n.* poisonous substance produced by chemical changes in plant and animal tissue

toy *n.* object designed for the enjoyment of children; a small trinket; a bauble

trace *n.* visible mark or sign of a thing, person, or event; something left by some past agent or event

track *n.* mark, as a footprint, left by the passage of anything; a regular course; a set of rails on which a train runs; a circular or oval course for racing

tract *n.* extended area, as a stretch of land

trac-tor *n.* diesel or gasoline-powered vehicle used in farming

trac-tor trail-er *n.* large truck having a cab and no body

trade *n.* business or occupation; skilled labor; a craft; an instance of selling or buying; a swap **trader** *n.*

trade-mark *n.* brand name which is legally the posses-

sion of one company and cannot be used by another

tra-di-tion *n.* customs passed down from one generation to another **traditional** *adj.*

tra-duce *v.* to betray

traf-fic *n.* passage or movement of vehicles; trade, buying and selling

trag-e-dy *n., pl. -ies* extremely sad or fatal event or course of events

trail *v.* to draw, drag, or stream along behind; to follow in the tracks of

trail-er *n.* one who trails; a large vehicle that transports objects and is pulled by another vehicle

trait *n.* quality or distinguishing feature, such as one's character

trai-tor *n.* person who betrays his country

tra-jec-to-ry *n., pl. -ies* curved line or path of a moving object

tram-mel *n.* long, large net used to catch birds or fish

tramp *v.* to plod or walk with a heavy step

tram-ple *v.* to tread heavily; to stomp; to inflict injury, pain **trampler** *n.*

tram-po-line *n.* canvas device on which an athlete or acrobat may perform

trance *n.* stupor, daze, mental state, or condition, such as produced by drugs or hypnosis

tran-quil *adj.* very calm, quiet

trans-act *v.* to perform, carry out, conduct, or manage business in some way **transaction, transactor** *n.*

tran-scend *v.* to pass beyond; to exceed; to surpass

tran-scribe *v.* to make copies of something; to adopt or arrange

tran-script *n.* written copy

tran-scription *n.* process or act of transcribing

trans-fer *v.* remove, shift, or carry from one position to another **transferable** *adj.*

trans-fig-ure *v.* change the

outward appearance or form **transfiguration** *n.*

trans-fix *v.* to pierce; to hold motionless, as with terror, awe or amazement **-ion** *n.*

trans-form *v.* change or alter completely in nature, form or function **-ation** *n.*

trans-fuse *v.* transfer liquid by pouring from one place to another

trans-gress *v.* to go beyond the limit or boundaries

tran-sient *adj.* not staying or lasting very long; moving from one location to another **transiently** *adv.*

tran-sit *n.* passage or travel from one point to another

trans-late *v.* change from one language to another while retaining the original meaning **-ion, -or** *n.*

trans-lu-cent *adj.* diffusing and admitting light but not allowing a clear view of the object

trans-mis-sion *n.* act or state of transmitting *Mech.* gears and associated parts of an engine which transmit power to the driving wheels of an automobile or other vehicle

trans-mit *v.* dispatch or convey from one thing, person, or place to another

trans-mute *v.* change in nature, kind, or substance

tran-som *n.* small, hinged window over a doorway

trans-par-ent *adj.* admitting light so that images and objects can be clearly viewed; obvious **transparency** *n.*

tran-spire *v.* to happen; to take place **-ation** *n.*

trans-plant *v.* remove a living plant from where it is growing and plant it in another place; to remove a body organ from one person and implant it in the body of another, as a kidney transplant

trans-port *v.* carry or move from one place to another

trans-pose *v.* reverse the place

or order of

trans-sex-u-al *n.* person whose sex has been changed surgically

trap *n.* device for holding or catching animals; anything which deliberately catches or stops people or things *v.* catch in a trap

tra-peze *n.* short horizontal bar suspended by two ropes, used for acrobatic exercise or stunts

trau-ma *n., pl.* **-mas** *or* **-mata** severe wound caused by a sudden physical injury; an emotional shock causing lasting and substantial damage to a person's psychological development

tra-vail *n.* strenuous mental or physical exertion

trav-el *v.* journey or move from one place to another

tra-verse *v.* pass over, across, or through

trawl *n.* strong fishing net which is dragged through water

tray *n.* flat container having a low rim, used for carrying, holding, or displaying something

treach-er-ous *adj.* disloyal; deceptive **treachery** *n.*

tread *v.* to walk along, on, or over; to trample

treas-ure *n.* hidden riches; something regarded as valuable

treas-ur-y *n., pl.* **-ies** place where public or private funds are kept

treat *v.* behave or act toward; regard in a given manner; provide entertainment or food for another at one's own expense or cost

treat-ment *n.* manner or act of treating; medical care

tre-foil *n.* any of various plants having three leaflets with red, purple, yellow, or pink flowers

trek *v.* make a slow and arduous journey **trekker** *n.*

trel-lis *n.* latticework frame used for supporting vines

trem-ble v. shake involuntarily, as with fear or from cold **-er** n., **-ly** adj.

tre-men-dous adj. extremely huge, large, or vast Slang wonderful

trem-or n. quick, shaking movement; any continued and involuntary trembling or quavering of the body

trench n. ditch; long, narrow excavation in the ground

trend n. general inclination, direction, or course; a fad

tres-pass v. infringe upon another's property

tres-tle n. bar or beam supported by four legs

tri-al n. in law, the examination and hearing of a case before a court of law

tri-an-gle n., Geom. plane figure bounded by three sides and having three angles **triangular** adj.

tribe n. group of people composed of several villages, districts, or other groups which share a common language, culture, and name

trib-u-la-tion n. great distress or suffering

tri-bun-al n. decision making body

trib-ute n. action of respect or gratitude to someone

tri-ceps n., Anat. large muscle at the back of the upper arm

trick n. action meant to fool, as a scheme; a prank; a feat of magic **tricky** adj.

trick-er-y n. deception

trick-le v. flow in droplets or a small stream **trickle** n.

tri-col-or n. the French flag having three colors

tri-cy-cle n. small vehicle having three wheels, propelled by pedals

tri-dent n. long spear with three prongs, used as a weapon

tried adj. tested and proven reliable or useful

tri-fle n. something of little value or importance; a dessert made with cake, jelly, wine, and custard

trig-ger n. lever pulled to fire a gun; a device used to release or start an action

v. to start

trim v. clip or cut off small amounts in order to make neater; to decorate

adj. neat **trim** n.

trin-ket n. small piece of jewelry

tri-o n. set or group of three

trip n. travel from one place to another; a journey; a loss of balance

tri-ple adj. having three parts

trip-let n. one of three born at the same time

tri-pod n. three-legged stand

trite adj. used too often; common

tri-umph v. be victorious n. victory **triumphantly** adv.

triv-i-al adj. insignificant; of little value or importance

trol-ley n. streetcar powered by electricity from overhead lines

tro-phy n., pl. -ies prize or object, such as a plaque, awarded to someone for his success, victory, or achievement

troth n. good faith; the act of pledging one's fidelity

trou-ble n. danger; affliction; need; distress; an effort v. bother; to worry; to be bothered **troubler** n.

troupe n. group, especially of the performing arts

trou-sers pl., n. outer garment that covers the body from the waist down

trous-seau n. wardrobe, linens, and other similar articles of a bride

tru-ant n. person who is absent from school without permission **truancy** n.

truce n. agreement to stop fighting; a cease fire

trudge v. walk heavily and wearily; plod

true adj. in accordance with reality or fact; not false; real; loyal; faithful

trunk n. main part of a tree; the human body, excluding

the head, arms and legs; a sturdy box for packing

trust n. confidence or faith in a person or thing

trust-y adj. reliable

truth n., pl. **truths** facts corresponding with actual events or happenings; sincerity or honesty **-ful** adj., **-fully** adv.

try v. make an attempt; to make an effort; to strain; to hear or conduct a trial; to place on trial **-ing** adj.

tub n. round, low, flat-bottomed, vessel with handles on the side

tu-ba n. large, brass wind instrument having a low range

tu-ber-cu-lo-sis n. contagious lung disease of humans and animals caused by microorganisms

tuck n. flattened fold of material, usually stitched in place

tug v. strain and pull vigorously n. hard pull

tu-i-tion n. payment for instruction, as at a private school or college

tu-lip n. bulb-bearing plant, having upright cup-like blossoms.

tum-ble v. fall or cause to fall; to perform acrobatic rolls, somersaults, and similar maneuvers

tum-ble-down adj. ramshackle; in need of repair

tum-brel n. cart which can discharge its load by tilting

tu-mor n., Pathol. swelling on or in any part of the body; an abnormal growth which may be malignant or benign

tu-mult n. confusion and noise of a crowd; a riot

tu-na n., pl. **-na** or **-nas** any of several large marine food fish

tune n. melody which is simple and easy to remember; agreement

tu-nic n. loose garment extending to the knees, worn by ancient Romans and Greeks

tun-nel n. underground or underwater passageway

tur-bu-lent adj. marked by a violent disturbance

turf n. layer of earth with its dense growth of grass and matted roots

tur-moil n. state of confusion or commotion

turn v. to move or cause to move around a center point; to revolve or rotate

turn-over n. process or act of turning over; an upset; a change or reversal

tur-pen-tine n. thick sap of certain pine trees; a clear liquid manufactured from this sap

tusk n. long, curved tooth, as of an elephant or walrus

tu-tor n. person who teaches another person privately

tux-e-do n. semiformal dress suit worn by men

twice adv. double; two times

twinge n. sudden, sharp pain

twin-kle v. gleam or shine with quick flashes; to sparkle

twirl v. to rotate or cause to turn around and around

twist-er n., Slang tornado; a cyclone; one that twists

twit v. tease about a mistake

twitch v. move or cause to move with a jerky movement

two-bits n. twenty-five cents

two-faced adj. double-dealing

ty-coon n., Slang business person of wealth and power

tyke n. small child

type n. class or group of persons or things

ty-phoid n., Path. acute, infectious disease caused by germs in drink or food, resulting in high fever and intestional hemorrhaging

ty-phoon n. tropical hurricane

typ-i-cal adj. exhibiting the characteristics of a certain class or group **-ly** adv.

typ-i-fy v. be characteristic or typical of

typ-ist n. operator of a typewriter

ty-rant n. absolute, unjust, or cruel ruler control unfairly

U, u the twenty-first letter of the English alphabet

ubiq-ui-tous *adj.* being in all places at the same time **-ness** *n.*, **-ly** *adv.*

U-boat *n.* the submarine of the Germans

ud-der *n.* milk-producing organ pouch of some female animals, having two or more teats

ugh *interj.* used to express disgust or horror

ug-li-fy *v.* to cause or to make something or one ugly

ug-li-ness *n.* the state of being ugly; that which is ugly

ug-ly *adj.* offensive; unpleasant to look at **-ily** *adv.*

uh *interj.* to express hesitation.

u-ku-le-le *n.* small, four-stringed musical instrument

ul-cer *n.* festering, inflamed sore on a mucous membrane or on the skin that results in the destruction of the tissue

ul-cero-gen-ic *adj.* inclined to develop ulcers

ul-na *n.*, *Anat.* one of the two bones of the forearm **-nar** *adj.*

ul-ti-mate *adj.* final; ending; most extreme **-ly** *adv.*

ul-ti-ma-tum *n.*, *pl* **-tums, -ta** final demand, proposal, or choice

ultra- *prefix.* beyond the scope, range, or limit of something

ul-tra-mod-ern *adj.* extremely advanced or modern in style

ul-tra-son-ic *adj.* relating to sound frequencies inaudible to humans

ul-tra-vi-o-let *adj.* producing radiation having wavelengths just shorter than those of visible light and longer than those of X rays

um-bil-i-cal cord *n.* structure by which a fetus is attached to its mother, serving to supply food and dispose of waste

um-brel-la *n.* collapsible frame covered with plastic or cloth, held above the head as protection from sun or rain

um-pire *n.* in sports, the person who rules on plays in a game *v.* act as an umpire

ump-teen *adj.*, *Slang* indefinitely large number

un- *prefix* reverse or opposite of an act; removal or release from

un-a-ble *adj.* not having the mental capabilities

un-ac-com-pa-nied *adj.* alone; without a companion *Mus.* solo

un-ac-count-a-ble *adj.* without an explanation; mysterious; not responsible

un-ac-cus-tomed *adj.* not used to or in the habit of; not ordinary

u-nan-i-mous *adj.* agreed to completely; based on the agreement of all

un-armed *adj.* lacking means for protection

un-as-sum-ing *adj.* modest and not showy

un-at-tached *adj.* not engaged, going steady, or married

un-a-void-able *adj.* inevitable; unstoppable **-ly** *adv.*

un-a-ware *adj.* not realizing

un-bear-a-ble *adj.* not possible to endure; intolerable

un-be-com-ing *adj.* unattractive; not pleasing; not proper, polite or suitable for the situation

un-be-known *or* **unbeknownst** *adj.* not known; without one's knowledge

un-be-liev-able *adj.* incredible; hard to accept; not to be believed **unbelievably** *adv.*

un-called for *adj.* not necessary or needed; not requested

un-can-ny *adj.* strange, odd, or mysterious; exceptional

un-cer-tain *adj.* doubtful; not sure; not known; hard to predict

un-changed *adj.* having nothing new or different

un-civ-i-lized *adj.* without culture or refinement; without an established cultural

un-cle *n.* brother of one's mother or father

un·clean *adj.* immoral; dirty; not decent

un·clothe *v.* uncover or undress

un·com·fort·a·ble *adj.* disturbed; not at ease physically or mentally

un·com·mon *adj.* rare; odd; unusual; extraordinary

un·com·pro·mis·ing *adj.* firm; unwilling to give in or to compromise

un·con·cern *n.* lack of interest; disinterest; indifference

un·con·di·tion·al *adj.* without conditions **-ly** *adv.*

un·con·scious *adj.* not mentally aware; done without thought; not on purpose

un·con·sti·tu·tion·al *adj.* contrary to the constitution or the basic laws of a state or country

un·couth *adj.* acting or speaking crudely, unrefined; clumsy or awkward

un·cov·er *v.* remove the cover from something; to disclose

un·de·cid·ed *adj.* unsettled; having made no firm decision; open to change

un·de·ni·a·ble *adj.* not open to doubt or denial; not possible to contradict

un·der *prep.* below, in place or position; in a place lower than another; less in degree, number, or other quality; inferior in rank, quality, or character; during the reign or period; in accordance with; less than the required amount; insufficient

under *prefix.* location beneath or below; lower in importance or rank

un·der·brush *n.* small bushes, vines, and plants that grow under tall trees

un·der·clothes *pl., n.* clothes worn next to the skin; underwear

un·der·de·vel·oped *adj.* not fully mature or grown; lacking modern communications and industry

un·der·foot *adj.* underneath or below the feet; being so close to one's feet as to be in the way

un·der·go *v.* to have the experience of; to be subjected to

un·der·grad·u·ate *n.* college or university student studying for a bachelor's degree

un·der·hand *adj.* done deceitfully and secretly **underhandedly** *adv.*

un·der·line *v.* to draw a line directly under something

un·der·mine *v.* to weaken; to make less strong

un·der·neath *adv.* beneath or below; on the under side; lower

un·der·pass *n.* road or walk that goes under another

un·der·priv·i·leged *adj.* deprived of economic and social advantages

un·der·rate *v.* rate or value below the true worth

un·der·score *v.* emphasize

un·der·sell *v.* sell for less than a competitor

un·der·side *n.* side or part on the bottom

un·der·stand *v.* comprehend; to realize

un·der·stand·a·ble *adj.* able to comprehend **-ly** *adv.*

un·der·state *v.* make too little of the actual situation **understatement** *n.*

un·der·stood *adj.* agreed upon by all

un·der·stud·y *v.* to learn another person's part or role in order to be able to replace him if necessary

un·der·take *v.* set about to do a task; to pledge oneself to a certain job; to attempt

un·der·tak·er *n.* person who prepares the dead for burial

un·der·tone *n.* low, quiet voice; a pale or subdued color visible through other colors

un·der·tow *n.* underwater current which runs in the opposite direction of the surface current

un·der·wa·ter *adj.* occurring, happening or used beneath the surface of the water

un-der-write v. sign or write at the end of something; to finance; to assume a risk by means of insurance assume responsibility for; to undertake to pay a written pledge of money **underwriter** n.

un-de-sir-a-ble adj. offensive; not wanted **-ly** adv.

un-do v. cancel; to reverse; to loosen or unfasten

un-done adj. not finished; unfastened; ruined

un-du-late v. to move from side to side with a flowing motion; to have a wavy shape **undulation** n.

un-dy-ing adj. without end

un-earth v. dig up from the earth; to find or discover

unearthly adj. strange; not from this world

un-eas-y adj. feeling or causing distress or discomfort; embarrassed

un-em-ployed adj. without a job; without work **unemployment** n.

un-e-qual adj. not even; not fair; not of the same size or time

un-e-ven adj. not equal; varying in consistency or form; not balanced

un-e-vent-ful adj. lacking in significance; calm

un-expect-ed adj. surprising; happening without warning **unexpectedly** adv.

un-fail-ing adj. constant, unchanging

un-fair adj. not honest; marked by a lack of justice

un-faith-ful adj. breaking a promise or agreement; without loyalty

un-fa-mil-iar adj. not knowing; strange; foreign

unfavorable adj., not desired; harmful; unpleasant

un-feel-ing adj. without sympathy; hardhearted; with-out sensation

un-fit adj. not suitable; not qualified; in poor body or mental health

un-fold v. open up the folds of and lay flat; to reveal gradually **unfoldment** n.

un-fore-seen adj. not anticipated or expected

un-for-get-ta-ble adj. impossible or hard to forget; memorable **-ly** adv.

un-for-tu-nate adj. causing or having bad luck, damage, or harm

un-found-ed adj. not founded or based on fact; groundless; lacking a factual basis

un-friend-ly adj. showing a lack of kindness; not friendly

un-furl v. unroll or unfold; to open up or out

un-fur-nished adj. without furniture

un-god-ly adj. wicked; evil; lacking reverence for God **ungodliness** n.

un-grate-ful adj. not thankful; no appreciation

un-guent n. healing or soothing salve; ointment

un-happy adj. sad; without laughter or joy; not satisfied or pleased

un-heard adj. not heard; not listened to

un-heard--of adj. not known or done before; without precedent

un-hook v. release or undo from a hook

u-ni-corn n. mythical animal resembling a horse, with a horn in the center of its forehead

u-ni-cy-cle n. one wheeled vehicle with pedals

un-i-den-ti-fied flying object n. flying object that cannot be explained or identified

u-ni-form n. identical clothing worn by the members of a group to distinguish them from the general population **uniformly** adv.

u-ni-fy v. come together as one; to unite

un-in-hab-it-ed adj. not lived in; empty

un-in-ter-est-ed adj. having no interest or concern in; not interested

un-ion n. act of joining

together of two or more groups or things; a group of countries or states joined under one government; a marriage; an organized body of employees who work together to upgrade their working conditions and wages **Union** The United States

u-nique *adj.* unlike any other; sole

u-ni-sex *adj.* adaptable and appropriate for both sexes

u-ni-son *n.* in music, the exact sameness of pitch, as of a tone

u-nit *n.* any one of several parts regarded as a whole; an exact quantity that is used as a standard of measurement; a special section

u-nite *v.* join or come together for a common purpose

United Nations *n.* international organization formed in 1945; comprised of nearly all the countries of the world whose purpose is to promote security, economic development, and peace

United States of America *n.* country bordering the Atlantic and Pacific Oceans, Mexico, and Canada

u-ni-ty *n.*, *pl.* -ies fact or state of being one; accord; agreement; harmony

u-ni-valve *n.* mollusk having a one-piece shell, such as a snail

u-ni-ver-sal *adj.* having to do with the world or the universe in its entirety

u-ni-verse *n.* the world, stars, planets, space, and all that is contained

u-ni-ver-si-ty *n.*, *pl.* -ies educational institution offering undergraduate and graduate degrees in a variety of academic areas

un-just *adj.* not fair; lacking justice or fairness

un-kempt *adj.* poorly groomed; messy

un-kind *adj.* harsh; lacking in sympathy, concern, or understanding

un-known *adj.* strange; unidentified; not known; not familiar **unknown** *n.*

un-lead-ed *adj.* containing no lead

un-like *prep.* dissimilar; not alike; not equal in strength or quantity

un-lim-it-ed *adj.* having no boundaries or limitations

un-load *v.* take or remove the load; to unburden; to dispose or get rid of by selling in volume

un-lock *v.* open, release, or unfasten a lock; open with a key

un-loose *v.* loosen or undo; to release

un-luck-y *adj.* unfortunate; having bad luck; disappointing or unsuitable **unluckily** *adv.*

un-manned *adj.* designed to operate or be operated without a crew of people

un-men-tion-a-ble *adj.* improper or unsuitable

un-mis-tak-a-ble *adj.* very clear and evident; understood; obvious

un-mor-al *adj.* having no moral knowledge

un-nat-u-ral *adj.* abnormal or unusual; strange; artificial

un-nec-es-sar-y *adj.* not needed; not appropriate **unnecessarily** *adv.*

un-nerve *v.* frighten; to upset

un-num-bered *adj.* countless; not identified by number

un-oc-cu-pied *adj.* empty; not occupied

un-pack *v.* remove articles out of trunks, suitcases, or boxes

un-pleas-ant *adj.* not agreeable; not pleasant

un-pop-u-lar *adj.* not approved or liked

un-pre-dict-a-ble *adj.* not capable of being foretold; not reliable

un-pre-pared *adj.* not equipped or ready

un-pro-fes-sion-al *adj.* contrary to the standards of a profession; having no professional status

un-prof-it-a-ble *adj.* showing or giving no profit; serving no purpose

un-qual-i-fied *adj.* lacking the proper qualifications; unreserved

un-rav-el *v.* to separate threads; to solve; to clarify; to come apart

un-re-al *adj.* having no substance or reality

un-rea-son-a-ble *adj.* not according to reason; exceeding all reasonable limits

un-re-li-a-ble *adj.* unable to be trusted; not dependable

un-re-served *adj.* done or given without reserve; unlimited

un-re-strained *adj.* not held back, forced, or affected

un-ru-ly *adj.* disorderly; difficult to subdue or control

un-sat-is-fac-to-ry *adj.* unacceptable; not pleasing

un-screw *v.* to loosen or unfasten by removing screws from

un-scru-pu-lous *adj.* without morals, guiding principles, or rules

un-seat *v.* cause to lose one's seat; to force out of office

un-sel-fish *adj.* willing to share; thinking of another's wellbeing before one's own

un-set-tle *v.* cause to be upset or excited; to disturb

un-sheathe *v.* draw a sword from a sheath or other case

un-sight-ly *adj.* not pleasant to look at; ugly

un-skilled *adj.* having no skills or training in a given kind of work

un-sound *adj.* having defects; not solidly made

un-speak-a-ble *adj.* of or relating to something which can not be expressed

un-sta-ble *adj.* not steady or firmly fixed; having the tendency to fluctuate or change

un-stead-y *adj.* not secure; unstable; variable

un-sub-stan-tial *adj.* lacking strength, weight, or solidity

un-suit-a-ble *adj.* unfitting; not suitable; not appropriate for a specific circumstance

un-tan-gle *v.* free from snarls or entanglements

un-thank-ful *adj.* ungrateful

un-think-a-ble *adj.* unimaginable

un-ti-dy *adj.* messy; showing a lack of tidiness

un-tie *v.* unfasten or loosen; to free from a restraint or bond

un-til *prep.* up to the time of *conj.* to the time when; to the degree or place

un-time-ly *adj.* premature; before the expected time

un-told *adj.* not revealed; not told; inexpressible; cannot be described

un-touch-a-ble *adj.* cannot be touched; incapable of being obtained or reached

un-true *adj.* not true; contrary to the truth; not faithful; disloyal

un-truth *n.* something which is not true **untruthful** *adj.*

un-used *adj.* not put to use; never having been used

un-u-su-al *adj.* not usual; uncommon **unusually** *adv.*

un-ut-ter-a-ble *adj.* incapable of being described or expressed; unpronounceable

un-veil *v.* remove a veil from; to uncover; to reveal

un-war-y *adj.* not cautious or careful; careless

un-whole-some *adj.* unhealthy; morally corrupt or harmful

un-will-ing *adj.* reluctant; not willing **unwillingly** *adv.*

un-wind *v.* undo or reverse the winding of; to untangle

un-wise *adj.* lacking good judgment or common sense

un-wor-thy *adj.* not deserving; not becoming or befitting; lacking merit or worth; shameful **unworthiness** *n.*

up *adv.* from a lower position to a higher one; on, in, or to a higher level, position, or place; to a greater degree or amount; in or into a specific action or an excited state, as they stirred up trouble; under consideration, as up for discussion; in a safe, protected place; totally, completely, as the building was burned up

up-beat n., Mus. relatively unaccented beat preceding the down beat adj. optimistic; happy

up-bring-ing n. process of teaching and rearing a child

up-com-ing adj. about to take place or appear

up-date v. revise or bring uptodate; to modernize

up-draft n. upward current of air

up-grade v. increase the grade, rank, or standard of

up-hill adv. up an incline adj. hard to accomplish; going up a hill or incline

up-hol-ster v. cover furniture with fabric covering

up-keep n. cost and work needed to keep something in good condition

up-land n. piece of land which is elevated

up-on prep. on

up-per adj. higher in status, position or location n. the part of a shoe to which the sole is attached

up-per--class adj. economically or socially superior

up-right adj. having a vertical direction or position; honest n. something standing vertically

up-ris-ing n. revolt; a rebellion; an insurrection

up-roar n. confused, loud noise; a commotion

up-root v. detach completely by pulling up the roots

up-set v. capsize; to turn over; to throw into confusion or disorder; to overcome; to beat unexpectedly adj. capsized; overturned; distressed; troubled -ter n.

up-stage adj. & adv. toward or at the back part of a stage

up-start n. one who has risen quickly to power or wealth

up-tight adv. nervous, or tense

up-ward or **upwards** adv. from a lower position to or toward a higher one

u-ra-ni-um n. hard, heavy, shiny metallic element that is radioactive

urge v. encourage, push, or drive; to recommend persistently and strongly

ur-gent adj. requiring immediate attention

urine n. in man and other mammals, the yellowish fluid waste produced by the kidneys

Us pl., pron. objective case of we; used as an indirect object, direct object

us-a-ble or **useable** adj. fit or capable of being used **usability** n., usably adv.

us-age n. way or act of using something; the way words are used

use v. put into action; to emply for a special purpose; to employ on a regular basis; to exploit for one's own advantage

u-su-al adj. ordinary or common; regular; customary **usually** adv., usualness n.

u-surp v. take over by force without authority. **usurpation**, usurper n.

u-ten-sil n. tool, implement, or container

u-ter-us n. organ of female mammals within which young develop and grow before birth **uterine** adj.

u-til-i-ty n., pl. -ies state or quality of being useful; a company which offers a public service

u-til-ize v. make or put to use

ut-most adj. of the greatest amount or degree; most distant **utmost** n.

u-to-pi-a n. condition or place of perfection or complete harmony

u-vu-la n. fleshy projection which hangs above the back of the tongue **uvular** adj.

V, v the twenty-second letter of the English alphabet

va-cant *adj.* empty; not occupied; lacking an occupant

va-cate *v.* leave; to cease

va-ca-tion *n.* period of time away from work for pleasure, relaxation, or rest

va-ca-tion-er *n.* one who takes a trip or vacation

va-ca-tion-ist *n.* one who goes on a vacation

vac-ci-nal *adj.* referring or relating to a vaccination

vac-ci-nate *v.* inject with a vaccine so as to produce immunity to an infectious disease

vac-ci-na-tion *n.* inoculation with a vaccine

vac-cine *n.* solution of weakened or killed microorganisms, as bacteria or viruses, injected into the body to produce immunity to a disease

vac-il-late *v.* oscillate; sway -tor *n.*, -ingly *adv.*

vac-u-ole *n.* small space in the tissues having fluid or air

vac-u-um *n.*, *pl.* -ums, -ua space which is absolutely empty

vag-a-bond *n.* homeless person who wanders from place to place

va-gar-y *n.*, *pl.* -ies eccentric or capricious action or idea vagarious *adj.*

va-gi-na *n.*, *pl.* -nas, -nae *Anat.* canal or passage extending from the uterus to the external opening of the female reproductive system

va-gi-ni-tis *n.* inflammation of the vagina

va-grant *n.* roaming from one area to another without a job vagrancy *n.*

vague *adj.* not clearly expressed; not sharp or definite vaguely *adv.*

vain *adj.* conceited; lacking worth or substance -ly *adv.*

val-ance *n.* decorative drapery across the top of a window

vale *n.* a valley

val-e-dic-to-ri-an *n.* student ranking highest in a graduating class

val-en-tine *n.* card or gift sent to one's sweetheart on Valentine's Day, February 14th

val-et *n.* man who takes care of another man's clothes and other personal needs; a hotel employee

val-iant *adj.* brave; exhibiting valor valiance, valor *n.*

val-id *adj.* founded on facts or truth *Law* binding; having legal force

val-ley *n.*, *pl.* -leys low land between ranges of hills

val-or *n.* bravery -ous *adj.*

val-u-a-ble *adj.* of great value or importance -less *adj.*

val-ue *n.* quality or worth of something that makes it valuable; material worth

valve *n.* movable mechanism which opens and closes to control the flow of a substance through a pipe or other passageway

va-moose *v. Slang* leave in a hurry

vam-pire *n.* in folklore, a dead person believed to rise from the grave at night to suck the blood of sleeping persons; a person who preys on others

van *n.* large closed wagon or truck

va-na-di-um *n.* metallic element symbolized by V

van-dal-ism *n.* malicious defacement or destruction of private or public property

vane *n.* metal device that turns in the direction the wind is blowing

va-nil-la *n.* flavoring extract used in cooking and baking

van-ish *v.* disappear suddenly; to drop out of sight

van-i-ty *n.*, *pl.*, -ies conceit; extreme pride in one's ability

van-tage *n.* superior position; an advantage

va-por *n.* moisture or smoke suspended in air, as mist or fog -ish, -ous *adj.*

var-i-a-ble *adj.* changeable; tending to vary; inconstant

variableness n., **variably** adv.

var-i-ance n. state or act of varying; difference; conflict

var-i-a-tion n. result or process of varying; the degree or extent of varying

var-i-e-gat-ed adj. having marks of different colors **variegate** v.

va-ri-e-ty n., pl., -ies state or character of being varied or various; a number of different kinds; an assortment

var-i-ous adj. of different kinds **variousness** n.

var-mint n., Slang a troublesome animal; an obnoxious person

var-nish n. solution paint used to coat or cover a surface with a hard, transparent, shiny film

var-si-ty n., pl., -ies best team representing a college, university, or school

var-y v. change; to make or become different; to be different

vas-cu-lar adj., Biol. having to do with vessels circulating fluids, as blood

va-sec-to-my n., pl. -ies method of male sterilization

vast adj. very large or great in size **vastly** adv., **vastness** n.

vault n. room for storage and safekeeping, as in a bank, usually made of steel; a burial chamber

veg-e-ta-ble n. plant, as the tomato, green beans, lettuce, raised for the edible part

veg-e-tar-i-an n. person whose diet is limited to vegetables

veg-e-ta-tion n. plants or plant life which grow from the soil

ve-hi-cle n. a motorized device for transporting goods, equipment, or passengers

veil n. a piece of transparent cloth worn on the head or face for concealment or protection

vein n., Anat. vessel which transports blood back to the heart after passing through the body **vein** v.

ve-lour n. soft velvet-like woven cloth

vel-vet n. fabric made of rayon, cotton, or silk

vend-er or **vendor** n. person who sells, as a peddler

ven-det-ta n. fight or feud between blood-related persons

ven-er-a-ble adj. meriting or worthy of respect by reason of dignity, position, or age

venereal disease n. contagious disease, as syphilis, or gonorrhea, which is typically acquired through sexual intercourse

ve-ne-tian blind n. window blind having thin, horizontal slats

ven-i-son n. edible flesh of a deer

ven-om n. poisonous substance secreted by some animals, as scorpions or snakes **venomous** adj.

ve-nous adj. of or relating to veins

vent n. means of escape or passage from a restricted area; an opening which allows the escape of vapor, heat, or gas

ven-ti-late v. expose to a flow of fresh air for refreshing, curing, or purifying purposes   -ion, -or n.

ven-ture n. course of action involving risk, chance, or danger, especially a business investment

ven-ue n. place where a crime or other cause of legal action occurs; the locale of a gathering

verb n. part of speech which expresses action, existence, or occurrence

ver-bal adj. expressed in speech; expressed orally; not written **verbally** adv., **verbalize** v.

ver-ba-tim adv. word for word

ver-be-na n. American garden plant

verge n. extreme edge or rim; margin; the point beyond which something begins

ver-sa-tile adj. having the

capabilities of doing many different things; having many functions or uses

verse *n.* writing that has a rhyme; poetry; a subdivision of a chapter of the Bible

ver-sion *n.* an account or description told from a particular point of view; a translation from another language, especially a translation of the Bible

ver-so *n.*, *pl.* **-sos** left-hand page

ver-sus *prep.* against; in contrast to; as an alternative of

ver-te-bra *n.*, *pl.* **-brae, -bras** one of the bony or cartilaginous segments making up the spinal column

ver-tex *n.*, *pl.* **-es, -tices** highest or topmost point; the pointed top of a triangle

ver-ti-cal *adj.* in a straight up-and-down direction

ver-y *adv.* to a high or great degree; truly; absolutely; exactly

ves-per *n.* evening prayer service; a bell to call people to such a service

ves-sel *n.* hollow or concave utensil, as a bottle, kettle, container, or jar; a hollow craft designed for navigation on water

vest *n.* sleeveless garment open or fastening in front

ves-tige *n.* trace or visible sign of something that no longer exists **vestigial** *adj.*, **vestigially** *adv.*

ves-try *n.*, *pl.* **vestries** room in a church used for meetings

vet *n.*, *Slang* veterinarian; a veteran

vet-er-an *n.* person with a long record or experience in a certain field; one who has served in the military

vet-er-i-nar-i-an *n.* one who is trained and authorized to give medical treatment to animals

vet-er-i-nar-y *adj.* pertaining to or being the science and art of prevention and treatment of animals

ve-to *n.*, *pl.* **vetoes** power of a government executive, as the President or a governor, to reject a bill passed by the legislature

vex *v.* to bother or annoy

vi-a *prep.* by way of; by means of

vi-a-duct *n.* bridge, resting on a series of arches

vi-al *n.* small, closed container used especially for liquids

vi-brate *v.* move or make move back and forth or up and down **vibration** *n.*

vi-car-i-ous *adj.* undergoing or serving in the place of someone or something else; experienced through sympathetic or imaginative participation in the experience of another

vice *n.* immoral habit or practice; evil conduct

vi-ce ver-sa *adv.* with the order or meaning of something reversed

vi-chy-ssoise *n.* soup made from potatoes, chicken stock, and cream, flavored with leeks or onions and usually served cold

vi-cin-i-ty *n.*, *pl.* **-ies** surrounding area or district; the state of being near in relationship or space

vi-cious *adj.* dangerously aggressive; having the quality of immorality **-ly** *adv.*

vic-tim *n.* person who is harmed or killed by another **victimize** *v.*

vic-tor *n.* person who conquers; the winner

vic-to-ri-ous *adj.* being the winner in a contest **victoriously** *adv.*

vic-to-ry *n.*, *pl.* **-ies** defeat of those on the opposite side

vid-e-o *adj.* being, related to, or used in the reception or transmission of television

vid-e-o disc *n.* disc containing recorded images and sounds

vid-e-o game *n.* computerized game displaying on a display screen

vid-e-o term-in-al n. *Computer Science* computer device having a cathoderay tube for displaying data on a screen

vie v. strive for superiority

view n. act of examining or seeing; a judgment or opinion

vig-il n. a watch with prayers kept on the night before a religious feast; a period of surveillance

vig-or n. energy or physical strength; intensity of effect or action   vigorous adj.

vile adj. morally disgusting, miserable, and unpleasant vilely adv., vileness n.

vil-la n. a luxurious home in the country; a country estate

vil-lage n. incorporated settlement, usually smaller than a town   villager n.

vil-lain n. evil or wicked person -ous adj., -y n.

vin-di-cate v. to clear of suspicion; to set free vindication n.

vin-dic-tive adj. showing or possessing a desire for revenge; spiteful

vine n. plant whose stem needs support as it climbs or clings to a surface

vin-e-gar n. a tart, sour liquid derived from cider or wine

vin-tage n. the grapes or wine produced from a particular district in one season

vi-nyl n. variety of shiny plastics, similar to leather, often used for clothing and for covering furniture

vi-o-la n. stringed instrument, slightly larger and deeper in tone than a violin

vi-o-late v. break the law or a rule; to disrupt or disturb a person's privacy violation n.

vi-o-lence n. physical force or activity used to cause harm, damage, or abuse

vi-o-let n. small, low-growing plant with blue, purple, or white flowers; a purplish-blue color

vir-gin n. person who has never had sexual intercourse adj. in an unchanged or natural state

vir-ile adj. having the qualities and nature of a man; capable of sexual performance in the male -ity n.

vir-tu n. love or knowledge of fine objects of art

vir-tue n. morality, goodness or uprightness; a special type of goodness   -ous adj.

vi-rus n. any of a variety of microscopic organisms which cause diseases

vis-cid adj. sticky; having an adhesive quality

vis-i-bil-i-ty n., pl. -ies degree or state of being visible; the distance that one is able to see clearly

vis-i-ble adj. apparent; exposed to view

vi-sion n. power of sight; the ability to see; an image created in the imagination; a supernatural appearance

vis-it v. journey to or come to see a person or place n. a professional or social call *Slang* to chat -or, -ion n.

vi-su-al adj. visible; relating to seeing or sight

vi-tal adj. essential to life; very important   vitally adv.

vi-ta-min n. any of various substances which are found in foods and are essential to good health

vit-re-ous adj. related to or similar to glass

vi-va-cious adj. filled with vitality or animation; lively

viv-id adj. bright; brilliant; intense; having clear, lively, bright colors vividly adv.

viv-i-fy v. give life to

vo-cab-u-lar-y n., pl. -ies list or group of words and phrases, usually in alphabetical order; all the words that a person uses or understands

vo-cal adj. of or related to the voice; uttered by the voice; to speak freely and loudly n. vocal sound   vocally adv.

vo-ca-tion n. career, occupation, or profession

vo-cif-er-ate v. utter or cry out loudly; to shout

vogue n. leading style or fashion; popularity

voice n. sounds produced by speaking; the ability or power to produce musical tones v. to express; to utter

void adj. containing nothing; empty; not inhabited

voile n. a fine, soft, sheer fabric used for making light clothing and curtains

volt-age n. amount of electrical power, given in terms of the number of volts

vol-ume n. capacity or amount of space or room; a book; a quantity; the loudness of a sound

vol-un-tar-y adj. done cooperatively or willingly; from one's own choice

vol-un-teer n. one who offers himself for a service of his own free will adj. consisting of volunteers

vo-lup-tu-ous adj. full of pleasure; delighting the senses; sensuous; luxury

vom-it v. eject contents of the stomach through the mouth

vo-ra-cious adj. having a large appetite; insatiable

vote n. expression of one's choice by voice, by raising one's hand, or by secret ballot **voter** n.

vo-tive adj. performed in fulfillment of a vow

vouch v. verify or support as true; to guarantee

vow n. solemn pledge or promise, especially one made to God; a marriage vow

vow-el n. sound of speech made by voicing the flow of breath within the mouth; a letter representing a vowel

vul-gar adj. showing poor manners; crude; improper; immoral or indecent

vul-ner-a-ble adj. open to physical injury or attack

vul-ture n. large bird of the hawk family, living on dead animals; a greedy person

W, w the twenty-third letter of the English alphabet

wad n. small crumpled mass or bundle **wad** v.

wad-ding n. the material used for stuffing and filling

wad-dle v. walk with short steps and swing from side to side **waddle, waddler** n.

wade v. walk through a substance as mud or water which hampers one's steps

wad-er n. the waterproof trousers used for wading

wad-ing pool n. a small pool

wa-fer n. small, thin, crisp cracker, cookie, or candy

waf-fle n. pancake batter cooked in a waffle iron

waft v. drift or move gently, as by the motion of water or air **waft** n.

waf-ture n. a wavelike motion or movement

wag v. move quickly from side to side or up and down n. playful, witty person **waggish** adj.

wage n. the payment of money for one's labor or services v. to conduct

wa-ger v. make a bet

wage scale n. levels of wages paid to an employee

wag-gish adj. being done for sport or fun **-ness** n.

wag-on n. four-wheeled vehicle used to transport goods; a station wagon; a child's four-wheeled cart with a long handle

wag-on-er n. one who drives or guides a wagon

wag-on train n. group of wagons traveling the land

waif n. abandoned, homeless, or lost child

wail n. loud, mournful cry or weep

waist n. narrow part of the body between the thorax and hips **waisted** adj.

wait v. stay in one place in expectation of; to await; to put off until a later time or date

wait-er n. man who serves food at a restaurant

wait-ress n. woman who serves

food at a restaurant

aive v. forfeit of one's own free will; to postpone or dispense with

ake v. come to consciousness, as from sleep

n. vigil for a dead body.

alk v. move on foot over a surface; to pass over, go on

alk-out n. labor strike against a company

all n. vertical structure to separate or enclose an area

v. to provide or close up, as with a wall

al-la-by n. small or medium-sized kangaroo

al-let n. flat folding case for carrying paper money

al-lop n. powerful blow; an impact v. to move with disorganized haste   -er n.

all-pa-per n. decorative paper for walls, usually having a colorful pattern

al-nut n. edible nut with a hard, light-brown shell; the tree on which this nut grows

al-rus n. large marine mammal of the seal family, having flippers, tusks, and a tough hide

altz n. ballroom dance

am-pum n. polished shells, once used as currency by North American Indians *Slang* Money

and n. slender rod used by a magician

an-der v. travel about aimlessly; to roam; to stray **wanderer** n.

ane v. decrease in size or extent; to decrease gradually   n. gradual deterioration

an-gle v. resort to devious methods in order to obtain something wanted -er n.

ant v. wish for or desire; to need; to lack; to fail to possess a required amount

ar n. armed conflict among states or nations

ard n. section in a hospital v. to keep watch over someone or something

are n. manufactured items of

the same general kind; items or goods for sale

ware-house n. large building used to store merchandise

warm adj. moderate heat; neither hot or cold

warn v. give notice or inform beforehand; to call to one's attention; to alert

warp v. become bent out of shape; to deviate from a proper course

war-rant n. written authorization giving the holder legal power to search, seize, or arrest   -able adj.

war-ri-or n. one who fights in a war or battle

war-y adj. marked by caution; alert to danger

wash v. cleanse by the use of water; to remove dirt

wash--and--wear adj. requiring little or no ironing after washing

wash-board n. corrugated board on which clothes are rubbed in the process of washing

washed--out adj., *Slang* tired

wash-er n. small disk usually made of rubber or metal having a hole in the center, used with nuts and bolts; a washing machine

wash-ing n. clothes and other articles that are washed or to be washed; cleaning

was-n't contr. was not

wasp n. any of various insects, having a slim body with a constricted abdomen, the female capable of inflicting a painful sting

waste v. to be thrown away; to be available but not used completely   -ful adj.

watch v. view carefully; to guard; to keep informed

watch-dog n. dog trained to guard someone or his property

watch-ful adj. carefully observant or attentive **watchfully** adv.

watch-man n. person hired to keep watch; a guard

wa-ter n. clear liquid making

up oceans, lakes, and streams; the body fluids as tears or urine

water moccasin *n.* venomous snake

water polo *n.* water game between two teams

water power *n.* power or energy produced by swift-moving water

wa-ter-proof *adj.* capable of preventing water from penetrating.

wa-ter-shed *n.* the raised area between two regions that divides two sections drained by different river sources

wa-ter-ski *v.* travel over water on a pair of short, broad skis while being pulled by a motorboat

wa-ter-spout *n.* tube or pipe through which water is discharged

water table *n.* upper limit of the portion of the ground completely saturated with water

wa-ter-tight *adj.* closed or sealed so tightly that no water can enter

wa-ter-way *n.* navigable body of water; a channel for water

wa-ter-y *adj.* containing water; diluted; lacking effectiveness   **wateriness** *n.*

watt *n.* unit of electrical power represented by current of one ampere, produced by the electromotive force of one volt

wave *v.* move back and forth or up and down; to motion with the hand

wa-ver *v.* sway unsteadily; to move back and forth; to weaken in force   **waver** *n.*, **waveringly** *adv.*

wax *n.* natural yellowish substance made by bees, solid when cold and easily melted or softened when heated   **waxy** *adj.*

way *n.* manner of doing something; a tendency or characteristic

way-far-er *n.* person who travels on foot

way-lay *v.* attack by ambush

way-ward *adj.* unruly; unpredictable

we *pl., pron.* used to refer to the person speaking and one or more other people

weak *adj.* having little energy or strength; easily broken; having inadequate skills   **weakness** *n.*, **weakly** *adv.*

wealth *n.* abundance of valuable possessions or property

wean *v.* accustom an infant or small child to food other than a mother's milk or bottle

weapon *n.* device which can be used to harm another person

wear *v.* to have on or put something on the body; to display   **wearable** *adj.*

wea-ri-some *adj.* tedious; boring or tiresome

wea-ry *adj.* exhausted; tired; feeling fatigued   **wearily** *adv.*, **weariness** *n.*

wea-sel *n.* mammal with a long tail and short legs; a sly, sneaky person

weath-er *n.* condition of the air or atmosphere in terms of humidity, temperature and similar features

weath-er-man *n.* man who reports or forecasts the weather

weather vane *n.* device that turns, indicating the direction of the wind

weave *v.* make a basket, cloth, or other item by interlacing threads or other strands of material   **weaver** *n.*

web *n.* cobweb; piece of interlacing material which forms a woven structure

wed *v.* take as a spouse; to marry

we'd *contr.* we had; we should

wed-ding *n.* marriage ceremony; an act of joining together in close association

wedge *n.* tapered, triangular piece of wood or metal used to split logs, to add leverage and to hold something open or ajar

weed *n.* unwanted plant which interferes with the growth of grass, vegetables, or flowers

week *n.* period of seven days, beginning with Sunday and ending with Saturday

week-day *n.* any day of the week except Saturday or Sunday

week-end *n.* end of the week from the period of Friday evening through Sunday evening

weep *v.* to shed tears; to express sorrow, joy, or emotion

wee-vil *n.* small beetle having a downward-curving snout

weigh *v.* determine the heaviness of an object by using a scale; to consider carefully in one's mind

weight *n.* amount that something weighs; heaviness; a heavy object used to hold or pull something down

weight-less *adj.* lacking the pull of gravity; having little weight

weight-y *adj.* burdensome; important

weird *adj.* having an extraordinary or strange character

weirdly *adv.*

weird-o *n., Slang* person who is very strange

wel-come *v.* extend warm hospitality; to accept gladly

weld *v.* unite metallic parts by applying heat and sometimes pressure, allowing the metals to bond together

wel-fare *n.* state of doing well; governmental aid to help the disabled or disadvantaged

well *n.* hole in the ground which contains a supply of water; a shaft in the ground through which gas and oil are obtained

we'll *contr.* we will; we shall

well--be-ing *n.* state of being healthy, happy, or prosperous

well--done *adj.* completely cooked; done properly

well--groomed *adj.* clean, neat, and properly cared for

well--known *adj.* widely known

well--man-nered *adj.* polite; having good manners

well--mean-ing *adj.* having good intentions

well--to-do *adj.* having more than enough wealth

welsh *v., Slang* cheat by avoiding a payment to someone; to neglect an obligation

welt *n.* strip between the sole and upper part of a shoe; a slight swelling on the body

wel-ter-weight *n.* boxer weighing between 136 and 147 pounds

went *v.* past tense of go

wept *v.* past tense of weep

were *v.* second person singular past plural of be

we're *contr.* we are

were-n't *contr.* were not

west *n.* direction of the setting sun **western** *adj.*

whack *v.* strike with a hard blow, to slap *n.* an attempt

whale *n.* very large mammal resembling a fish which lives in salt water

wharf *n.* pier or platform built at the edge of water so that ships can load and unload

what *pron.* which one; which things; which type or kind

what-ev-er *pron.* everything or anything *adj.* no matter what.

what's *contr.* what is

wheat *n.* grain ground into flour, used to make breads and similar foods

wheel *n.* a circular disk which turns on an axle

wheel-bar-row *n.* vehicle having one wheel, used to transport small loads

wheel-chair *n.* a mobile chair for disabled persons

wheel-er *n.* anything that has wheels

wheeze *v.* breathe with a hoarse whistling sound *n.* high whistling sound

whelk *v.* any of various large water snails, sometimes

edible

when *adv.* at what time; at which time

pron. what or which time

conj. while; at the time that

whence *adv.* from what source or place; from which

when-ev-er *adv.* at any time; when

conj. at whatever time

where *adv.* at or in what direction or place; in what direction or place

where-a-bouts *adv.* near, at, or in a particular location

n. approximate place

where-as *conj.* it being true or the fact; on the contrary

where-by *conj.* through or by which

wher-ev-er *adv.* in any situation or place

whet *v.* to make sharp; to stimulate

wheth-er *conj.* indicating a choice; alternative possibilities; either

whet-stone *n.* stone used to sharpen scissors, knives, and other implements

whew *n., interj.* used to express relief; or tiredness

whey *n.* clear, water-like part of milk that separates from the curd

which *pron.* what one or ones; the one previously; whatever one or ones; whichever

which-ev-er *pron.* any; no matter which or what

whiff *n.* slight puff; a light current of air; a slight breath or odor

while *n.* length or period of time

conj. during the time that; even though; at the same time

whim *n.* sudden desire or impulse

whim-per *v.* make a weak, soft crying sound

whim-si-cal *adj.* impulsive; erratic; light and spontaneous

whimsically *adv.*

whine *v.* make a squealing, plaintive sound; to com-

plain in an irritating, childish fashion

whin-ny *v.* neigh in a soft gentle way

whip *v.* spank repeatedly with a rod or stick; to punish by whipping *n.* flexible stick or rod used to herd or beat animals   **whipper** *n.*

whip-lash *n.* injury to the spine or neck caused by a sudden jerking motion of the head

whip-poor-will *n.* brownish nocturnal bird of North America

whir *v.* move with a low purring sound

whirl *v.* rotate or move in circles; to twirl; to move

whirl-pool *n.* circular current of water

whirl-wind *n.* violently whirling mass of air; a tornado

whirl-y-bird *n., Slang* helicopter

whisk *v.* move with a sweeping motion;   move quickly or lightly

whisk-er *n.* hair that grows on a man's face; the long hair near the mouth of dogs, cats, and other animals

whiskers man's beard

whis-key *n.* alcoholic beverage distilled from rye, barley, or corn

whis-per *v.* speak in a very low tone; to tell in secret

whis-tle *v.* make a clear shrill sound by blowing air through the teeth, through puckered lips, or through a special instrument

white *n.* color opposite of black; the part of something that is white or light in color, as an egg or the eyeball; a member of the Caucasian group of people

white-cap *n.* wave having a top of white foam

white--col-lar *adj.* relating to an employee whose job does not require manual labor

white-wash *n.* mixture made of lime and other ingredients and used for whitening

pose, or reason for which

interj. expressing surprise or disagreement

wick *n.* soft strand of fibers which extends from a candle or lamp

wick-er *n.* thin, pliable twig used to make furniture and baskets

wick-et *n.* wire hoop in the game of croquet

wide *adj.* broad; covering a large area; completely extended or open

adv. over a large area; full extent

wide-spread *adj.* fully spread out; over a broad area

wid-ow *n.* woman whose husband is no longer living

wid-ow-er *n.* man whose wife is no longer living

width *n.* distance or extent of something from side to side

yield *v.* use or handle something skillfully; to employ power effectively

wie-ner *n.* frankfurter; a hot dog

wife *n.* married female

wig *n.* artificial or human hair woven together to cover baldness or a bald spot on the head

wig-gle *v.* squirm; to move with rapid side-to-side motions **wiggler** *n.*

wig-wam *n.* Indian dwelling place

wild *adj.* living in a natural, untamed state; not occupied by man; not civilized; strange and unusual

adv. out of control

n. wilderness region not cultivated or settled by man

wild-cat *n.* medium-sized wild, feline animal; one with a quick temper

wil-der-ness *n.* unsettled area; a region left in its uncultivated or natural state

wild-life *n.* animals and plants living in their natural environments

will *n.* mental ability to decide or choose for oneself; strong desire or

fences and exterior walls

whith-er *adv.* what state, place, or circumstance; wherever

whit-tle *v.* cut or carve off small shavings from wood with a knife; to remove or reduce gradually

who *pron.* which or what certain individual, person, or group

who'd *contr.* who would; who had

who-ev-er *pron.* whatever person; all or any persons

whole *adj.* complete; having nothing missing; not divided or in pieces

whole-heart-ed *adj.* sincere; totally committed

whole-sale *n.* sale of goods in large amounts to a retailer

whole-some *adj.* contributing to good mental or physical health **wholesomely** *adv.*, **wholesomeness** *n.*

whole wheat *adj.* made from the wheat kernel with nothing removed

who'll *contr.* who shall; who will

whol-ly *adv.* totally; exclusively

whom *pron.* form of who used as the direct object of a verb or the object of the preposition

whom-ev-er *pron.* form of whoever used as the object of a preposition or the direct object of a verb

whooping cough *n.* infectious disease of the throat and breathing passages

whooping crane *n.* large bird of North America, nearly extinct

whoosh *v.* make a rushing or gushing sound, as a rush of air

whop-per *n.* something of extraordinary size *Slang* a lie

whore *n.* prostitute

who's *contr.* who is; who has

whose *pron.* belonging to or having to do with one's belongings

why *adj.* for what reason or purpose *conj.* cause, pur-

determination; a legal document stating how one's property is to be distributed after death

wil-low *n.* large tree, usually having narrow leaves and slender flexible twigs

wilt *v.* cause or to become limp; to lose force; to deprive of courage or energy

win *v.* defeat others; to gain victory in a contest; to receive *n.* victory; the act of winning **winner** *n.*

winch *n.* apparatus with one or more drums on which a cable or rope is wound, used to lift heavy loads

wind *n.* natural movement of air **windy** *adj.*

wind *v.* wrap around and around something; to turn, to crank *n.* turning or twisting

wind-bag *n., Slang* person who talks excessively without saying anything of importance

wind-fall *n.* sudden or unexpected stroke of good luck

wind instrument *n.* musical instrument which produces sound when a person forces his breath into it

wind-mill *n.* machine operated or powered by the wind

win-dow *n.* opening built into a wall for light and air; a pane of glass

win-dow-shop *v.* look at merchandise in store windows without going inside to buy

wind-pipe *n.* passage in the neck used for breathing; the trachea

wine *n.* drink containing 10-15% alcohol by volume, made by fermenting grapes

wing *n.* one of the movable appendages that allow a bird or insect to fly; one of the airfoils on either side of an aircraft

wing-spread *n.* extreme measurement from the tips or outer edges of the wings of an aircraft, bird, or other insect

wink *v.* shut one eye as a signa or message

win-ning *adj.* defeating other captivating *n.* victory

win-some *adj.* very pleasant charming

win-ter *n.* coldest season, com ing between autumn and spring *adj.* relating to o typically of winter

win-ter-green *n.* small plan having aromatic evergree leaves

wipe *v.* clean by rubbing; t take off by rubbing *n.* act o instance of wiping

wire *n.* small metal rod used t conduct electricity; thi strands of metal twisted together to form a cable; th telephone or telegraph sys tem

wis-dom *n.* ability to under stand what is right, true, o enduring; good judgmen knowledge

wise *adj.* having superi intelligence; having gre learning; having a capaci for sound judgment marke by deep understanding **-ly** *adv.*

wise-crack *n., Slang* wit remark or joke usuall showing a lack of respect

wish *v.* desire or long fo something; to command request *n.* longing or desir

wish-bone *n.* bone of a bir which, according to the su perstition, when broke brings good luck to the pe son who has the longer en

wish-ful *adj.* having or expre ing a wish; hopeful **wishfully** *adv.*

wish-y-wash-y *adj., Slang* purposeful; indecisive

wisp *n.* tuft or small bundle hay, straw, or hair; a th piece **wispy** *adj.*

wit *n.* ability to use words in clever way; a sense of hum

witch *n.* person believed have magical powers; mean, ugly, old woman

with *prep.* in the company

near or alongside; having, wearing or bearing

ith-draw v. take away; to take back; to retreat

ith-draw-al n. process of with-drawing; a retreat; the act of removing money from an account

iither v. dry up or wilt from a lack of moisture; to lose freshness or vigor

th-hold n. hold back or keep

thholding tax n. tax on income held back by an employer in payment of one's income tax

th-in adv. inside the inner part; inside the limits; inside the limits of time, distance, or degree

th-out adv. on the outside; not in possession of

rep. something or someone lacking

th-stand v. endure

t-ness n. person who has seen, experienced, or heard something; something serving as proof or evidence

t-ty adj. amusing or cleverly humorous

z-ard n. very clever person; a person thought to have magical powers *Slang* one with amazing skill

b-ble v. move unsteadily from side to side, as a rocking motion

e n. great sorrow or grief; misfortune

k n. convex metal cooker for stir-frying food

ke v. past tense of wake

lf n. carnivorous animal found in northern areas; a fierce person v. eat quickly and with greed

olfish adj., wolfishly adv.

man n. mature adult human female; a person who has feminine qualities

manhood n. state of being a woman

mb n. uterus; place where development occurs

n v. past tense of win

n-der n. feeling of amazement or admiration v. feel admiration; feel uncertainty

won-der-ment n. feeling or state of amazement

won-drous adj. wonderful; marvelous

won't contr. will not

won-ton n. noodle dumpling filled with minced pork and served in soup

wood n. hard substance which makes up the main part of trees

wood-chuck n. rodent having short legs and a heavyset body, which lives in a burrow

wood-en adj. made of wood; resembling wood; stiff; lifeless; lacking flexibility

wood-peck-er n. bird which uses its bill for drilling holes in trees looking for insects to eat

wood-wind n. group of musical instruments which produce sounds when air is blown through the mouthpiece, as the clarinet

wool n. soft, thick hair of sheep and other such mammals; a fabric made from such hair

word n. meaningful sound which stands for an idea; a comment

word pro-cess-ing n. system which produces typewritten documents with automated type and editing equipment

work-er n. person who works for wages; an employee; a bee or other insect which performs special work in the colony in which it lives

work-ing adj. adequate to permit work to be done; assumed to permit further work

work-man-ship n. skill or art of a craftsman; quality given to something in the process of making if

world n. planet Earth; the universe; the human race

worn adj. made weak or thin from use; exhausted

wor-ry v. oncerned or troubled; to tug at

repeatedly; to annoy; to irritate

wor-ship *n.* reverence for a
sacred object; high esteem
or devotion for a person
v. revere; attend a religious
service **worshiper** *n.*

worst *adj.* bad; most inferior;
most disagreeable

worth *n.* quality or value of
something; personal merit

wor-thy *adj.* valuable or useful;
deserving admiration or
honor

would-n't *contr.* would not

wound *n.* laceration of the skin
v. injure by tearing, cutting,
or piercing the skin

wow *interj.* expression of
amazement, surprise, or excitement

wran-gle *v.* quarrel noisily

wrap *v.* fold in order to protect
something; encase or
enclose

wrath *n.* violent anger or fury

wreak *v.* inflict punishment
upon another person

wreath *n.* decorative ring-like
form of intertwined flow-
ers, bows, and other articles

wreck *v.* ruin or damage by accident or deliberately

wrest *v.* twist or pull away in a
violent way

wretch *n.* extremely unhappy
person; a miserable person

wrig-gle *v.* squirm; move by
turning and twisting

wring *v.* squeeze and twist by
hand or machine; press
together

wrin-kle *n.* small crease on the
skin or on fabric

writ *n., Law* written court
document directed to a
public official or individual
ordering a specific action

writhe *v.* twist, as in pain; suffer greatly with pain

wrong *adj.* incorrect; against
moral standards; not
suitable **wrongly** *adv.*

wrote *v.* past tense of write

wrought *adj.* fashioned;
formed; beatened or ham-
mered into shape

wrung *v.* past tense of wring

X, x the twenty-fourth letter
the English alphabet

xan-thate *n.* salt of xanthic a

xan-thic *adj.* colors that ten
be yellow and yellows
flowers

xan-thip-pe *n.* wife; fem
which is like a shrew

xan-tho-chroid *adj.* lig
haired, Caucasion people

x-axis *n.* in Cartesian co
dinate system, the horizo
tal line of a two-dimension
plane

X chro-mo-some *n.* sex fem
chromosome, associat
with female characteristic
occurs paired in the fem
and single in the ma
chromosome pair

xe-non *n.* colorless, odorl
gaseous element found
small quantities in the a
symbolized by Xe.

xen-o-phobe *n.* person w
dislikes, fears, and mistru
foreigners or anythi
strange

xenophobia *n.*

X-Ra-di-a-tion *n.* treatm
with X-rays

X ray *n.* energy that is radia
with a short wavelength a
high penetrating power;
black and white negat
image or picture of the in
rior of the body

xy-lo-phone *n.* musical
strument consisting
mounted wooden ba
which produce a ring
musical sound when str
with two small wood
hammers **xylophonist**

Y, y the twenty-fifth letter
the English alphabet

yacht *n.* small sailing ves
powdered by wind or mo
for pleasure cruises

yak *n.* longhaired ox of Ti
and mountains of cent
Asia

yam *n.* edible root; a variety
the sweet potato

yap *v.* bark in a high pitch
sharp way *Slang* talk in
loud, or stupid manner

yard *n.* unit of measure that equals 36 inches or 3 feet; ground around a house

yarn *n.* twisted fibers, as of wool, used in knitting or weaving *Slang* involved tale or story

yawn *v.* inhale a deep breath with the mouth open wide

Y-Chro-mo-some *n.* sex chromosome associated with male characteristics

ye *pron.* you, used especially in religious contexts, as hymns

yea *adv.* yes; indeed; truly

yeah *adv., Slang* yes

year *n.* period of time starting on January lst and continuing through December 31st

yearn *v.* feel a strong craving

yeast *n.* fungi or plant cells used to make baked goods rise or fruit juices ferment

yell *v.* cry out loudly *n.* loud cry; cheer to show support for an athletic team

yel-low *n.* bright color of a lemon; the yolk of an egg *v.* make or become yellow *adj.* of the color yellow *Slang* cowardly

yellow fever *n.* acute infectious disease of the tropics, spread by the bite of a mosquito

yeo-man *n.* owner of a small farm; a petty officer who acts as a clerk

yes *adv.* express agreement

yes-ter-day *n.* day before today; a former or recent time *adv.* on the day before the present day

yew *n.* evergreen tree having poisonous flat, dark-green needles and poisonous red berries

yield *v.* bear or bring forward; give up possession

yo-del *v.* sing in a way so that the voice changes from normal to a high shrill sound and then back again

yo-ga *n.* system of exercises which helps the mind and the body in order to achieve tranquillity and spiritual insight

yo-gurt *n.* thick custard-like food made from curdled milk and often mixed with fruit

yoke *n.* wooden bar used to join together two animals working together, as oxen

yo-del *n.* very unsophisticated country person; a bumpkin

yolk *n.* yellow, nutritive part of an egg

Yom Kip-pur *n.* Jewish holiday observed with fasting and prayer for the forgiveness of sins

you *pron.* person or persons addressed

you all *pron., Slang* y'all southern variation used for two or more people in direct address

you'd *contr.* you had; you would

you'll *contr.* you will; you shall

young *adj.* of or relating to the early stage of life *n.* offspring of an animal -ster *n.*

your *adj.* belonging to you or yourself or the person spoken to

you're *contr.* you are

your-self *pron.* form of you for emphasis when the object of a verb and the subject is the same

you've *contr.* you have

yowl *v.* make a loud, long cry or howl **yowl** *n.*

yt-ter-bi-um *n.* metallic element symbolized by Yb.

yule *n.* Christmas

yule-tide *n.* Christmas season

Z, z the twenty-sixth letter of the English alphabet

za-ny *n., pl* -nies clown; person who acts silly or foolish *adj.* typical of the being clownish **zaniness** *n.,* zannily *adv.*

zap *v., Slang* destroy; do away with

zeal *n.* great interest or eagerness

zeal-ot *n.* fanatical person; a fanatic

zeal-ous *adj.* full of interest; eager; passionate

zealously adv.

ze-bra n. African mammal of the horse family having black or brown stripes on a white body

zeph-yr n. gentle breeze

ze-ro n., pl. -ros, -roes number or symbol "0"; nothing; point from which degrees or measurements on a scale begin; the lowest point v. aim, point at, or close in on adj. pertaining to zero; nonexisting

zest n. enthusiasm; a keen quality **zestful** adj., **zestfully, zesty** adj.

zig-zag n. pattern with sharp turns in alternating directions adv. move in a zigzag course or path

zilch n., Slang nothing; zero

zil-lion n., Slang extremely large number

zinc n. bluish-white crystalline metallic element, used as a protective coating for steel and iron, symbolized by Zn

zip n. act or move with vigor or speed v. move with energy, speed, or facility; open or close with a zipper Slang energy; zero; nothing

zip code n. system to speed the delivery of mail by assigning a five digit number, plus four to each postal delivery location in the United States

zip-per n. fastener consisting of two rows of plastic or metal teeth that are interlocked by means of sliding a tab

zir-co-ni-um n. metallic element symbolized by Zr

zit n., Slang pimple

zo-di-ac n. unseen path followed through the heavens by the moon, sun, and most planets; area divided into twelve astrological signs, bearing the name of a constellation

zom-bie n. person who resembles the walking dead

zone n. area or region set apart from its surroundings by some characteristic

zonk v., Slang stun; render senseless with alcohol or drugs

zoo n., pl. **zoos** public display or collection of living animals

zo-ol-o-gy n. science that deal with animals, animal life, and the animal kingdom **zoologist** n.

zoom v. move with a continuous, loud sound; move upward sharply

zuc-chi-ni n., pl. -ni summe squash that has a dark-green, smooth rind

zwie-back n. sweetened brea which is baked to make i crisp

zy-mur-gy n. chemistry o fermentation processes